Surfer Girls in the New World Order

Surfer Girls in the New World Order

Krista Comer

Duke
University
Press

*Durham &
London 2010*

© 2010
Duke University Press
All rights reserved
Printed in the
United States of America
on acid-free paper ∞

Designed by Jennifer Hill
Typeset in TheSerif by
Tseng Information Systems, Inc.

Library of Congress
Cataloging-in-Publication
Data appear on the last
printed page of this book.

For my father

Contents

Acknowledgments

Traveling the world to study surfing is not exactly a hardship and over the course of a ten-year project I have happily accumulated many debts that are a pleasure to acknowledge. I am fortunate to have received support from Rice University's Mosle Fellowship from 2001 to 2004, and generous support thereafter from the dean of the School of Humanities at Rice, Gary Wihl. I am also very grateful to have worked with Reynolds Smith, Duke's senior acquisitions editor. This is one of the final books Reynolds saw through to its end before pursuing his own projects in retirement. From his first solicitation of the book to the final production phase, Reynolds offered me wisdom as well as an old-fashioned kind of friendship between editor and writer. I am glad to have had him as my editor for a time.

I have named many surfers over the course of the book, but I would offer particular thanks here. In California, appreciations go to Jane MacKenzie (Jane at the Lane), who initially introduced me around the Santa Cruz scene. The filmmaker and photographer Elizabeth Pepin of San Francisco brought her insider's sense of subcultural life to my questions and I was saved many errors of judgment by her helpful corrections and no-nonsense analytic mind. We commiserated about gender politics, surfing, and big business over sushi lunches and time at Pacifica—the most female-friendly and gender-bent surf spot on the planet (where else does one find Drag Surfing?). Pepin's photographs of women are featured throughout these pages and the black-and-whites from Pacifica are among the most beautiful I've ever seen. I look forward to collaborative projects we have in the works.

The community that collects around Paradise Surf Shop in

Santa Cruz generously shared themselves and the vision for their shop and town with me in over a decade of conversations. Sarah Gerhardt and I met when she was still a PhD student of chemistry at the University of California, Santa Cruz, and just coming off the enormous feat (a few months earlier) of being the first woman to surf Mavericks. I was deeply admiring of her and (not alone here) anxious on her behalf since she intended to surf it again the very next day. Anyone who has contemplated Mavericks will appreciate its appeal and terrifying challenge. But for a woman to think of that singular spot as a terrain of her own possibility: even after a decade of getting used to Gerhardt's presence in the Mavericks lineup, I still find it tremendously inspirational. Izzy Tihanyi, of Surf Diva in San Diego, gave of herself when she had a new baby daughter—and her business smarts, self-possession, and travel between sites of "fun" and feminism are models for effective community-building today. When Izzy says, as a throwaway line, that she'd like to teach Hillary Clinton to surf, or Chelsea, one imagines picking up a newspaper at some future time that covers the story.

In Mexico, I greatly appreciate the time and accessibility of Bev Sanders, the owner of Las Olas surf camps, to answer my questions. Not many business owners will open their internal workings to researchers and I hope to have done her political commitments some justice. I have talked over the years to many surfers who worked at Las Olas as instructors—formally on tape and informally as we sat in the time warp familiar to people who gaze a lot at waves and their riders. All of these conversations informed my sense of what it means to travel the world today as local and global female citizens, and though I do not quote everyone, each woman individually, I appreciate the time and thoughts they shared. I also would thank Patty Southworth of Captain Pablo's, and the owners of Villa Amor, especially Mary Ingram. All of them showed me gracious hospitality, and I wish my final political assessments of the economy underwriting Villa Amor could have been more affirming of this kindness. I also thank the Mexican women and girl surfistas at Sayulita, for it takes a particular courage and self-regard to enter a sea of images and real-time Cali girls, and to talk to a researcher (potentially critically) about these topics when she herself calls the Cali-girl image to mind.

I also wish to thank surfers and their friends living in Jeffrey's Bay, South Africa, where I did ethnographic work in 2006, having gone to Cape Town as a member of a Mellon Foundation U.S. delegation. The classic surf film

The Endless Summer (1966) invented Jeffrey's Bay as a global surf spot—
now one of the world's great surf meccas. I was eager to investigate it. The
Mellon trip was organized by Roland Smith, vice provost at Rice University.
It offered the opportunity for African American educators and allies like
me involved with Mellon to meet with Bishop Tutu, tour Robbin Island, and
talk with University of Cape Town people about affirmative action in the
New South Africa. I managed to tear myself away from Cape Town and also
spend time in Jeffrey's Bay. From safari outdoorsman Paul Versfeld I heard
stories about Mickey Dora, who stayed at Paul's home. The lifelong surfer
Andy Thuysman told me tales of J-Bay's early surf museums housed in his
leather shop. Cheron Kraak, managing director of Billabong, South Africa,
fit me into her day on a moment's notice and told me about her life as a
South African hippie and seamstress, longtime female surfer, and eventual
entrepreneur. She has a keen sense of local and global girls' and women's
surf culture. It became instantly clear to me why she was named businesswoman of the year for the Eastern Cape Province in 2000. Rupert Chadwick,
curator of the present-day J-Bay Surf Museum and contest director of the
first event held at Supertubes in 1982 (the prototype for the Billabong Pro
today), told me incredible stories of his days as a "black sheep" surfer and
white African National Congress party activist.

Brenton Williams of South Coast Surf School provided much insight into
white surfers' efforts to reach across the chasm of apartheid in the new
South Africa in the federally-sponsored Surfing Development Initiative. For
Williams, the effort was up close and personal as he is also the adoptive
father of fifteen-year-old Samuel Mabetshe (b. 1991), one of the luminary
young surfers born in the adjacent shantytown of Tokyo Sewale, who came
up through the ranks at J-Bay and about whom a television documentary
aired in September 2005 on South Africa BC3, *The Healing Power of Nature:
Perfect?* Samuel also shared with me tales of his life and his transformation
through surfing from a five-year-old street boy to a young man with prospects for education and a surfing career. Though a few local women—Kim
Meyer, local longtime surfer, and her teenage daughter, Wanda Meyer—
surf Supertubes and have surfed the world with the surfer and shaper (and
husband and father) Mikey Meyer, there was not on the ground a girl localist presence sufficient for me to investigate and include in the present volume. Kim Meyer and Williams both noted the male bias of local surf culture. I have included in the bibliography a record of these oral histories in

the event other researchers might find them helpful. I thank both the locals there and the Mellon delegation for all they taught me about African race politics, gender, and surfing.

When it wasn't clear in the early years of the project that anyone in academia believed surfing was a serious topic, and some referred none too admiringly to "that Gidget book," I received letters and e-mails from generous people in different parts of the world who sent material, commented on work in progress, suggested grad students contact me, and provided general encouragement. These gestures of recognition—from Alice Echols, Robin Weigman, Eric Lott, Patrick Moser, George Lipsitz, Lawrence Buell, José David Saldívar, Mike Willard, and James Clifford—sustained me, allowing me to hold on a bit longer. At a crucial point I attended a conference in Brisbane, "On the Beach," sponsored in 2000 by the Cultural Studies Association of Australia. I wish to thank my colleagues there who, being not so alienated from water culture, delighted in this work and did not find it so foreign to scholarly pursuits, including especially Ian Buchanan, Margaret Henderson, P. David Marshall, Clifton Evers, and Paul Scott. At a later crucial moment I attended the "A New Girl Order?" Conference in London in 2002. There, I was exposed to work on contemporary girlhood that completely outstripped any thinking happening about girls in the United States, and I particularly want to thank Angela McRobbie and Rosalind Gill for conversations about surfing and girls, and also Valerie Walkerdine.

Talks given over the years helped me figure out the interface between globalization and surfing. I would thank the American Cultures and English Department at the University of Michigan, Ann Arbor, and Phil Deloria, Maria Cotera, and Penny Von Eschen; also, Priscilla Ybarra and Baird Callicott at the University of North Texas, Denton, and Patrick Moser of Drury University. I also thank Donna Kabalen of Monterrey Tech, in Monterrey, Mexico. It was a generous opportunity and a challenge to be invited to present my work on Mexican surfing and tourism to Mexicans in English and Spanish (their bilingualism more sophisticated than mine). Such conversations between U.S. Studies and Mexican Studies opened new collaborations with Latin Americanists at Rice, including the distinguished Beatriz Gonzalez-Stephan and a recent wonderful addition to the Rice faculty, Luis Duno-Gottberg. Their encouragement and thoughts about surfing as a border epistemology have allowed us all to imagine new routes of intellectual travel between Latin American Studies, studies of the United States and the Mexico borderlands, and U.S. Western Studies.

Also at Rice University I am grateful for the community of interdisciplinary feminist scholars who are my daily companions in the Center for the Study of Women, Gender, and Sexuality. Feminist resources at Rice are exceptionally deep and strong. I presented both early and nearly-finished work on this project over a ten-year period and appreciate the comments and encouragements of Lynne Huffer, Colleen Lamos, Betty Joseph, Susan Lurie, Helena Michie, Rosemary Hennessey, Melissa Forbis, and Elora Shehabuddin. Elizabeth Long and Cecilia Balli read the manuscript word for word more than once. From non-Rice contexts, Nöel Sturgeon offered formal comment that aided my final revisions. Melani McAlister and Nan Alamilla Boyd, friends from graduate school in American Studies at Brown University, have been especially encouraging. I have also enjoyed an abiding sense of community in the Western Literature Association for fifteen years, and have been giving papers out of this book for at least ten years now. I thank Neil Campbell, Susan Kollin, Susan Bernardin, Nancy Cook, Melody Graulich, Chad Allen, Bill Handley, Nat Lewis, Bonney MacDonald, and especially Stephen Tatum, whose friendship and scholarly work mean the world to me.

I deeply thank my husband José F. Aranda Jr., who I believe has been almost as interested in this project as I, and who brought me additional materials on surfing out of his huge appetite for reading newspapers, long after I wished never again to read anything about surfing. He sat with me through a very long three-week intensive writing period that saw the completion of the first draft, a gift no one else could or would have given me. From her travels and avid readings, my mother, Jean H. Comer, has supplied me with important newspaper clippings from San Francisco, San Diego, London, and Australia. My sons, Benito and Jesse, have gone to surf school and supported their mom's research as boogie boarders in the waters of California and Mexico but most often in Galveston near our Houston home. Two of my four sisters surf, all of us are ocean swimmers, and one memorable day several years ago all five of us Comer sisters with our kids, our partners, and my mom were out in San Diego, in full wet-suited familial force. My mother raced us all to the water and won, lording her win without apology. That day no doubt owes an unpayable debt to my late father, xiv

Stuart Comer, to whom this book is dedicated. Although not a surfer, he was my first exposure to bohemian Western men: a swimmer, diver, skier, dancer, golfer, cardplayer, and singer. He was also ever the businessman. While difficult to have as a father, he breathed life into the everyday and offered up a legacy of creative restlessness.

Critical Localisms in a Globalized World

In the fall of 2002—hurricane season—I left Houston for a research trip to Sayulita, Mexico, a fishing village turned surf town on the Pacific coastline, north of Puerto Vallarta. Sayulita's beach is modest by Mexican resort standards: it's rocky in patches, the sand a grainy gray. The northern point remains an active fishing venture with small boats pushing off and returning to shore, leaving gasoline rainbows trailing behind in the water. In fact, Sayulita is not a resort. It's an internationalist surf town, and at its center is a single surf spot, a consistent and clean reef-breaking wave that gamey beginners will more or less be able to manage. I wanted to go to Sayulita to study a women's surf camp, Las Olas, specifically to study transnational athletic play (fig. 1). Las Olas is owned by an American woman surfer from northern California and has been in operation since 1997. At the time I visited, travel and sport media were just beginning to widely profile it as "the world's premier surf safari for women," or "the Golden Door of surfing camps."[1]

To use the word *camp* to describe the environment in which women learn to surf in Sayulita is a bit like calling teatime in Meryl Streep's away-tent in *Out of Africa* a form of wilderness refreshment. One weighs the distant roar of lions against the sterling tea service. Las Olas headquarters are housed in "la Casita," a small bricked building distinguished by a mural of a woman in the curl of a wave. This is where classes are held and where surfboards and other gear are stored. The building sports a single bathroom, a private room for massage, a gravity shower rigged via PVC pipe, and a small kitchen. Exiting the headquarters one finds the amenities of town: some shops, a few one-story inns with rooms opening onto courtyards, and restaurants serving tequila, ginger shakes,

1 "We make girls out of women," Las Olas promotional postcard.

and fish tacos—surfer food. Rising behind the town proper is so-called Gringo Hill, a collection of a hundred single-family homes bought as get-away places by retirees and surfers whose principal residences remain in the United States.[2] Built following the inauguration of NAFTA, the neigh-borhood mixes styles: beach bungalows and mountain houses uniquely held together with Mexican colored-cement work. If simplicity charac-terizes the Las Olas headquarters and the town of Sayulita, the nighttime accommodations of "campers" have more in common with Gringo Hill. The price of the package, about $2,250 per week inclusive, puts people at Villa Amor, a cluster of beautifully appointed villa spaces built directly into coastal mountains.[3] Each villa (like the homes on the Hill) makes for an architectural work of art. The colorful whole of them, terraced up the mountainside amid bougainvillea and hibiscus, affects an elegant moun-tain treehouse.

On the particular early evening of our arrival, dark thunderheads hung back offshore. From the terrace of my own villa's open-air living room I saw a world of infinite blue sea. At dusk the local fishermen and boys waded in the shore break to drag up onto the sand by thick ropes and bare hands their small boats for the night's tie-up. There was mild talk of a hurricane somewhere in the Pacific. I took a quick dip in the living room's soaking pool and marveled. About a half mile down the beach the surf spot was going off—a bit of a storm wave, I speculated, sloppy but strong. More than a few surfers took the opportunity. For all of us recent arrivals, mostly Californians, the wide eyes and unconscious exclamations of "wow!" and "my God!" indicated that we jointly experienced this moment as having journeyed to paradise.

In the context of surf camps currently in international operation—upwards of one thousand across the globe, training several hundred thousand would-be surfers in the past five to ten years[4]—I had chosen to visit Las Olas because it advertises itself as a "reverse finishing school" that makes "girls out of women." Given the hard-won second-wave feminist victory by which adult females had come to be understood in U.S. culture at large as women and *not* girls, I wondered: what were the political causes and effects of this cheeky new vernacular? If the renunciation of woman for girl might be read as a depoliticization of previous gains, there was also something more going on. The Las Olas "Manifesta" explicitly frames the camp's purpose as an effort to foster female political consciousness and power.[5] The founder of Las Olas, Bev Sanders, a middle-aged American surfer and ecoactivist, believes that environmentalist action necessitates human connection to the natural world as a precursor. By playing in the ocean, "developing a friendship with the ocean," Sanders claims that women better manage "to speak up for what we believe in, the rights of our families and communities, or on behalf of an abused ocean or forest."[6] As we shall see, this transformation from environmental to other politicized consciousnesses occurs in subcultural daily life more frequently all the time. If closing the gap between humans and nonhuman nature constitutes a familiar environmental ideal, the Las Olas strategy for nurturing it is new. Empowerment lies specifically in the link between girlhood and play: "[Our] strength can be discovered by the little girl inside who just loves to play in the waves."[7]

That October the camp comprised twenty-five campers, about a dozen of them middle-aged women who called themselves the "Hot Flashes." Their name refers to a group of thirty or so Bay Area women who play soccer, basketball, and softball in various northern California sports leagues. They also serve as extended family to one another. Most are divorced, single mothers who have helped raise one another's children. What unites these women beyond sport and motherhood is their extremely loud humor, spontaneous skits, song, dance, theme parties, and girlish intense teasing. These women travel with costumes (nuns' habits, clogs, feather boas) "just in case" circumstances arise in which masquerade should come in handy.

In style and behavior the Hot Flashes cut a strikingly different generational profile than did the Las Olas surf staff. Ranging in age from twenty-five to thirty-three, the staffers' belly shirts, bikinis, long hair, and pedicures called attention to them as young, hetero-sexy, definitely "hip and cool." In addition to teaching surfing during the Southern Hemisphere surf season, these younger women formed their own network, trading among each other (as well as providing for guests) massage therapy, yoga instruction, chiropractic knowledge, and know-how about surfing the world's best breaks as women.

In the past decade Sayulita has seen a parade of surfing women pass up and down its cobblestone streets, heavy longboards balanced atop their heads. Such a sight, with local variation, has become common in other places where female-only surf camps make their homes: Costa Rica, Nicaragua, Brazil, California, Florida, Hawaii, Australia, Bali. To be sure, these constitute new forms of contemporary femininity *and* of surf culture, even as they invoke, for me personally, the sense of coming home to a familiar world. I spent much of my younger life in California surf and beach subcultures, not as a surfer or even a wannabe but as an ocean swimmer whose everyday world was structured by the water, its people, and its economies. I had my home base on Silver Strand Beach in Oxnard (an hour north of Los Angeles), a tiny community of bohemians, surfers, and Vietnam veterans living cheaply in beach bungalows. In feeling, the Strand had that "wrong side of the tracks," dogtown kind of defiance captured so memorably in the skateboarding documentary *Dogtown and Z-Boys*.[8] During summers as a young teen, one of the mothers would drive my girlfriends and me from town out to the beach. Over time I came to know the local surf crew, a rough bunch of working-class guys with a deep-rooted group ethic and a reputation for territoriality. They looked out for each other. As I got older and discovered the heavy hostilities directed against rebel girls by suburban neighborhoods like mine, I claimed the Strand as an alternative home. When I dropped out of the University of California, Berkeley, after a year-long stint begun in 1975 when I was sixteen, I returned.

For the next ten years I came and went between the Strand and other coastal towns, sometimes in college, always working jobs related to growing flowering plants. I lived inside what today I would call a string of West Coast countercultures. At the time I believed my life was more real and responsible (in a cosmic sense) than were the aspiring lives of my college-bound middle-class peers who seemed to be living according to plans someone else had made for them. Eventually I got a real estate license and with my boyfriend (a working-class surfer/carpenter-turned-contractor) made a living by building and selling beach houses. We planned to make enough money to start a farm.

But with the Reagan era in the 1980s the countercultural edge started to disappear from Oxnard's everyday scene. Surfers who had become real estate agents now worried over the prime rate and stopped surfing. Some faded away or bottomed out; a few turned up dead. Like so many places up and down the coast, Oxnard's beach spaces began their conversion into tourist destinations, debating a name change to Channel Islands and inaugurating the annual Strawberry Festival to draw visitors. The money to be made by selling pieces of this new scene's edge moved to the front of collective local attention, a response to the dilemma of how locals were to remain on a beach getting more expensive by the day. In an agony of mixed feelings, I followed the advice of a family friend and went east to Wellesley College. There people would not (as they had in Oxnard) hate the "stuff about women" that I espoused. I matriculated in my mid-twenties as a paying-my-own-way continuing education student, suffering a culture shock that had no name.

By all indications I had left behind a personal "local scene" with no profound relationship to anything beyond its borders—until the mid-1990s, when surf culture, female surfers, and the language of surfing the Web became instant and widespread features of twenty-first-century life in the global village. When I arrived in Sayulita nearly twenty years after I had left California, I already had a deep feeling for the everyday lifeways of surfing subculture, its self-understanding as a collective stitched together by international surf breaks even while a sense of some specific local home served to center individual identity. But the nature of this local/global subculture and its implications for large-scale social transformation had dramatically changed. Females, especially girls, were now crucial to the public face and overall currency of the subculture, as was its leadership in issues of coastal environmentalism and the new "responsible tourism" movement.[9] Surfing claimed new kinds of "new social movement" activities.[10] As I saw it,

2 Surfing the new world order, *Cricket Magazine* for children.

the subculture had experienced a rocket launch into global prominence because new, globe-altering technologies had become harnessed to surfing as both a lifestyle and a structure of feeling. That is, in the spirit of the great C. L. R. James's (1963) work on cricket and empire, surfing was about far more than sport.[11] Of all of the metaphors that might have served to describe computer users' relationships to cyberspace, "surfing" had caught on. People all over the world today surf the Internet; they do not fly or sing or paint it. Nearly overnight this particular way of "doing" cybertechnology became normalized.[12]

The present book grew out of my need to understand the various implications of "surfing" for surf subculture and well beyond it. Since the end of the Cold War the values and language associated with surf culture have articulated some of the most consequential changes in both local and global cultural and economic life. The practice and metaphor of surfing mutually inscribe the comings and goings of travels in the new world order with the relaxed Hawaiian "Aloha" spirit of surf subculture (fig. 2). The structures of feeling that historically underwrote surf subculture—to relax the work mandates of Protestant masculinity and to bridge racial divides and connect with peoples of the world on pacifist terms—have been adopted and

3   Kuta tourist district in the aftermath of the Bali bombing by al-Qaeda, 2002.

adapted to serve in more official capacities as among the governing cultural logics of mobility and desire in the new world order. Surfing as a language for imagining contemporary global mobility suggests pleasurable, creative, and freeing outcomes.

But such celebratory rhetorics linking surfing and the techniques of governance associated with postindustrial freedoms and pleasures gloss over a hornet's nest of subcultural contradictions and histories of domination — not the least of which concerns surf "surfari." The terrorist bombing in 2002 by al-Qaeda of The Sari, a nightclub in the heart of the Kuta tourist area of Bali well known as an internationalist hangout of surfers, indexed from a different point of approach surfing's coming of age as a metaphor for Western culture.[13] Via headlines that read, "Surfboards Used as Stretchers," chilling reports arrived of nearly 200 people (in addition to 346 wounded) killed in Bali, many of whom were Australians and Americans on surfari (fig. 3).[14] A second attack in Kuta in 2005 killed 20 and injured more than

200. Whether discourses that join surfing and freedom are defensible as arguments either about globalization or about the subculture of surfing in its global dispersions will be among the thorny subjects to follow.

In the time it's taken to research and write this book (I began in 1998), images of surfer girls in U.S. popular culture have gone from being occasional and exotic visual anomalies to having become mainstay figures of desirable, global twenty-first-century womanhood. Much of this book grapples with how and why this change came to be and why any of us should invest intellectual and political efforts in the topic. At my project's beginning materials about surfing came from surfers and subcultural media outlets like surf magazines and films or videos, select surf museums, individual oral histories and personal collections, as well as a few popular histories.[15] I gratefully catalogued each newspaper clipping or attic-box memento sent to me by the women and girls who participated in the project. A sense of feminist social movement characterized our time together as it became clear that interviews and conversations with me formed part of larger efforts underway in women's surfing to create new public cultures able to counter the raunchy masculinism of surf media and to transform women's in-water everyday experience.[16] All of us commented with surprise as surfing females began to cross over from subculture to mainstream.

At around the time the Hollywood blockbuster surf film *Blue Crush* appeared in 2002, the cataloguing work entirely got away from me—"ran away," I want to say, in the sense in which Anthony Giddens uses the term to describe globalization.[17] The surf archive produced by subculturalists exploded to include some few hundred mass-market paperback books, many of which documented surfing history and some of which now overtly dealt with female surf issues.[18] In popular visual culture especially, surf-girl images began to proliferate in ways that no individual researcher could hope to track. Suddenly everywhere one looked—on big city billboards, in mall stores, in McDonald's "Happy Meals," in advertising culture across many media, in newspapers' "Life" and "Travel/Leisure" sections, TV awards programs, reality shows and children's programming, in bookstores' "how to" areas, on video shelves, and in a variety of sports media in languages from English to Portuguese, Japanese, French, German, Spanish, Dutch, and Afrikaans—the clear-eyed and superfit female surfer (including the toddler) stood as the poster child for all that young women might be-

4 Kia'i Tallett, daughter of Sally Lundburg and Keith Tallett, on the Big Island of Hawaii.
Photograph by Elizabeth Pepin.

come in the twenty-first century (fig. 4). The figure even inspired parodist critique (figs. 5 and 6).

But if in popular culture and print media the imagery and rhetorics of surfing have become ubiquitous, little of an intellectual or critical nature has been written about surfing—and (with a few exceptions) nearly nothing has come from U.S. universities about the U.S. scene.[19] To be sure, surfing has been written about extensively and well by surfers turned popular historians and journalists like Matt Warshaw, Drew Kampion, and Nat Young.[20] Indeed, the English-speaking world has read about surfing for two hundred years from literary pens as different as those of Captain James Cook, Mark Twain, Isabella Bird, Jack London, James Michener, Thomas Wolfe, and Kem Nunn.[21] As a topic of critical inquiry, however, surfing has barely registered. Two anthropological studies of surfing produced in the mid-twentieth century—one focused on Hawaii, the other on Australia and New Zealand—remain sources for most recent popular histories.[22] Scattered journal articles exist as well. The New Zealander Douglas Booth has been publishing on Australian beach culture, the pleasure and discipline of competitive surfing, and gender since the mid-1990s, as have the Australians Margaret Henderson and Leanne Stedman.[23] Two essays—one by

5 Lonely Surfer Squaw (1997).
By Lori Blondeau, Cree,
Saulteaux-Gordon First Nation.

6 Hula girls holding hand grenades. From "Aloha Oe." Surfer/Artist Kevin Ancell,
Yerba Buena Center for the Arts, San Francisco, May 2000.

Rob Shields, the other by Robert Preston-Whyte—emphasized global spaces of touristic play and specific subcultural sites like Durban, South Africa.[24]
Kurungubaa: A Journal of Literature, History, and Ideas for Surfers put out its first issue (again from Australia) in 2008.[25]

To date, however, just a single scholarly book has appeared, *Surfing and Social Theory* by the surfer and geographer Nick Ford and the sociologist of sport David Brown, both at the University of Exeter.[26] Theorizing from a growing body of ethnographic and social science scholarship about surfing in the U.K., Oceania, South African, and Pacific contexts, including a number of unpublished dissertations, Ford and Brown evaluate the evolving social geographies of seascapes and beachscapes, enumerate types of surfing bodies, assert a particular surfer's gaze, and deal variously in the gender, culture, history, and media of surfing. Their work is synthetic, designed to make surfing intelligible to social theorists. For Ford and Brown the topic of surfing focuses a discussion of the mind-body interface, and through it they forward forms of living knowledge with the potential to rewrite the mind-body dualisms of Western scholarly tradition.

Like most engaged in this developing transdisciplinary scholarship on surfing, I, too, work between textuality, media, global tourism, and subcultural material life. I also use ethnography as a form of cultural analysis attuned to questions both of representation and of lived reality. By analyzing real existing identities (in the ethnographic sense), reflexively locating issues of authorship in relation to that archive, I hope to attend with greater reliability to the voices of others and to what they tell us (as James Clifford might say) about travel, dwelling, and the translation between them.[27] But if *Surfing and Social Theory* serves as a companion text to my own, alert to putting analytic pressure on "surfing," I am less interested than its authors are in the experience of actual surfing or in theorizing what Ford and Brown call "the dream glide." Nor will readers find an emphasis on Hawaii, though recent work to theorize a New Pacific and Pacific Orientalism bodes well for future research.[28] My own project prioritizes *onshore* social life and its relation to gender. I place my emphasis on gender and politics, the gender of globalization, and tracking the global implications of the influential local California surf scene. Most important, I am interested in the production of contemporary girlhood and in tracking it "from below."

The visibility of surfer girls, I will argue, forms part of a much larger discourse about First World girlhood and the future of the Western world. The articulations of this discourse are many and contradictory. Psychological literature of the last decade addressed anorexic "Ophelias," back-stabbing "queen bees," gangbanging "locas," and poor "ghetto girls," as well as high-achieving "alpha girls," emotionally balanced "gamma girls," and strong, sporty girls able to wear the athlete's "game face."[29] Feminist educational organizations like the U.S. National Women's Studies Association (NWSA) and the American Association of University Women (AAUW) founded special projects and advisory committees to assess the status of girls' mental and physical health, as well as to advocate broadly for girls' life flourishing.[30] The Feminist Majority Foundation, National Organization for Women, and the National Council also developed outreach initiatives for young women. Australian, Canadian, and British Youth Councils, public commissions, the Council of Europe, YMCAs and YWCAs, and countless transnational NGOs were charged with similar tasks.[31] A host of transnational activist organizations—most devoted broadly to "teen empowerment"—were established, often led by girls or young women.[32] Organizations focused on young women in media were set up in the United States for example, the Center for New Words, Women in Media and News, and the Women's Media Center. Feminist blogs such as "Feministe" and "Feministing" were also initiated. The social import of these combined activities suggested not just new opportunities for girls in the wake of feminism but also Western girlhood as one masthead of journeys into a new world order.

In a fundamental way the crossover phenomenon of surfers into mass culture has served as confirmation of arguments I had been formulating about surfing as a diasporic public culture visible on the ground in many outpost surf breaks around the world, as well as about surfing as an emergent keyword of globalization processes and practices. Surfing as a globalist trope suggests that the social possibilities generated by the circulation of international capital, new information technologies, and people in transit will prove freeing, much as board surfing is popularly understood to be freeing. Surfing thus constitutes a rhetoric of optimism about the potential of globalization to advance the global good. Since women are surfing's most advertised global fresh face—national and international icons for all that is ostensibly "free" about Western gender conventions—the topic of surfing calls out for commentary to feminists in particular. To "surf" the Web or the new world order is to be in the midst of an argument, an ideological project, about the ethics, gender, and regional Hawaiian and California borderlands style of globalization. What particular local history has permitted such global designs?[33] What possibilities and disciplining mechanisms go with surfing territory?

Not long ago Fredric Jameson and Masao Miyoshi edited a set of impressive essays in what became for me an important entry point into the emerging field of global studies: *The Cultures of Globalization.*[34] Some of globalization's most prominent theoreticians made appearances—David Harvey, Walter Mignolo, Enrique Dussel, Leslie Sklair, Noam Chomsky. Jameson prefaced the volume by noting that the essays' ranging perspectives on globalization showed "this area up, not as a new field of specialization, but rather as a space of tension, in which the very 'problematic' of globalization still remains to be produced."[35] I had come to the text hoping to learn how better to identify defining dynamics of the new globalized economy and world political system. Like many people I could murmur something about expanded communications technologies, new financial markets, new forms of mobility (whether of people, capital, or information). Surfing had emerged as one possible expression of the problematic of globalization, I believed. Surfing had set people, money, goods, and ideas into motion in ways that created new forms of identity, sociality, commerce, and politics. Jameson's sense of globalization as a topic that confounds traditional academic disciplines—"[it] concerns politics and economics in immediate ways, but just as immediately culture and sociology, not to speak of information and the media, or ecology, or consumerism"—to my mind could have easily been taken as a statement about surfing.[36] But how did one devise an approach to go after Jameson's "untotalizable totality?"[37]

What I ultimately took away from *Cultures of Globalization* were lessons in and examples of the production of the problematic itself, what Jameson calls the "intervention of a practical relationship to it [globalization]."[38] Such an intervention, he thought, if done successfully, would force a new theoretical practice that might close the gap between "sciences and cultural sciences, as well as theory and practice, the local and the global, the West and its Others, but also postmodernity and its predecessors and alternatives."[39] In particular, I was drawn to Jameson's notion that this new theoretical practice would go hand in hand with the creation of a new culture and a new politics.[40] What I had observed in surfing were precisely new global/local cultures and political formations in emergence, ones related to gender, race, the environment, and global citizenship. Persuaded that one key to mapping theories of globalization would be creating "practical" relations to it, I began to imagine a method that could grasp, alongside surfing as global discourse, the simultaneous fact of surfing as a global/local subculture. But mine was a project about women, feminism, and gender, not typically the concerns of global theory or subcultural or youth studies. In *Cultures of Globalization* Jameson acknowledges as much by noting that the global dilemmas lying afield of the essays' frameworks include "the conflicted strategies of feminism in the new world system."[41]

No doubt because gender so often remains unmarked in global theory, it would take some time before it dawned on me that I had been thinking in global studies directions all along by way of women's studies and its theorization of the role of capitalism and imperialism in exploiting global sexism to create new sources of cheap labor. A special issue of *Signs*, "Globalization and Gender" (2001), recalled the feminist work of the 1970s and early 1980s and of what was then called "the new international division of labor," as well as more recent work on migration and diaspora, all of which examine relations between gender and political economy to point out the conspicuous inattention in recent theories of globalization to issues of gender.[42] If the more influential of globalization approaches focus on "the effects of new kinds of capitalist accumulation, such as structural adjustment, expansion of markets, technologies of media and finance, and neocolonialism," gender analysis has simply not figured. Carla Freeman questions why, when feminism so persuasively demonstrates the centrality of gender to all networks of production, consumption, distribution, we get so much gender-neutral macroanalysis and history of new economic forms alongside microanalyses of women's "fit" into structures as supposedly gender-free workers or nationals.[43] The problem with such oversight, as the *Signs* special issue makes clear, is a failure to consider questions of agency in relation to women, to consider "whether and why globalization can also provide opportunities for certain groups of women to leave the worst excesses of patriarchal oppression behind," even as "globalization exemplifies capitalism's worst tendencies of expansion and domination."[44] Situating gender at the center of theorizing globalization puts the specificity of gender in conversation with issues of agency and social movements, political economy and identity formation.[45]

Recently, feminist scholars in girls' studies have taken up precisely this theoretical challenge to argue that an emphasis on First World girlhood offers one way to investigate the global and its dominant regimes of subject production. In 2001 a conference in London titled "A New Girl Order?" put the expanded presence of girls in the public sphere of Western societies in recent years into overt dialogue with large-scale social and economic change. That conference initiated a flourishing of scholarly activity.[46] Girls are being constructed not only as a "vanguard of new subjectivity," the sociologist Anita Harris argued sweepingly in *Future Girl*, but also as ideal late modern subjects on whose choices and powers of self-regulation could be modeled the future of the Western world.[47] Drawing on Ulrich Beck, Harris emphasized the concepts of risk and individualization when coining the term *can-do girl* to stand in for the popularized figure able to make good on the gains of feminism and thus meet the demands of a new historical moment for change-adaptive and self-inventing citizens.[48] The can-do girl looks after her personal and economic development without recourse to the state or civil society, certainly a much-needed skill given the privatization of services formerly assumed to form part of the modern welfare state. But if this attention suggests the celebration of girlhood, Harris (following Michel Foucault) sees a regulatory process underway, one that constructs girls into these very same roles. The feminist sociologist Angela McRobbie, the so-called godmother of girls' studies, concurs: "'Girls,' including their bodies, their labour power, and their social behaviour, are now the subject of governmentality to an unprecedented degree."[49] Subject to greater forms of regulation still is the opposite of the can-do girl, the "at-risk girl," that other figure of late modern anxiety. But if her life circumstances (class or race especially) create obstacles to success in work, schooling, or consumption, any failure to achieve will be understood as a case of poor planning and personal irresponsibility, not of structural disadvantage. The notion of structured opportunity or disability, like the former safety net function of the liberal welfare state, has been superseded by a neoliberal world order centered ideologically on already liberated individuals.[50]

The claim for girlhood as a late modern social space in which neoliberal definitions of national and global citizenship are achieved finds a kind of echo in the activist organizations and bodies of writing associated with U.S. third-wave feminism. In the confusions of the immediate post–Cold War period, and like so many university intellectuals and public policy makers trying in those years to understand the rapid and uneven expansion of global free trade, third-wave young women beginning in about 1995 sought to narrate for themselves and older women their own feminist evolution as well as a collective sense of a generational political project. But they faced intergenerational problems: charges from second wavers that younger women were politically lazy and took for granted the feminist gains of the 1960s and 1970s; the mistaken conflation of their own feminisms with those of so-called postfeminism, the cultural dominant that sees the battle against sexism as won and therefore over.[51] It didn't help that young women's political coming of age occurred at the very same moment that young feminism itself (most notably "girl power" and feminist hip hop and punk) was appropriated by global mass media and turned into a depoliticized commodity. The anthology of first-person essays emerged as the most widely circulated genre that spoke to the anxiety of anticipated censure, yet holding on to characteristic generational shrewdness about the layered image battles at issue: Rebecca Walker's *To Be Real*, Barbara Findlen's *Listen Up!*, Ophira Edut's *Body Outlaws*, Daisy Hernández's and Bushra Rehman's *Colonize This!*, Vickie Nam's *YELL-Oh Girls!*[52] These set out such third-wave concerns as the fashioning of the self in relation to expanded global media, the contradictions of multiply located subjects, the problem of white racism for U.S. feminist coalition building, attention to sexuality and the body as they intersect with expanded pornography and beauty industries, and conversations between U.S. critical race studies and postcoloniality, global migration, and youth.

If, as arguments or political philosophy, this work could be said to be "in process," sometimes ill-informed in its characterizations of second-wave feminist politics, history, and ideals (the backlash against feminism circulating in global media contributed to third-wave confusions), still, the collective generational call was clear. There was an urgent need to understand the life contexts of these young women as quite distinct from those that had transformed their civil rights–influenced foremothers into feminists. Younger scholars like Leslie Heywood and Jennifer Drake made this case in *Third Wave Agenda*, as did Edne Garrison in an article in *Feminist Studies*.[53] One of the points at issue was the hyperimperative of the new social order to continually reinvent a flexible self. In the new global service economy, such self-packaging abilities represented a crucial skill set for workplace survival. If second-wavers saw in the third wave a politics of the self that was all personal and no political, this was not so much

7   Peace work at Maui Surfer Girls.

plainly wrong (though it required overlooking the classic as well as new forms of political engagement most were involved in) as a criticism that missed the point. The kinds of political paradigms that would need to be devised to exploit the more diffuse and constrained political opportunities of the present were under construction, and they brought home, ever more clearly, the political light years traveled in the interim.

Surfer Girls in the New World Order makes use of the claim for girlhood as a constitutive feature of the new global order and links it to third-wave calls for intergenerational conversation to frame a larger thesis about surfing girls' and women's politics. I concur with Harris and others that young women's new ways of doing politics may not be recognizable under older paradigms but that they nonetheless merit recognition as engaged. At the same time, they reflect the possibilities and limits of this era of globalized youth culture in which the market absorbs rebel youth styles and reorganizes power from the national to the global.[54] But if power has diffused globally, struggles over it show themselves in intensely localist ways.[55] The new world-space of global capital simultaneously grows more localized as it grows more globalized.[56] This study forwards the concept of "girl localism"—a feminist critical regionalism—as a way to merge theories of the Global Girl with those about the local/global dialectic.[57] For surfing girls, the realm of the "local" surf break and the social life of coastal towns in which breaks are situated is always in dialogue with the "global." Such has been the case, moreover, since the end of the Second World War. The concept of girl localism argues that girls and women surfers have brought critical perspective not just to norms of femininity but to understandings of the material places (oceans, beaches) in which counterfemininities are enacted. Girl localism provides one productive means of understanding how new forms of local/global political engagement occur both inside and outside conversations with more familiar forms of mobilized politics.[58] The political imaginations that have arisen from girls' local/global exchanges inform surfing as a global contemporary social movement with feminist environmental, pacifist, and antipoverty commitments in particular (fig. 7). Such imaginations underwrite surf subculture's efforts at what we might characterize as grassroots globalization, drawing from Arjun Appadurai's sense of the importance of vernacular attempts (like those of so many sub-cultural businesses) to meet the anxieties of the global through real-time actions that globalize from below.[59]

Alert to Walter Mignolo's reminder in *Local Histories/Global Designs* that only some local histories are in a position to imagine or implement global designs, my current project argues that there would *be* no glamour or cultural power to rhetorics of surfing without the simultaneous west-ern American meanings that have attached to surfing in the United States and without the historical ability of "America's West" to signal a colonial discourse about Western civilization.[60] Although the origins of modern surfing have distinct histories in nations like Australia, South Africa, Bra-zil, Japan, or Vietnam, and I could list others, surfing's status as a meta-phor depends on a renewable western American regional identity. Here the "western regional" must be understood as including the West's outermost horizons of California and, beyond it, colonized Hawaii, as well as the bor-der regions between Mexico and the United States.[61] What we might want to call regional identity more than ever travels the circuits of global capi-talism, suggesting to viewers and to consumers of durable and nondurable goods that they are engaged in the production of some kind of Western meaning. At the same time local contexts and environments play crucial roles in producing a range of subregional identities and social formations related to race, gender, nation, and so on, conditioning how people engage and disengage all matters related to the political. How, then, shall we make sense of these "everyday regionalisms," as Matt Herman wonderfully calls the structures of feeling and doing that get articulated through the performance of local/global vernaculars?[62]

Surfer Girls in the New World Order continues an argument I began in *Landscapes of the New West* about the concepts of place and space and their relation to gender, race, representation, and contemporary power.[63] I concluded *Landscapes* in a period when the concept of "the regional" had come to the fore of social theory because it suggested political and cultural formations in excess of the nation-state and described the new flux, flows, and frictions of global capital, technology, production, labor, people, and culture.[64] Regionalism in the 1990s became one way to map, according to Christopher Connery, "the materiality of new capitalist spaces."[65] For scholars working on representation and the American West, the innovation of regionalism as a critical category produced provocative openings related in particular to the theorization of postwestern identities and of transnational cultural forms. Neil Campbell conceptualized the twenty-first-century West as a Deleuzian or rhizomatic third space, an imaginative "home" not to settled notions of Western place as much as to its mutation across global media.[66] Stephen Tatum's work on Frederic Remington and western art as well as postwestern literature and theory addressed questions of being, knowing, community, and aesthetics in tension with contemporary technologies and colonial hauntings of western space.[67] Chad Allen's multilingual comparative work on western American Indian and Maori literary and activist texts clarified incompatibilities between global indigenous aesthetics and extant postcolonial theories.[68] The critical impulse shared by us all concerns the move away from notions of a western region as a subcategory of nation toward region or postregion as a power player in global political economies, activist movements, and media and aesthetic marketplaces.[69]

Surfing circulates in this historical moment as a postwestern or globalist keyword even as it invokes and retains familiar meanings linked to the regional or local American West. Consider, for instance, how familiar a *western* figure the surfer—including surfer girls—cuts across many media. Think about classic "old western" visual and cultural tropes such as the lone white male framed against a redemptive, unpeopled landscape. He might

8 South Padre Island, Texas.
Photograph by Kenny Braun.

be a mountain man or a pioneer overlooking "virgin" territories; cowboy riding into the cinematic distance against a backdrop of open range; or today, a solitary surfer against a seascape at sunset (fig. 8). Surfers are recent enactments of an older set of western characters who negotiated transitions to other new world orders. Such characters and the large and small dramas of empire they staged have traveled the world for nearly two hundred years producing profit and various knowledges about the borders of masculinity, femininity, and white racial formation in New World political economies.

With regard to racial formation, the subculture's renovation of white masculinity has sent surfers in global pursuit of "the perfect wave" for half a century now, establishing an international or diasporic surfing public along the way and with it, many a postcolonial conundrum.[70] To scholars of the American West these will prove familiar dilemmas.[71] The white western protagonist of so many cultural tales co-opts features of indigeneity (he "goes native") and becomes a border crosser to critique normative WASP discourse. But that process compromises the very places and people he admired and needed to formulate different visions of white manhood. Surfing's love affair with Hawaiian native manhood and islander "Aloha" spirit (and women) is no exception; neither are surf culture's forays into Mexico and its embrace of Mexican structures of everyday feeling and doing. The argument here goes to the structures of colonial and racialized feeling attached to western and California *spaces*, and to the historical and present-day global export of those structures of feeling to other places around the world.

By the same token—and here I may bring less political or critical pressure to bear than some readers wish—I would not dismiss these border-crossing efforts as mere appropriation, cultural primitivism, or racial masquerade. It makes no sense to condemn people for the contradictions they face, even while the responses charted in efforts to address contradictions must be held to account.[72] While it is true that surfing today as a world phenomenon is associated with privileged forms of whiteness, it is also true that the subculture's sympathy for nonwhite spatialities grew from its disaffection from and critique of mid-century U.S. racial formations and from its openness to alternative lifeways. White surfers have usually been in search of much more than perfect waves; they've been in pursuit of fundamentally better ways of everyday living, including living more interracial and flexibly gendered lives and with relative compatibility with the non-human natural world.

The double duty surfers perform in contemporary culture—invoking a familiar Western American iconographic past to comment on and intervene in a changed present—emerges most tangibly in the figure of the white California surfer*girl*. If the trope of the singular figure in contest with the depopulated western wild is one we might read as typically productive of individualist, imperial, and masculinist national subjectivity, what happens when we now put in place instead the figure of the youthful *female* surfer? Her appearance as the subject, not the object, of these masculinist visual economies suggests that even wilderness ("extreme" landscapes)—the ultimate proving ground of the national masculine past—are open to young female navigation. Heir not only to the pioneer's or cowboy's rugged individualism but also to the pioneer *woman*'s or cow*girl*'s scrappy toughness, the girl who can surf knows historic opportunity when she sees it and takes pride in being no man's fragile flower. At the same time we must remember that the western woman's relationship to histories of empire is comparatively tentative. She is dragged into "the adventure," trailing behind the men. While her ambivalence in no way disqualifies the privileges of race and citizenship she embodies or exploits on the nineteenth-century frontier, the political imaginations of westering women should not be conflated uncritically with those of men.[73] Such distinctions, with many caveats, find analogies in the present.

So far I have conceptualized girl localism as a constellation of critical femininities that evolve in tandem with critical sensibilities related to specific materialities—like surf breaks. I will continue to use the concept in this catchall way to describe a process of political consciousness formation related both to gender and to local/global place. But social dynamics involving race relations and critical whiteness operate through the notion of girl localism as well, for it describes how female-gendered versions of the "western local" travel elsewhere, by no means traveling light, and then root, adapt. Sometimes these performances of the western local meet challenges from other girl localisms. In the exchanges between groups, conflicts over race and coloniality sharpen. Sometimes local female surf communities have not developed to a point where a collective pushback occurs against the arrival of the western local, and in such cases the new twenty-first-century social formations under construction show all the power struggles and radical disjunctions of life on the ground of the new world order. Of course all the various subtribes of male surfers also exist on the ground and must be negotiated.

If girl localism denotes a self-conscious gender location in relation to specific places, let me forward a parallel concept, "related-locals," which suggests most broadly how the social imagination informing the subculture conceives of being in place. In the world map of surfing, the regard for or contest over any singular local place will be understood against the whole, meaning the set of "related local" surf spots that characterize surfers' sense of a planet of local/global surfing breaks. The language of related locals names for this project how we might talk about place or the local in an era of traveling cultures. As Clifford argues, "place" in late modernity involves mobility, dwelling, and the translations between them.[74] Indeed, since the mid-twentieth century, surfers' everyday culture of the local has been imaginatively formed in the spirit of the translocal: Malibu linked to Rincon (Santa Barbara), linked to Waikiki (Hawaii), to Jeffrey's Bay (South Africa), to Burleigh Heads (Australia). Surfing's earliest and most identifiably "local" of surf legends—native Hawaiian Duke Kahanamoku of Waikiki Beach, the father of modern surfing who in the 1920s popularized the sport on the U.S. mainland and in Australia—is revered as Hawaii's ambassador to the world.[75] Contemporary global surf subculture conceives of itself in the vein of a diasporic traveling culture of peoples who have been scattered about the world by corrupt economic forces that have ruined their homeland (local surf breaks) and left them reluctant if inventive exiles. This diasporic sense of place is mobile, busy, and constituted, as Clifford would have it, as much by displacement as by dwelling. Yet I want to point out that the stories that have set the diaspora into motion, those stories that relate local places to one another and that create the backbone logic of today's global subculture, were born very explicitly in the Cold War militarist contexts linking Southern California and Hawaii. The process of place affinity at work in this project is thus quite local, at the same time that the very sense of local occurs across larger global and transregional networks that are economic, military, cultural, technological, gendered, generational, and touristic.

Nowhere is the concept of related locals and their global articulations more influentially on display than in the subculture's premier canonical text, the film *The Endless Summer* (1966).[76] Produced as a furious if unconscious rebuke to the crowding of surf breaks and the popularization of surfing as a sport and lifestyle following the popular film *Gidget* (1958) and the popular genre of Beach Blanket movies it set in motion, *The Endless Summer* took the subculture's troubles on the road. In addition to narrating the larger global subculture as it would ultimately unfold with Malibu as its point of origin, the film laid down the founding trade routes for the massive expansion of surfing activities from the mid-1960s to the late 1980s. From the cinematic surfari grew economic networks and social relations as transnational cottage industries—selling boards, other equipment, travel information, lodging, ground and water transportation, local water know-how and so on—formed to service the new markets created by the film and its eccentric clientele. All the social exchanges these processes require created, piecemeal, the infrastructure of surfing as an eventual extensive internationalist public culture. Such networks came to bear all the more powerfully once the international professional tour was established in 1976. It is not too much to say that *The Endless Summer* produced both the initial economy and the foundational structures of feeling that today underwrite surfing as an international public culture of some 6 million participants.[77] To be truly "inside" the subculture, surfers must demonstrate some working sense of surfing's important places, of its related locals.

Who are these several million travelers? They are most likely to come from places with very developed water cultures: 2 million each from the

United States (especially California) and Australia, 1 million from Brazil, 750,000 from Japan, and sizeable groups from New Zealand (100,000), France (80,000), South Africa (50,000), the United Kingdom and Mexico (30,000 each).[78] The surf spots they seek are often elsewhere—Bali, for example, has tens of thousands of annual surf visitors but only about 1,000 native surfers. Coming from all walks of life, surfers no longer fulfill the stereotype of the unemployable "bum." They might be rock stars, professionals, tradespeople, pink-collar workers, students, young people not yet obliged to work, or those who work less to surf more. About 15 percent were estimated in 2002 to be female (I believe these to be inflated numbers, but doubtless female surfing is up from less than 5 percent in the late 1990s).[79] The age of surfers spans the life cycle. Their politics run the spectrum, though it would be rare for someone to disclaim environmentalism. Most surfers, as I already noted, are white. The majority have daytime jobs. But those who form the core of the subculture are often employed in one of the surf industry's many microeconomies—industry profits from the early 1980s to the end of the decade went from tens of millions to $2 billion dollars; by 2002 they soared to $4.5 billion, and by 2006 to $7.5 billion.[80] In the economic downturn of 2008–9, industry sales figures remained remarkably stable with but a slight dip in 2008.[81] Men and women alike have followed "subcultural careers" (as McRobbie designates such labor niches) since the 1950s.[82] They have opened surf shops and schools, designed new technologies and lifestyle products related to surfing, founded magazines and film or video companies, created photography portfolios, and built whole resort communities. New digital technologies have reinforced this trend and allowed surfers to further engage in subcultural work and global mobility.[83] Benefits of subcultural employment have always been flextime for surf and travel between local breaks and elsewhere. The best surfers work the global competitive circuit as professionals—Kelly Slater, surfing's premier competitor, reportedly brings in $1 million annually. Others globetrot the surf circuit for periods of their lives, as do, for example, the five surf instructors at Las Olas in Sayulita.

What social formations and political imaginations have come out of such movements between related places? Are surfers expatriates, nomads, tourists, venture capitalists, or global citizens? And what kind of group formation characterizes subcultural identity today, in an era of fragmentation and individualization, as opposed to subcultural life before neoliberalism? Subcultural studies in recent conversation with global theory has changed its understanding of subcultural affiliation, using the language of "scapes," "neotribes," "networks," and "scenes" to describe the relatively more diffuse social identities and structures of the present.[84] Of particular relevance to this project are the findings and theorizations of Irena Guidikova and Lasse Siurala who see in postcolonial youth music subcultures in Europe new forms of citizenship, social spaces for the debate of issues, imagined alternative lifeworlds that enable the performance of transitional politics in alternative public spheres.[85] So, in response to the above question about surfers as expatriates, nomads, and the like, the provisional answer is, yes, to some degree they are all of these. But most often surfers travel the world today as subcultural workers according to a logic resembling global citizenship. Surfing gives citizenship geographical dimension ("homelands" are surf breaks), political coherence (global green politics as a shared philosophy), and a ready-made group of generally like-minded citizen-friends. If this claim for surfers as global citizens stretches credulity given that the image of surfers-on-surfari might as easily call to mind bad boys on a global romp, we should not forget that to be inside *any* subculture is to be subject to a variety of disciplining communal standards.

In surfing the most fundamental communal ethics have to do with "surf etiquette"—a system of widely observed subcultural rules that I forward here as a bill of rights and responsibilities of global surf citizenship. At first glance, surf etiquette has to do with rights of way in the water: don't surf alone; relinquish the right of way to the surfer deeper into the wave; share waves; help surfers in distress; keep the beach green.[86] But surf etiquette also governs social relations in the water. In a general context of crowds, surf etiquette adjudicates pecking order and attempts to control environmental health. Before there were crowds, what surfers call "the spirit of Aloha" structured group behavior. Hawaii still centers surfing's social imagination as both a geography of specific surf spots and a *cultural* geography characterized by individual generosity and community service, as well as knowledge of nonhuman nature.[87] As a map to surfing's unconscious, surf etiquette suggests a deeply localist politics, deferential to locals' priority rights of access. Such localism is globalist in its conception for it aims to redress the postcolonial conundrums of a subculture built on expansion and growth.

Indeed, surfing has changed, lessons have been learned, and today its public causes are many. The biggest is the environment—and the initiatives and organizations running through the surf world seem countless. The Surfrider Foundation alone has sixty U.S. chapters and branches in seven nations.[88] But "advocacy" also has been redefined. Some for-profit businesses, like Patagonia, provide products as much as they sponsor educational projects with social missions funded by profits.[89] Others, like the Indonesian surf ecoresort Nihiwatu, on the island of Sumba near Bali, have funneled profits into humanitarian initiatives for children's health, education, and clean water.[90] Joining forces with the "responsible tourism" movement to use tourism as an economic development tool that might combat poverty and foster peace and conflict resolution in areas of political instability, ecofriendly commerce is *the* industry trend.[91]

Yet it may be in its less officially political dimensions that surfing has made its deepest impact on the long-term development of alternative lifeways. Always a path for living the everyday *differently*, surfing implicates lifestyle behaviors in oppositional politics. In the reproduction of subcultural life, surfing from the beginning has been an *onshore* practice performed amid the communities in which surfers go about daily life. Surfers' investments in various world places might have begun as bohemian rebellion, an "adventure" and love affair of sorts that landed rebels in this or that place in part by expedient accident. But these loves have turned out to be not so accidental—no one-night or one-summer stands after all. Connections to surf breaks have translated into specific kinds of links to the towns, cities, and ecosystems in which surf breaks are located. Surfers-as-community have found themselves linked, by way of the global subculture, to place-based surfing communities elsewhere. In the transnational communities surfers have created, they bring together a loosely organized set of mobile identities and special interests that make up one kind of international civil society that can be brought to bear on specific political struggles over water quality, public health, coastal development, sustainable tourism, humanitarian aid, and even battles against al-Qaeda.[92]

Such efforts work from a savvy sense of the local, one always tied to other global/local places and their political contexts and formations, which Arif Dirlik characterizes via the term "critical localisms."[93] By claiming actual places in the world, banding together with others in attempts to define the sociality of those spaces and defending those socialities, forwarding them as better than those of the overworked, unsustainable mainstream, subcultural sociality of the past fifty years has turned out to actually be *about* something tangible. Surf culture has found itself implicated in non-surf issues, and in the tension and translations between the sociality of these related places, a new global/local politics has become possible.

We are at a crossroads on the ground on which global/local political imaginations can be built. Too much contemporary thought about "the political" continues to be nostalgic for oppositional strategies formulated to address the welfare state and made famous by the global civil rights movements of the 1960s. Surf culture was never self-consciously beholden to these political imaginations, enabling it to implement new political practices when global restructuring began. The way surfing as a subculture "does politics" today has everything to do with the changed macro- and political-economic contexts of globalization, as well as with the changed functions of the local in a globalist marketplace. Put simply, surf subculture makes money. The presence of surfing and surfers in many global coastal places draws the revenue of not only or even especially surfers but that of people for whom surfing is tourist spectacle. That is, surfing, for nonsurfers, is a spectator sport. As such, surf subculture and its own productions of the local today provide sources of economic *value* both to the state and to global economies.[94] Political concessions related particularly to the environment have been leveraged from that new location. Like other subcultural movements (hip hop comes to mind), surfing should be understood as neither a simple continuation nor betrayal of previous subcultures, countercultures, or social movements. Especially the differences, as Alain Touraine has noted about subcultural politics more generally in *Can We Live Together*, issue from the questions: To whom, in a neoliberal world, is political grievance addressed?[95] The state? The global economy? In an environment in which reform has become more challenging, what protest strategies prove effective?

Such questions seem especially timely to girls. The absence of a dominating civil rights identity to surf subcultural politics has no doubt been one reason why surf culture has magnetized younger people's attention. For them, civil rights political imaginations appear dated—they represent the political and coming-of-age contexts of their parents, teachers, and other authority figures who tell them what politics "should be." Born after 1960 and 1980, respectively, Generation X and Generation Y are the children of postmodernity in the sense in which Jameson uses the term to name the official hip culture of late capitalism and its affects of irony, distancing, and fleeting intensities.[96] They came of age during the years of an emergent and then consolidated neoliberal ideological transformation of the planet. Many civil rights–inspired politics and identities of resistance arrived at their doorsteps already normalized: feminism is official discourse, nonwhite racial pride is the Disney Channel's everyday, deconstruction is passé since contingency is all that's ever been, sexuality is another niche market. This constitutes the dominant reality for girls in the First World, and if second-wave feminists are to be committed to younger women's liberation, a cross-generational feminist politics of the present must recognize this reality and find new ways to fashion a response to it.

The figure of the surfer girl has the potential to teach older feminists much about the current conditions of girlhood in the First World, and these conditions, as well as a better understanding of them by older feminists, make for urgent matters. Anyone actively close to young women can see that girlhood has become a public topic in North America, Australia, and the United Kingdom like never before. A business such as the Mexican surf camp Las Olas, with its call to a reverse finishing school makeover in which women become girls, makes cultural sense only in this larger context. Young women athletes (surfer girls serving as the case in point) should not be dismissed, especially not by feminists, in attempts to formulate a response to the challenges of neoliberalism for feminist activism. Even if these young women do not claim the political designation "feminist," they should face neither dismissal nor criticism. Instead, new cross-generational conversations and activisms must be developed that speak to the places at which women struggle against current forms of sexism, but also against "feminism" as it has come to be popularly represented. Until second-wavers learn to speak effectively to the fact that young women often see feminism as a discourse of gender surveillance, a self-defeating political generation gap will persist.

I began this introduction via my ethnographic work in Sayulita because it shows interesting moments of intergenerational female solidarity even as U.S. women's surfaris in Mexico pose tangled dilemmas about efforts to globalize from below. Surfing has claimed many homes over the past fifty years, but only recently have any of them been places where, as one magazine article approvingly noted about Sayulita, "women rule."[97] Of course feminist scholars will want to know, which women? Do the place-claims of surfers displace other place-claims (Gringo Hill comes to mind)? If so, when and why do locals find it in their interests to consent? Is "consent" an appropriate language if no alternative exists? What does it mean that women as a group, not just the rare individual, now might go on surfari or run capitalized businesses dependent on female travel? Do *women's* travels and the trope of the surfer girl, to revise Clifford a bit, suggest the comings and goings of an unfinished female modernity? And how might we measure improvements to women's lives when female surf activism so regularly embraces essentialist discourse (women's "natural" caretaking tendencies applied to the environment) to create political consciousness?

I will address such questions in what follows by way of many women and girls from different social, geographical, and age locations, all of whom are called at this moment in history into the discourse or category of "girl." Already we have encountered a toddler and a preadolescent, as well as adolescent girls and young women. We will encounter others soon: tourists on surfari, gray-haired surf "pioneers," professionals whose pictures in fashion and sports media advertise a Western-world version of femininity beyond the limits of sexism. There will be entrepreneurs, globetrotters, aloof soul surfers, activists, and legions of the anonymous rank and file. Clearly, however, as the questions above suggest, exclusions and hierarchical selection processes order the evolving story of contemporary subcultural life. The question of which women "rule" Sayulita bends toward questions about which girls count or don't count in discussions of girlhood. Not all girls or women today are called to this dominant, can-do girl formation. These, too, will be encountered—the not-blonde surfers, the girls and women of internationalist surf towns whose maternal or other gendered duties, whose poverty and burdens of everyday labor, make the self-development philosophy embedded in neoliberal girl discourse seem a joke or a Hollywood fantasy.

I would also alert readers to methodological and tonal differences that will become apparent as the chapters progress. I move from theory, history, and textual analysis increasingly toward ethnography. These different argumentative registers and style conventions no doubt contribute to a certain restraint I discovered as I moved through my own evaluation of my subject matter, which eventually included an extended cast of real and living characters. A few of them made it clear that, especially regarding issues of lesbian sexuality, they wished their privacy to be respected. The first part, "California Goes Global," takes up the export of the western local and considers its global designs via Hawaii's Cold War militarization and then, more recently, via the work of the "California girl" to embody idealized global femininities. I lay out the framing gender formation of surfing subculture across two historical moments—the mid-twentieth century and the present. At the center of this part of the book is the Gidget legacy, because the "true inside" of surfing subculture, I argue, has been constructed repeatedly in and through it. Working from films, magazines, novels, and ethnographic materials, as well as from feminist and globalization theory, chapters 1 and 2 chart the subculture's evolving implication in global security matters, alternative gender, emerging social change and girl power, issues of embodiment in everyday life, and local/global networks. Girl localism is revealed both as a product manufactured by the surf industry to create female markets and as a feminist politics formulated by on-the-ground girls which answers industry "bikini babe" images with personal skepticism, public retort, or coordinated counterattack. Girl localism implements a body politics of strength and courage, an ecopolitics blending stewardship with social justice issues of public health, and a vision of subcultural labor as a site of female possibility and flourishing.

The second part of the book, "Globalization from Below," spins out, in multi-sited contexts, institutionalized expressions of the subculture—businesses, organizations, foundations, initiatives—that enact what I have called "new" new social movement intentions. By way of these institutions I map cross-generational conversations about work, play, and sexuality. Chapter 3 pulls the Mexican townswomen and girls of Sayulita into ethnographic conversation with mainly non-Mexican surf staff and campers and the related local surf communities of San Diego and the Bay Area. The ethnographies survey, from varied transnational perspectives, the predicaments and possibilities of Las Olas as an ecofeminist and girl-powered instance of globalization from below. If the girl localism of Las Olas in chapter 3 is best understood against more heavy-capital attempts to develop Sayulita as a First World tourist destination, so too are the girl localisms of California surf shops in chapter 4 best understood against the arrival of the global surf industry (and the return of the western local transformed by its global travels) to surf-intensive communities like Santa Cruz and San Diego. This chapter situates a study of two female-focused surf shops, one in Northern and the other in Southern California, in the larger context of the consolidation of the global surf industry. The feminist projects of these shops have come under heavy assault, I argue, putting at risk the important generational transfers of regionalist knowledge and alternative gendered visual economies these shops facilitate. Taking stock of surfing as global big business, chapter 5 asks about what is next for girl localisms. How might feminist work in the future be staged through critical localist girl movements? With an eye toward suggesting work on girl localist networks and political sites of the future, this chapter comparatively considers strong communities in the Hawaiian islands founded by established women surfers against emergent communities in Bali, nurtured principally by surf-industry giants. Bringing the legacy of Gidget to the fore of our understanding of "surfing the new world order" indexes not just a half century of subcultural development but also a larger process regarding the relation of non-normative gender identities to global decolonization, world wars, and the current war on terror, as well as to feminism and its uneven reconstitution within the global economic restructuring activities of the past twenty years.

As a multiply signifying rhetoric, a traveling subculture, and a cosmopolitan recreational and social practice, surfing is fully implicated, indeed serves as a linchpin, in the larger imaginative process by which globalization has rushed into twenty-first-century everyday life and speech. Emblematic of contemporary pleasures and agencies, surfing maps wave-riding leisure activities conducted in the liminal offshore spaces of nation-states, while also mapping a world in which mobility and migration, as well as post national cultural border crossing, constitutes a given and a positive value for peoples of various genders, ages, classes, races, and national origins. None of the above analogies to ocean surfing would be culturally viable were there no actual subculture of surfing on whose edgy identity and popular rebel history an emergent discourse could build. Though some other rhetoric surely could have worked as well, surfing has served as a vernacular lens in the evolving thematics of globalization. Its subcultural life has expressed features of globalization that are both "out there," as are the world financial markets, as well as "in here," meaning everyday life experienced in tension with altered structural circumstances.[98] Performing new ways of being and doing, new forms of political subjectivity, surf culture articulates the unevenness of the local/global dialectic, its continuing postcolonial conundrums. It identifies and exploits political openings.

Part I. California Goes Global

One

Californians in Diaspora

The Making of a Local/Global Subculture

Many [baby boomers] fondly remember their California
childhoods, regardless of whether they grew up in the state.
—Kirse Granat May, *Golden State, Golden Youth*

When the fictional surfer girl Franziska Lawrence is nicknamed
"Gidget" and admitted to the all-male Malibu crew in 1957, nobody
imagines this term of fond condescension (it means girl midget)
will grow into a way to think about the history or politics of local
and global surfing. This chapter works history backwards, so to
speak, through the *Gidget* novels and films that initially popularized surfing as lifestyle and identity, and by way of them looks to
actual teenage surfing girls in the 1950s of whom Gidget (or Kathy
Kohner) became representative. I am interested in historical contexts and mid-century versions of girl localism. While I attend in
some detail to subcultural masculinity, attributing women surfers' own alternative femininities in some measure to its inspiration and example, the intention is not to construct a bohemian,
beatnik, or surfy version of male history to then have someplace
from which to narrate female historical presence or agency. Prior
to the first *Gidget* novel in 1957, gendered power struggles, a kind
of leering anger at women in the water, did not characterize subcultural identity or behavior as sharply as it would thereafter.[1] Before the arrival of missionaries, ancient Hawaiians had surfed for
pleasure, religious ritual, competitive sport, and (in the case of the
royals) to court one another. Queens as much as kings were renowned for their surfing prowess—and the subculture thrived on
such lore.[2] But in a flash point of change, practically overnight,
popularization altered the subculture and its Hawaiian-derived

gender formation. Surfing's pre-Gidget "golden age" of harmony and co-operation were over. Gidget in all its/her implications locates the moving center of these changes.

Crowds. More than any other outrage, it was crowds glutting the favorite breaks (Malibu much mourned) that set in motion both the need and the conditions of possibility for the creation of subcultural magazines, artwork, and cinema. Crowds motivated the search for new "virgin" global surf spots and produced, eventually, a global public. No single cultural text did more to invent an "us" and a "them," a subcultural inside and outside than *The Endless Summer* (1966), southern Californian Bruce Brown's answer of sorts to *Gidget*. *The Endless Summer* made explicit what was at least one con-clusion of *Gidget*; it offered a response to crowds. Flee, *The Endless Summer* suggested as a solution. Escape, relocate, travel. Transport the western-local scene elsewhere. Imagining a series of places where surf and sun were easily available, a new dream took shape—the "surfari"—that ministered to the social pressures suggested by crowds.

It was a desperate solution. But the search for an endless summer was always about much more than waves. At mid-century, California ranked among the most coveted of national addresses: homeland to youth, orange blossoms, postwar opportunity, glamour. Few Californians left the prom-ised land without permanent ambivalence, a sense of betrayal or forced exile. Indeed, imaginations of exile have played winning hands in form-ing the cultural logic of surfing's global public. We see in the aftermath of *The Endless Summer* the out-movement of diasporic scattering. Californians in exile from crowds, seaside traffic, and suburban sprawl: the homeland spoiled, a paradise now in memory only. If the dream was invented by one generation of young, mostly white Californian men, the larger enactment of it was undertaken by another and for both groups of men the motivation was not so much adventure (though that was always on the surface) but despair. What goes under the sign of "crowds" for this generation of young baby boomers, and how did surfing the globe answer it? To what degree has the reappearance of surfing at the turn of the twenty-first century per-mitted a return to these questions?

One of the most difficult things to study in U.S. society is middle-class culture and its discontents. Barbara Ehrenreich some years ago named one mid-century discourse of discontent a battle for "the hearts of men."[3] The "hearts" to which she refers concern masculine social purpose, as well as physical health and well-being—both of which were popularly understood, Ehrenreich shows, as under assault from the gray-suit ideals of postwar manhood. Ehrenreich reads into this discourse a large permission for men to flee commitment to others. As I see it, surf subculture of the 1950s understood itself as a player in that battle. The subculture served as an everyday locus for struggles over the expectation that male coming-of-age meant lives organized around breadwinning for a nuclear family. Ehrenreich's *The Hearts of Men* persuasively argues for the dire implications of that battle for homemaking women and for children whose life possibilities depended on the family wage. Yet my work in this chapter on mid-century subcultural battles over manhood comes at the male-female power imbalance differently, since surfing women generally saw in subcultural revisions of male gender roles an expansion of gender norms related to femininity. Further, alternative subcultural masculinity has always been tied to the production of a rebel girl discourse and to actual rebel girls. That is, the alternative femininity of the surfer girl enabled countermasculinities.

I begin by way of what surfers consider "the scene of the crime," meaning surfing's initial popularization in the late 1950s. I bring critical attention to the *Gidget* novels and films—fictionalized tales based on the efforts of Kohner ("Gidget") to surf and join the iconic Malibu crew—that initially publicized surfing as lifestyle and identity.[4] Ethnographic materials I have collected from women surfers of this period expand the evidence of surfing's mid-century gender formations. By way of ethnography and of *Gidget* and its formulation of the beach bum "Kahoona" figure, I then approach subcultural masculinity and its most canonized artifact of alternative masculine purpose: *The Endless Summer*. My ultimate interest is not (as the Beach Boys sang) "surfing in the U.S.A.," however, but the gender and racial formations generated by the influential local Southern California subcultural scene, their export to other world places, and their eventual evolution into something else, something altered and differently "local" in new locations. In later chapters I consider the political imaginations and social activisms that have emerged by way of this local/global movement. But here I set the stage, detailing the specific problems that would lead to the critical localist consciousness pervasive in local/global surf culture today and into which girl localism offers such an important intervention. These problems have to do with how surfers understood work and history, the kinds of non-academic educations they valued and pursued, and the everyday culture and social geography of the many relatively sleepy beach towns up and down the coast of Southern California (Malibu being the exception) out of which the global subculture grew.

The *Gidget* Legacy

Women's history most often tells the story of contemporary women's liberation through "bright and committed" young activists, Freedom Rides to register voters in the American South, Students for a Democratic Society (SDS), and northeastern feminist "cells" like Redstockings or the Combahee River Collective.[5] Reliable tellers of women's liberation tales will include these political players and events in the overall representation of feminist consciousness, practice, and history. For this chapter, however, we must begin by noticing that the historical memories invoked through such supposedly reliable narratives pose problems for identifying, and understanding, the politics of surfer girls. As the official or most canonized memories of second-wave feminism, they typically do not put us in the mind of the countercultural rebellion happening on the West Coast, a movement with likely several thousand times more members. Nor of top-down radical civil rights reforms enacted by Congress or the Supreme Court,[6] nor, perhaps most unthinkable to veteran civil rights activists then and now, does it speak to the impact of changing images in television and film on viewers' performance of gender, racial, sexual, and class identities.[7] To fathom the story of female liberation told here, we will need to steer clear of a mandate to be committed only to "the bright and committed." By contrast, I imagine rebel female history through the Gidget phenomenon, a televised B-movie and "body phenomenon" that might seem to indicate the height of the nonbright, the noncommitted.

My discussion of Gidget and what clearly are Cold War ideological projects framing her as a female icon and historical figure grows from the recent post–Cold War fascination with surfing that we observe in popular culture in many parts of the world. The hallmark of surfing's global renaissance is often visualized via girls and women; the phenomenon of women in surfing makes news. Women far more often than men appear in newspaper visuals reporting on what's different or interesting, what has changed, or what is possible and should be celebrated. As consumers and influential ideas people, women are seen to have jump-started the renais-

9 Sandra Dee as Gidget (1958).

sance by providing new markets, products, and business leadership.[8] A young women's surf video is local news,[9] women's international surf camps are travel news,[10] women's surf shops sponsoring women's surf films are arts and entertainment news,[11] moms who surf are special interest news,[12] a teenage girl who surfs competitively again after losing a limb to a tiger shark is all-category news.[13] If surfing wants to be part of the current news cycle (and it does), it has found itself invested like never before in recovering and promoting the history of women's surfing. Women's history sells.

In this flurry of media, commercial, and public history activity, Gidget has reentered the American vernacular, appearing in many guises. The first, and continuing, Gidget is *not* the real life surfer girl of the 1950s, Kathy "Gidget" Kohner Zuckerman, a skiing, tennis-playing, "nice Jewish girl from Brentwood" as she has often been quoted describing herself, who today works as a hostess in a Los Angeles restaurant, but the film character Gidget played by Sandra Dee in 1958 (fig. 9). This cinematic Gidget's adventures were adapted to the screen by the real Gidget's father Frederick Kohner, a Czech Jewish former professor of psychology at the University of Vienna who left Europe for Hollywood as Nazism spread. Kohner became a Hollywood screenwriter and penned this first novel drawing on his daughter's summertime adventures with the legendary all-male Malibu crew of the 1950s. That novel, reissued in 2001 with a foreword by Zuckerman as "the real Gidget herself," initially sold over a million copies and spawned seven additional Gidget novels reprinted in ten languages during the following decade:[14] *Cher Papa* (1960), *Gidget Goes Hawaiian* (1961), *Gidget Goes to Rome* (1963), *The Affairs of Gidget* (1963), *Gidget In Love* (1965), *Gidget Goes Parisienne* (1966), and concluding with *Gidget Goes New York* (1968) (fig. 10). Under such titles as "female surf bum," *The New York Times*, among others, reviewed *Gidget* favorably.[15]

But in visual culture Gidget left her most lasting cultural imprint. After the monumental success of the first novel and film, the film sequel *Gidget Goes Hawaiian* followed, which in turn inspired the spate of 1960s Beach Blanket films and fueled the popular musical career of the Beach Boys. On television, ABC debuted the comedy *Gidget* starring Sally Field in 1965 and tried again in the mid-1980s with *The New Gidget*. Other Gidget-related cultural productions have appeared over the years, including *Gidget* the comic book, made-for-TV movies, even a novelistic rant about overcrowded breaks titled *Gidget Must Die: A Killer Surf Novel*.[16] In 1997 the surfer girl magazine *Wahine* proclaimed, referring to the novel, "Gidget Turns Forty!"[17] The article also featured a story about Kohner Zuckerman (fig. 11). Also in 1997 *Surfer* magazine named Gidget the seventh most influential surfer (and the most important woman) in the history of the sport. Kohner Zuckerman herself in 1999 founded a Gidget line of postcards.[18] In 2000 Francis Ford Coppola cowrote *Gidget: The Musical*, a short-lived but sold-out theatrical production casting mainly unknown actors but including Dermot Mulroney as Kahoona. Coppola hopes to see it produced again (perhaps on Broadway) before making it a film.[19] And of course the original *Gidget* films continue in frequent reruns on TBS and elsewhere.

The point here is that as an actual person, an iconic figure of popular culture, or as both, Gidget is indexed not just everywhere in surf media but well beyond it, so much so that a 248-page reference book, *Cowabunga! Gidget Goes Encyclopedic*, appeared in 2001.[20] In discussions of surfing as a subculture *or* as a metaphor, there is no escaping the Gidget legacy, nor

10   The Gidget novels.

11.1 Wahine celebrates Gidget (1997).

11.3 First edition 1957 (reissued 2001).

11.2 Kathy "Gidget" Kohner Zuckerman, Los Angeles, 2001.

should feminist intellectuals permit themselves to dismiss it or evade its complex implications. "A lot of good came from Gidget" reported Jericho Poppler Bartlow, a cofounder of the Women's International Surfing Association (wisa) and a member of surfing's hall of fame.[21] Debbie Beacham, the 1982 women's surf champion, taught herself to surf after she watched Field as Gidget on television.[22] Matt Warshaw, the most prolific and best of surfing's popular historians, calls Gidget an "Eisenhower-era feminist."[23] And linking the mid-century with more recent surf developments for women, the Gidget encyclopedia begins with the emphatic, "Gidget became a teenage spokesperson for 'women's lib' . . . or should that be GIRL POWER!"[24] One teenage girl actually approached Kohner Zuckerman recently, after she had given a talk at the University of California, San Diego, on surf history, to stammer, teary-eyed, "you are my hero."[25]

On the Gidget legacy's moving foundation rests an ideology of female freedom, one based on bodily strength and perseverance, an ability to stand up to male threats, and the joy and power of athletic accomplishments realized in spite of sexist intimidation or distractions. Then and now Gidget as iconography encourages young women to script their bodies according to a narrative of female persistence, courage, and risk-taking. It writes them as *subjects* rather than objects of California beach stories—a revision of the social geography represented in Tom Keck's widely published photo of Mike Turkington surfing Oahu's west side in 1963 (fig. 12). In Gidget discourse, girls appear in a critical relationship to ideologies of gender and place, evidencing girl localism. Given what feminists know today about the importance of female sport and physical power to women's and girls' sense of competence and their ability to fight for themselves and other women, it should be possible to revisit the Gidget legacy and perceive in it the making of a bohemian female outdoorswoman and, by implication, to appreciate its importance to the history of the women's movement and the radicalization of postwar consciousness about women's social place.

Let me offer here a reading of the first *Gidget* film, one informed by the early *Gidget* novels. I work against the scanty critical opinion on the topic, which sees the film as evidence of Cold War normative femininity at its most contained, and none of which either mentions or is interested in the *Gidget* novel series, actual subcultural life, or the historical young woman who shouldered the popularization.[26] I will focus less on exhaustive readings than on forwarding my argument about the production of subcul-

12 Women watching a man. Tom Keck's classic shot of Mike Turkington at Yokohama Bay on Oahu's west side, 1963.

tural masculinity and its inseparability from the *Gidget* phenomenon—the emergence of a female rebel girl discourse is one of its crucial conditions of possibility. Moreover, *Gidget* is as much invested in producing what I see as an Americanized version of male European bohemianism (indebted as we will see to mid-century Beat culture) as it is in representing rebellious female athleticism. *Gidget* lays out the initial script of subcultural manhood, offers a set of talking points, and forwards a useable masculine past. *The Endless Summer* will then take what is implicitly the Kahoona type and will retool and systematize him, name his desire "surf surfari," and plot that desire's geographic coordinates along grids that eventuate in an international surfing circuit.

The film *Gidget* of 1958 concludes with its heroine (Dee) dancing on the shoreline, happily matched with one of the love objects she has desired over the course of the tale, Moondoggie (James Darren). She wears a party dress and twirls about the shore in a carefree, rapturous splendor. We might well assume that whatever opening the film has produced for athletic flat-chested young women has just been effectively contained. But this is not the all of it. Yes, Gidget has been removed from the water as an able surfer and appears on the brink of her female initiation into a prescribed relationship with the state, that of the consuming mother of a nuclear Cold War family. But if Gidget is not figured atop her board, neither do we see her within the domestic frame of the suburban home at movie's end, as is implicitly her mother. Gidget remains out of doors, playing at the edge of national femininity, dancing, twirling, embodied.

I owe part of my reading of the film's ending to my reading of the original novel's conclusion.[27] Both tales resolve by the consummation of a romance plot: Gidget is pinned to Moondoggie. But the novel, even while it realizes a romance plot, also subverts it. Moondoggie's pin provides Gidget relief from answering the "do you have a boyfriend?" question obsessively posed by her female peers who have "a few more inches upwards and sideways" (154). That is, being officially pinned frees Gidget from the gender norms and peer pressure enforced by *other girls* so that she can enact instead a different kind of femininity. The final page of the text proclaims Gidget's "big love is still out Malibuways with some bitchen surf going" (154). Gidget second-guesses the truth of her feelings for each of the text's male love objects and contrasts those "maybe" feelings with this statement: "But with the board and the sun and the waves it was for real" (154). In a text quite concerned with a young woman's coming of age, with being a woman in love, Gidget concludes: "Maybe I was just a woman in love with a surfboard" (154). This conclusion vindicates the repeated scenes of male hazing and harassment that Gidget has confronted in her efforts to learn to surf. She has won the battle to establish a female presence in very male social spaces on terms that concern her physical and mental abilities, not how she looks in a bikini. Girl localism is taking root. Gidget now owns a part of herself that women are routinely encouraged to underestimate or give up.

What is so telling about the Gidget novels as a series is their general disregard of the nation's Cold War "need" for mothers and soldiers. Often the rhetoric of Cold War aggression appears quite parodically. Several novels in their different opening gambits explicitly figure Cold War contexts. *Gidget*, for example, offers a description of a bay next to the Malibu pier, "where the waves coming from Japan crush against the shore like some bitchen rocket bomb" (2). In *Cher Papa*, the second book in the series, we learn that Gidget's family goes to the ski town of Sun Valley, "a yearly ritual in our family, come hell or sputnik."[28] The state of the nation and national discourse certainly are at issue in both texts; the opening scene of *Gidget* pivots on young Francie's humiliated rescue at sea by Moondoggie on the fourth of July.

But Gidget's response to the serious business of fighting the Cold War is to play. She surfs, skis, swims, laughs, kisses, cuddles. She longs. This a world that revolves around "some bitchen surf going," meaning a world driven by tides, swells, healthy air, and, above all, desire. And the desire envisioned here runs counter to that promoted for women by a militarist state. Female sexuality and the labor of reproduction, inseparable in Cold War equations, are not here harnessed in service to the nation, nation building, or the advancement of a new kind of empire dedicated to keeping the world safe for democracy. In her bodily love affair with the Pacific, Gidget engages in something like a traitorous international border crossing, for the ocean's waters do not obey the logic of geopolitical boundaries. Hers is a form of female subjectivity *not* based in the reproduction of Cold Warriors but on some rather vague but distinctly pacifist sense of female possibility, articulated through outdoorsy, sexual, internationalist, physically powerful, playful, and free female bodily experience. The globalist implications of girl localism exceed the nation-state and show the former's ability to situate a gender critique at Malibu as a site of intersection between U.S. and Pacific worlds.

Let me reiterate that the gender legacy I'm forwarding under the banner of Gidget is based on claims about the *combined* cultural work of the film and the novels, put into dialogue with subcultural life, actual surfers, and an evolving popular understanding of both. In the late 1940s and early 1950s the "young girl on the beach" figure at Malibu that underwrote *Gidget* had seen its real-life counterpart in surfer girls like Vicki Flaxman, Claire Cassidy, Darilyn Zinc, Marge Gleason, Robin Grigg, Patty O'Keefe, Shelley Merrick, Mary Lou Drummy, and Barbara Peterson (fig. 13).[29] Indeed, many of them could just as easily have served as the model for Gidget. As early as the summer of 1950 they were riding waves at Malibu's midpeak, traveling up and down the Pacific coast (including Baja, Mexico) in search of surf. They had formed Hele Nalu (Going Surfing), a girls' surf club: the beginnings of loose institutional bases for girl localist activity. "Localism" here invokes structures of feeling combining Mexican borderlands, the prestate Hawaiian islands, and California coastlines. They were not without female role models, having found encouragement in the reputation of

13 Women of Malibu. Clockwise: top left, Mary Ann Hawkins; Robin Grigg; Vicki Flaxman and Claire Cassidy; group comprises Claire Cassidy, Darilyn Zinc, Marge Gleason, Patty O'Keefe, and Vicki Flaxman; and Vicki Flaxman, *Longboard* (May–June 1999).

14 Doc Ball photograph of Mary Ann Hawkins surfing Redondo Beach stormflood, 1930s, *Longboard* (May–June 1999).

Mary Ann (Hawkins) Morrissey, who surfed expertly at Malibu through the 1940s and into the 1950s, perhaps the best body surfer on the local scene, an extraordinary all-around water athlete, legendary for her work as a Hollywood stuntwoman (fig. 14).[30]

Most of the young Malibu women rode light balsa "girl boards" specially made for them by the shaper and board innovator Joe Quigg, and the history of the reception of these boards and their girl riders reveals much about the gender politics of mid-century subcultural life. Recall that this is surfing's golden age. Women described male surfers as generous, open, and encouraging of girls who wanted to learn, even gentlemanly. They pushed female surfers to improve their skills in bigger surf. Girl boards ultimately revolutionized the design of all surfboards, permitting a new range of motion and control. That new ability became instantly observable and some young women, like Flaxman, now surfed better than many of the local male Malibu regulars. This is where the line was drawn and the golden age showed the limits of its hospitality. "They [the men] were jealous," Quigg asserts. "A lot of people don't want to admit that, but a lot of big name Malibu guys [Bob Simmons and Buzzy Trent] did not like women out there looking that good."[31] By the end of the summer of 1950, when girl boards came out, Quigg notes, all of the best guy surfers on the beach wanted one—for a "girlfriend," that is.

Women explain their motivation to surf rather simply—at least on the surface. They were in it for the fun, the play. "We all loved surfing, and loved the water," recalls Aggie (Bane) Quigg.[32] According to Kohner Zuckerman, "It was all about the wave, the tide, the sun and being free."[33] But behind this light language, typical for a subculture that prizes action and physical competence over speech or self-analysis, is a more serious investment in a practice that afforded women opportunities for both income and physical performance not found elsewhere. Most women turned their athleticism into a lifetime of paying work. Kohner Zuckerman was a skier, a swimmer, resumed surfing at sixty, and her livelihood has been tied to her athletic abilities and identity since the 1950s.[34] Drummy and Merrick both founded organizations to advance women's competitive surfing and today work with youth advocacy surfing organizations (Drummy) and surfing's most prominent eco organization, Surfrider Foundation (Merrick). O'Keefe, Flaxman, and Aggie (Bane) Quigg went on to become championship canoe paddlers in Hawaii. Grigg today owns a ranch on the Big Island, where she practices as a physical therapist.

While the film *Gidget* thus resolves its gendered mandates far more conservatively than do the novels, Gidget—both as rebel girl discourse and as representative real-life surf girl—anchored a developing male subcultural phenomenon. Emergent alternative or bohemian versions of maleness came about in tension with atypical femininities; they were produced simultaneously. The kind of young woman wishing to be around rebel men was herself taking risks, pushing the gendered boundaries. We are here of course squarely in the period about which Betty Friedan would break the silence: that of the problem with no name. The problem was intensified, in fact, by the popular music lyrics of the Beach Boys, as well as by the Beach Blanket film tradition (e.g., *Beach Party*, 1963; *Muscle Beach Party*, 1964; *Bikini Beach*, 1964; *Pajama Party*, 1964; *Beach Blanket Bingo*, 1965; *How to Stuff a Wild Bikini*, 1965; and the last of the series, *The Ghost in the Invisible Bikini*, 1966).[35] These popular film and music traditions contained rebel girl femininity ever more strenuously within Cold War domesticity, and the variety and urgency of that effort speaks to the degree to which the original Gidget discourse threatened the status quo. In such a narrowed context, it's no wonder that rebel girls made unspoken alliances with surfing men. The men's problems did have a name—conformity—and subcultural masculinity offered a study in the explication of its evils. Let me turn by way of illustration to the most powerful of the early versions of subcultural rebel men: the great Kahoona of the *Gidget* novels and films.

As the sage figure of the *Gidget* series, Kahoona is the local crew's leader, Gidget's mentor, and at nearly thirty, he is older and deeper into his days as a "surf bum" (his identification) than are the younger men around him. He introduces himself to Gidget and to readers as "Cass," but the others deferentially call him "Kahoona," a Hawaiian word that translates loosely to mean leader or respected elder. As a surfer figure, Kahoona is drawn from one of the local legends of the Malibu crew in the 1950s, Terry "Tubesteak" Tracy, whose celebrated seaside shack provided the model for Kahoona's bamboo-curtained and Gauguin-wallpapered hut.[36] The local crew that ultimately admits Gidget to its all-male ranks is none other than a fictionalized version of the most influential group of surfers of the period, Joe Quigg, Micky Dora, Kemp Aaberg, Bob Simmons, and Buzzy Trentsome, who would appear as stunt surfers in the *Gidget* films. This group set the tone of surfing up and down the California coastline during these formative years, indeed exporting it globally.[37]

If local Malibu legends and subcultural life provided one set of informing story lines and social logics for the creation of Kahoona as an explicitly Cold War literary and film hero, they did so by incorporating the styles and rebellions of Beat subcultures into surfing and by watering down, yet not jettisoning, beatnik intellectualism. In *Cher Papa*, Gidget's fictional father, finding that he admires Kahoona against his will, sees Kahoona as a beatnik surfer who at the same time suggests a much older and established figure of Western Civilization: "This bum was no bum at all. He was Diogenes, Lord Byron, and Heathcliff all rolled into one" (*CP*, 18). Kohner sounds much like Mark Twain and Jack London, who famously wrote about Islander surfers.[38] Even more than a Lord Byron or a Heathcliff, Kahoona recalls figures of *western* American historical memory (Leatherstocking, Ishmael, Hemingway's men, A.B. Guthrie's Dick Sommers). Described as a "superannuated Huckleberry Finn" whose skin is so dark that "you have never laid your eyes on a tan like that," Kahoona has gone native (*Gidget*, 26). Unlike the Beats whose figure of emulation was the African American man, western Americans historically emulate the indigenous man who, in the context of surf culture and mid-century representation, is native Hawaiian. The altered or mixed racial position of the white man gone native permits his critique of Anglo civilization. We might think of the Kahoona figure as a twentieth-century heir apparent to the most beloved and ambivalent masculine mythos of the American cultural imagination: that of the antimaterialist "natural man," the New World "authentic." One recurrent resolution to the troubles told by his tales is to take them on the road; to fix things by lighting out for the territories. But from what does this mid-century man "gone native" flee?

His troubles have to do with the kinds of lives to which young men are supposed to aspire in the postwar period. What is there to be, beyond the gray suit and the family-man social order that immediately tumbles from it? In the film Kahoona registers the problem by renouncing his former identity and duties as a pilot in the Korean War. "Too many rules," he tells Gidget as an implicit explanation for why he became a surf bum. This renunciation and its eventual recuperation (Kahoona converts wartime duties to civilian ones and becomes a commercial airline pilot) constitute the crucial development of the *Gidget* film and its most conservative reinscription of dominant gender ideologies. The novels, however, do not rein Kahoona in, and at the end of *Gidget*, he surfs as a way of life and can be found "pushing some green water down in Peru" (154). Unlike the film, the novels focus on mapping the everyday practices of lives lived in defiance of Cold War gender mandates, spelling out the logics that guide this group rebellion and that attract newcomer converts (like, potentially, readers) to the subculture's unconventional gender formation. As Kahoona tells Gidget's fictional father in *Cher Papa*, "It's not why a man lives that makes all the difference. . . . It's *how* he lives" (*CP*, 17).

The "how" makes for the books' general topic. We come to understand from Kahoona's crew that he "never loses a [surf] season on stupid things like trying to make a living or get a job" (*Gidget*, 41–42). One of them quotes Kahoona's economic philosophy: "The only way to get economic independence is to be independent of economics" (*Gidget*, 42). To get by, Kahoona feeds on local sea life: abalone steak, lobster, buttermouth, perch, giant clams—the kind "you can't order at [favorite Malibu spots] Jack's and King's" (*Gidget*, 42). He tells Gidget's father in *Cher Papa*, "I travel . . . I see the world. I lie on beaches. I surf. I catch my food from the sea. I go to the mountains. Ski my legs off" (17). Such a life is "hard work." Keeping his "shack . . . a going outfit. That's work" (*CP*, 17). Kahoona does not renounce work itself. He considers himself ambitious: He paints. He wants to get to know people. He reads; on his bookshelf readers find "Dostoevski, Plato, Buddha, Thomas Wolfe, and Joseph Conrad," even "a copy of [the contemporary philosopher William Macneile] Dixon's *The Human Situation*" (*CP*, 13). What he renounces is the ready-made identity that comes with professional work life in U.S. postwar economies and the immediate other social roles attached to it. From Kahoona's perspective, the real work of his life is that "it took a lot of hard thinking to find out about myself" (*CP*, 17). Surfing for Kahoona is about some larger sense of masculine human potential, one path by which to map a postwar masculine "real."

Unlike the "phony character" Gidget has seen on "some corny T.V. show with Irene Dunne" (*Gidget*, 40), Kahoona is an authentic surf bum, "the real article" (*Gidget*, 41). The crux of his authenticity, the bedrock on which his subcultural capital rests, is that he has surfed a zero break wave to shore, the only man to have done so besides the greatest *kahoona* of all, Duke Kahanamoku, the ambassador of Hawaii to the world, the popularizer of surfing on the mainland.[39] One of Kahoona's crew, Lord Gallo, recalling this story for Gidget, remarks: "Zero break comes up only once a year, during storm surf or when there's an earthquake. . . . now with all those H-bomb blasts you get them more often. But only in the islands" (*Gidget*, 41). Kahoona's amazing feat, then, is that he rides Cold War waves, playing in the sea of disturbance kicked up underwater by nuclear activity. And he does so in symbolic affiliation with the father of modern surfing, Duke Kahanamoku. Such a feat happens "only" in Hawaii, that former sovereign nation and now annexed territory about to be, according to the United Nations Declaration on the Granting of Independence to Colonial Countries and Peoples (UNGAR 1514), eligible for decolonization.[40]

In his life as a surf bum, Kahoona has found one way to beat the Cold War, or at least to beat the domestic-front expectations it levies on its able-bodied young American men. He does what the "American natural man" has so often done and what distinguishes his Beat bohemianism from its urbane, history-conscious European counterpart: he *embodies* the alternatives. Kahoona's life practice is one in which the Cold War male body is not dedicated to workplace ambition, to getting ahead, or to policing the world's geopolitical borders. Yet to maintain the practice Kahoona must

be on the move, for the conclusion of *Gidget* shows that the golden age of
surfing in Malibu has suffered some setbacks. In the aftermath of a fire on
the beach, Kahoona's shack has been dismantled by the Malibu police. The
summer is over, and many of the local crew have scattered. Moondoggie
has been drafted and is "shooting the curl at some bootcamp in Texas"
(*Gidget*, 153).

Now with all the guys gone, Gidget has the beach to herself; hers will
be the last word. Best of all, she has Moondoggie's pin, which shields her
from the pressures of normative girlhood or from any hint that she might,
as a female athlete, be other than heteronormative (her best friend LaRue
is suggestively butch and the subject of innuendo). Surfing as a subculture
and the evolving girl localism at Malibu have thus permitted Gidget to resist the peer pressure and gender norms enforced by other *girls* and to enact
instead a different kind of femininity. Her other influence in this evolution
has been Kahoona, and Gidget readily acknowledges herself "beholden"
to him (*Gidget*, 153). In the last scene of the text, she paddles into big surf,
imagining "that's the way it must look at Makaha at zero break" (*Gidget*,
146). This ritual recalls Kahoona's own authenticating moment. She tells
herself, "I have to come in standing" (*Gidget*, 148), and then yells to herself,
"Shoot it," meaning shoot the curl (*Gidget*, 148). She repeatedly "stood it,"
meaning she stays on her feet, one wave, another, another, until shoreline
is visible. Like Kahoona, she has learned to ride Cold War waves. But the
meaning of this feat to her, the meanings she makes of subcultural life,
always remain distinct from what the guys teach her. The particular challenges she faces as a young *female* surfer differ from those the young *men*
face, and the efforts of girl localism to identify these differences will be an
ongoing topic in this book. For now, let us follow through this discussion of
subcultural masculinity moving into canonical subcultural territory.

Malibu and Its Others: The Related Locals
of *The Endless Summer*

In the context of social compression, of the crowding of subcultural
men on landscapes they had perceived to be both deeply purposeful and
"theirs," the subculture discovered after *Gidget* that it had new enemies, a
new threatening edge to its center. To say "enemy," or to name "woman"
as the outside of an inside, is certainly too much. But if the ripple effect

brought to subcultural gender formation by *Gidget* moved gradually and unconsciously, it moved unmistakably. The real rub was not that Gidget or any of the surfer girls had taken for themselves any of the freedoms sub-cultural men enjoyed—somehow the guys expected that, even wanted it and helped it along, quietly admiring the young women who could actu-ally pull it off. That's what it meant to surf. The problem was that popular-ization symbolized so many confounding developments at once that it be-came hard to keep track of them, to discriminate between cause and effect. *Commercialization* became the catchword alongside *crowds*. Both brought distortions that spread and spoiled a tone about everyday life that had mat-tered. And then there was the heartbreak of Malibu, now overrun. Tube-steak and many other local heroes gave up on the spot, faded out of sight, went elsewhere. The loss of Malibu had struck a mortal blow. Critical surf localism—the imperative to distinguish between localist claims and side strategically with those that supported subcultural reproduction—was born.

The most powerful media available to answer the new disquiet, to nar-rate the licking of wounds, were subculturally sponsored magazines (ini-tially *Surfer*, founded in Southern California in 1960) and film. These forums invented the new narratives of the inside, of the new real opposing the fake, stupid stories offered by *Gidget* or the Beach Blanket knockoffs. Among the films, *The Endless Summer* stood out, offering the breakthrough visual nar-rative that brought a very different looking subculture to the mainstream (fig. 15). Its answer to *Gidget*, its critique, was light: it simply ignored her. A promotional poster for the film might have read, "This Is Not a Beach Blanket Movie." At the same time it changed the landscapes of the subcul-tural and consumer imaginations, so that surfing was now visualized most compellingly on an international stage. Using only a handheld Technicolor camera and no sound except voice-over narration, the young Bruce Brown directed and filmed two California surfers in 1964 following the summer season from its ending in California to its beginning in the Senegalese capi-tal, Dakar, then moving on to Accra, Lagos, Cape Town, and along the Indian Ocean coast to Durban. At telling moments we get flashbacks to Waimea Bay, Hawaii, to both the western and the eastern coasts of Australia, to Auckland, to Papeete (Tahiti), and finally back to summertime at Pipeline on Oahu, Hawaii, where the film ends. In this reconfigured global land-scape it seemed normal *not* to see women surfers, nighttime bonfires, or

15   *The Endless Summer* (1966).

heterosocial groups of young adults playing together. In the place of the older Hawaiian-modeled heterosocial communal formation, *The Endless Summer* inaugurated a new homosociality. The new inside celebrated men and masculinity on surfari. Surfer girls would become a visual spectacle associated with tamer, domestic commercial culture. Since the film ostensibly spoke to genre conventions of the documentary, the film's picture of the inside appeared to carry authority, the semblance of fact.

That *The Endless Summer* attracted mainstream attention made for part of its beauty. It brought high-art credentials to a subculture that was anything but. Called "the Fellini of the Foam" or the "Bergman of the Boards," Brown appealed to critics from coast to coast.[41] Instantly credentialed by reviewers from *The New York Times*, *The New Yorker*, and *The Washington Post*, Vincent Canby in particular became one of Brown's biggest fans. Canby called *The Endless Summer* "a very beautiful movie to look at . . . much less simple-minded than it originally sounded."[42] It captured "the joy of a sport that is part swimming, part skiing, part sky-diving, and part

Russian-roulette."[43] Critics celebrated the raw, healthy, masculine exuber-
ance that Brown both documented and embodied. Surfing "plugged [men]
in to life."[44] Critics applauded the film's commercial success.[45] Like Gidget's
father in *Cher Papa*, critics found themselves magnetized by Brown and
his men even as they registered the basic absence of any narrative line or
plot to his cinematic formula.[46] The corrective to this absence, I have been
arguing, the reason that such an absence did not prove fatal, was because
a narrative logic was implicit, supplied by both the Kahoona Beat figure of
the *Gidget* series as well as by all of those other western "natural men" in
American cultural memory.

As has so often held true for the literary and cinematic American West,
the story of *The Endless Summer* concerned a place, a cultural landscape,
as much as it did that place's human actors. *The Endless Summer* revisited
beloved places to eulogize them, to say goodbye. Priority access to Malibu
was no longer possible. (Does this not sound like the basic pathos of western tales: the "virgin" territory spoiled, the old days gone, and the moving
on?) Never again would surfers underestimate the vulnerability of their
most treasured resource: a perfect break. *The Endless Summer* grieved the
loss by establishing a new set of potential places to love.

To frame what I see as a mourning ritual, let us begin by asking what it
might mean, in the mid-1960s, to stage Malibu as the local departing site
for a film about global surfari? As the historian Kirse May shows, in the
postwar period, Southern California experienced one of the largest mass
migrations in U.S. history.[47] Between 1945 and 1965 the population growth
of Los Angeles surpassed that of any other city in the nation.[48] Significantly,
over 80 percent of those migrants were young *families*, the parents of the
baby boomers. The median age of Californians declined dramatically during these years: California went from being the state with the oldest median age in the nation in 1940 to a state thoroughly identified with youth-
fulness by the late 1950s. By the early 1960s Southern California was *the*
place to be young; the region had become the nation's preferred *family*
but also *teenage* cultural landscape. Surf culture, both the actual subcultural presence of surfers on local beaches and the popularization of surfing
in pop culture, became an important part of promoting the new postwar
paradise.

But the equation of youthful desirability and beach landscapes with Southern California had to be invented before it could be sold. The opening of *The Endless Summer* reads as a kind of docu-commercial advertising the concept of summertime. "Summer means many different things to different people," the narrator tells us as visuals roll by of potential consumer choices of leisure activities: catamaran sailing, sunbathing, dirt bike riding. Summertime as a social construct and a set of preferred consumer recreational activities must itself be established before the narrator can locate surf culture inside it as a cultural practice. For "us," the narrator tells viewers, invoking himself as a representative subcultural voice, summertime means the sport of surfing, the "thrill and fun" of surfing. Viewers receive instruction in modes of surfing: body surfing, body boarding, knee boarding, and finally stand-up surfing. A sequence of action shots in various sizes of surf follows. The narrator defines basic technical terms of longboard riding, schooling viewers to understand the maneuvers they see: turning, stalling, trimming, riding the nose, staying in the curl. The surf slang of wipeouts and stink-bug stances, as well as introductions to surf legends like Malibu's "Da Cat" Mickey Dora, Australia's Nat Young, or the big-wave surfer Butch Van Artsdalen—all these materials initiate viewers to the inside.

But no one is truly inside without knowing surf culture's "related locals," its important places. The opening of *The Endless Summer* establishes where one finds "authentic summertime," and here Hawaii, surfing's Mecca, comes into play. "No place represents summertime to surfers more than the Hawaiian islands," viewers learn, where conditions are "ideal" and locals "friendly." The narrator cuts to a contrasting shot of a place overtaken by scores of surfers on a day it isn't even breaking to observe dryly, "California has a lot of places that represent summertime to a lot of people, like this secret spot." The "secret" turns out to be Malibu. To find authentic summertime all year round, to escape the zoo conditions of Southern California and find warm water and big surf—"the ultimate thing for most of us"—surfers must go in search of an endless summer.

But what imperative actually existed to travel the globe in search of perfect all-season warm water waves when they could be found "at home," as the opening gambits on Hawaii decisively establish? And when, seasonally speaking, as Brown knew well, some of the world's best waves do *not* break. Cape Saint Francis in South Africa, which *The Endless Summer* discovered and put on film, is a winter break, for example, and the professional tour today convenes annually at nearby Jeffrey's Bay in July, wintertime in the Southern Hemisphere. Brown's representation of Cape Saint Francis as a spot that breaks perfectly three hundred days a year—a crucial moment since it consummates the film's desire sequence—is "overstated by about 285 days," as Warshaw has unceremoniously pointed out.[49] So what else besides a subcultural desire for ideal surf motivated *The Endless Summer*?

If Malibu's waves were crowded by the early 1960s, so too was the market for surf movies. Hollywood had hit on a sure-fire formula for making money: the Beach Blanket movie. It popularized ostensible summertime youth practices in Southern California: evening beach bonfires, the wild luau, frolicking at all hours in shorts on the sand. Based on a different formula, but a formula nonetheless, Brown himself had already made five films for the subculture's expanding base, *Slippery When Wet* (1958), *Surf Crazy* (1959), *Barefoot Adventure* (1960), *Surfing Hollow Days* (1961), and *Waterlogged* (1962). To make yet another that would prove competitive in a saturated market, Brown needed a new twist. A radical expansion of the California to Mexico to Hawaii trek, Brown's own formula, which had proved so winning but was becoming routine, might be just the thing. Hawaii by now was relatively known. So too was "Old Mexico" (fig. 16). Bud Brown (no relation), another early prominent surfing filmmaker, had taken to Australia a few years earlier his own Makaha footage in the film *Surfing in Hawaii* (1957) and that of Hawaiian Clarence Maki in *The Big Surf* (1962), introducing the Hawaiian big-wave scene down under.[50] He had not returned to the United States empty-handed, bringing back to U.S. surfers their first glimpses of Australian surfing and, in so doing, creating the first international surf film.

In a glutted market, Bruce Brown needed to show new spots, to generate new ideas. Already the Beach Boys and the Beach Blanket films had popularized for suburban consumption the logics of international travel and vacationing—the scripts were in cultural place and needed only to be angled, shifted.[51] Brown hit a nerve, judging by box-office receipts, when he moved U.S. surfing beyond national boundaries toward a global horizon. The *way* Brown represented the global, though indeed new in terms of its surfing protagonists, relied heavily on one of the oldest of Western colonial narratives: the adventure tale and the safari. But the spatial orientation of this global escapade showed something distinctly American and contem-

16.1 Movie poster, 1962.

16.2 Movie handbill, 1960.

porary: imaginative horizons mapped by the Second World War and the Cold War global power grab that followed. These blended orientations had clear consequences for how surf culture would conceive its related locals.

Hawaii, Australia, Southern California, and down the coast into Mexico: all were heavy surf spots, and all of them made for obvious strategic military sites for U.S. foreign operations and global security during the Second World War and the first decades of the Cold War. Far more than has been appreciated, the popularization of surf culture owed a great deal to military mobilization, networks, travel routes, new industrial technologies, and the accident of big surf in some of the forward-line hot spots on the Cold War frontier. Like the majority of young men of the era, most of surfing's best-known early design innovators, photographers, publishers, and filmmakers had served stints during the 1940s and 1950s in the air force, the army, and/ or the navy. Indeed, during the war, the famed surfboard design innovator Simmons (not inducted because of an arm handicap) claimed to be but "one of the few men surfing California . . . beaches were fortified borders and just about every other surfer was in the military."[52] Bud Brown served as a navy chief specialist in athletics, afterwards joining the Waikiki Surf Club.[53] Surfing's most respected photographer, LeRoy Grannis, enlisted in the air force. After the war, in the early 1950s as a high school teen, Bruce Brown himself had hopped a steerage passage aboard the Matson Liner steamship to Hawaii for a first surfing trip.[54] Following graduation he joined the navy, going to submarine school to ensure he could be stationed in Hawaii, where he shot his first 8mm movies. John Severson, the founding editor of *Surfer* magazine, filmed *Surf*, based on Makaha in the winter of 1957–58, while stationed in the army in Hawaii. He did so in between surf sessions with the Army Surf Team.[55]

Thus that early generation of surfing pioneers—the trendsetting leaders in the representation and equipment design innovation of the subculture—had more than surfing and Southern California in common. Their travels across the world's oceans and their group passion for Hawaii were deeply conditioned by wartime. The bombing of Pearl Harbor by the Japanese immediately transformed the islands into the chief Pacific base for U.S. forces, a staging ground for military incursions into Asia, as well as into a sacred national burial site. Several million young men passed through Hawaii during the war years.[56] To be in Hawaii in the decade following 7 December 1941 was to be in the obvious heart of nationalist fervor and military buildup. Not a state but nonetheless claimed as U.S. territory, the islands were considered by surfers to be unproblematically American. If many soldiers agreed with a comment recorded in the Military Censors' Files that "this is a strange land and they keep telling me I am in the US, but from the time I walked off the ship I have doubted it,"[57] few surfers would have despaired at the strangeness. For them, strangeness proved just the tonic. In their minds they were not consuming the prewar tourist industry picture of Hawaii; they had little interest in the royal Hawaiian, in coming across on luxury liners, or in hotel hula and fire-throwing spectacles. Bud Brown and Tom Blake had surfed with Duke Kahanamoku himself, had accepted the invitation to learn the ancient Polynesian tradition of open-ocean canoe voyaging, and saw themselves as allies in efforts to preserve historic Polynesian ritual and culture.[58] Through such activities they performed and secured their experiences of themselves as border crossers and as very influential subculturalists; they institutionalized a deep respect for native Hawaii in the everyday life of surfing.

The Endless Summer clearly had no concept of Hawaii as a colonized place, nor of the surfers themselves as complicated or unwitting agents of colonization. And only with historical retrospection is it clear that the decolonization processes in Africa played a pressuring role in fast-tracking Hawaii for statehood.[59] It's too glib to say that Hawaii served as a kind of suburb of Southern California for surfers, even while it clearly provided a bohemian getaway for Southern Californians who felt crowded or burned out by changing mainland local conditions. The regard for legendary Makaha, Sunset, North Shore, and Waimea was real, and some surfers (legendary John Kelly comes to mind, a generation older and an example to these younger men) stood against big development business to protect the environmental health and native residents of those places, participating also in Hawaiian sovereignty and indigenous reparation movements.[60] Surfing subculturalism thus fostered politicized critical localisms in Hawaii from the early 1950s on. Yet the concept of "authentic summertime" unquestionably linked Hawaii to Southern California in terms impossible to delink from their dominant meanings in youth leisure industries that not only invested heavily in white middle-class conformity and consumerism but also served to assimilate the colonial and racial difference of Hawaii into the mainstream postwar tourist and travel economy. If *The Endless Summer* expressed a localism critical of the commodification of surfing and of the overpopulation of Malibu, it ran up less critically against other locals—Hawaiians, white, mixed-race, or native—who worried about tourist incursions into Hawaiian space.[61] Surf culture, while hardly a direct power player in Hawaii's eventual incorporation into the union, nonetheless played a supporting role in the larger ideological work done by Hollywood Beach Blanket movies. Surfers brought up the rear guard in the battle to solidify Hawaii as the outer reach, the far hegemonic horizon of U.S. western geographic imaginations.

One sees in the California subculture's early claim to Hawaii the structuring features of surfing's political unconscious. It stakes claims not to systems of ideas as much as to particular places, often initially without much of a second thought. The belligerence of the claim on Hawaii, or on the African surf spots depicted in *The Endless Summer*, is that of possession by unconscious presumption. *The Endless Summer* casts the young men as very sure of their place in the world, of their right to travel the globe, and to do so casually, without anxiety. It does not occur to them that these social locations *are* social locations. Had just one of them been African American, and there were a few black surfers at the time, how keen might he have been to visit South Africa in 1963? Had the relatively few Hawaiians surfing at mid-century been less inclined to demonstrate "Aloha" in the islands, what limits might have stung the Californians into a new consciousness? Instead, the unspoken logic went: if waves are unridden, nobody is stopping me, and if I am bold enough to figure it out, why shouldn't I? In their Cold War innocence and arrogance about the world as their legitimate playground, surfers show, we can see in retrospect, enormous unaware privilege. At a time when the very spots to which the film crew traveled in Africa had just undergone the tumult of decolonization (Nigeria and Senegal in 1960, Ghana in 1957), the film never registers the international political terrain it navigates. Brown makes nonsensical cliché comments about primitives who have never seen a white man. Classic colonial stereotypes of African cannibalism, timeless village traditions, mask-wearing jungle men, and so forth, reign unchallenged. Besides the sophomoric racisms of the narrative, the film simply registers no sense of the history of colonial presence in Africa. If this is the place at which the reader, drawing back in shock, wonders about the worldview of surfers in these years, we might notice that the officially liberal and urbane reviewing corps of *The Endless Summer* was not itself scandalized by such representations.[62] No one took offense at the film's unselfconscious coloniality, its global confidence, or its unconcerned ignorance. Quite the opposite. Peter Bart of *The New York Times* finds "amusing" the scenes of "surfers and African natives who had never before seen either a white man or a surfboard."[63] The easygoing rebel masculinity of *The Endless Summer* seems to have offered a youthful model of national ambassadorship perhaps popularly associated with the Peace Corps. Except that these ambassadors had the appealing edge of a western American wilderness man.

As *The Sun Also Rises* did for the "lost generation," *The Endless Summer* freezes a moment in young baby boomers' development. The search for a perfect wave, that complicated hope that stages subcultural desire, is realized. The film's opening musical score, its romantic, sunlit beachscapes at dusk, its regard for male friendship, its documentation of longboard grace and style before the shortboard would radically change surfing in the late 1960s, its suggestion that sun-bleached white young men might roam the globe innocently in search of surf, and its ostensible "discovery" of its own paradisiacal hopes in the Cape Saint Francis wave footage, all these features at once captured and produced a generational hope and a Californian regional structure of feeling.

Without quite intending to, *The Endless Summer* invented what has since become surfing's greatest collective dream. This dream connects surf spots across the planet in a coherent narrative of potential world belonging, any of them possible "homes" to the surfer who can get there and manage them. At its core the collective dream suggested a fundamentally different vision of everyday life than, and one incompatible with, that found in the contemporary Western world, which provides one clue as to why, to realize it, a global landscape proved so enabling. The search for an endless summer went hand in hand with a search to live a *non*consumerist and postnational everyday life. To the question, "What is there to be, beyond the gray suit?" surfers answered, "surf." The answer implied a great deal. The collective dream invented in *The Endless Summer* was then as much about American domestic dissatisfaction as it was about "the world," a dissatisfaction ultimately displaced, deflected unevenly onto a global canvas. On that larger canvas the discontent had some chance of resolution. Other global spaces were less disciplined, less structured. Other places—Makaha, Papeete, even apartheid-tainted South Africa's Cape Saint Francis—were not yet as emplotted, storied, financed, patrolled.

Of course, they were not as patrolled if one were white. The race politics of South Africa during apartheid were to become instantly clear and problematic for native Hawaiian surfers, and the big-wave competitor Eddie Aikau's experiences there showed the limits of the subculture's collective dream. Spellbound by *The Endless Summer* and the promise of big waves in Durban and Jeffrey's Bay, Aikau traveled to South Africa with other celebrated (white) members of the Hawaiian surf team in 1971 to a major international contest. But once in Durban, Aikau was denied lodging at the pricey Malibu Hotel, where his teammates Jeff Hackman and Billy Hamilton stayed. Given that the Aikau family in Hawaii was regarded as near-royalty, Aikau was unprepared for this insult. It was not clear, additionally, whether he would be allowed to surf the contest since it was slated at a whites-only break. His teammates did nothing to stand up on his behalf; the Hawaiian team, anxious for its white members to compete, lodged no protest. Left to fend for himself, Aikau recalled how unsafe he felt on Durban streets, where he was stared at by circles of white children who did not understand his pidgin responses to their questions. Local anti-apartheid liberal press heard about and publicized the controversy, shaming public officials into allowing him access to whites-only space. He was befriended ultimately by a white South African family of surfers, who understood and could navigate local race politics. Back home in the islands, the experience drove a permanent wedge between him and his Hawaiian white countrymen; one of them had won the contest while, under the circumstances, Aikau's showing was poor.[64] The informal racialization of white, colored, and black beach geographies continues even though official segregation has been outlawed in the new South Africa.[65]

But in the 1960s such experiences did not trouble the subculture significantly, preoccupied as it was by other compromises. On the mainland, in Malibu, there was just no competing with the movie studios or the Malibu Colony types, the real players with real money. Surfers might get some bit parts in movies. Maybe, as Brown did with *The Endless Summer*, they might hit the jackpot and, with those earnings, drop out and relocate north to the exclusive Hollister Ranch surf enclave above Santa Barbara. From that private seaside retreat they might ride waves and motocross, live quietly among surfing friends, and refuse (as Brown explicitly did) to drain the subculture of every commercial possibility.[66] But the larger system running Southern California, with Malibu and Hollywood at the heart, seemed quite beyond the reach of surf culture's powers. It had to be faced that Malibu was gone, dead. In its place stood the everyday performance of global subcultural bohemianism, days spent surfing and days spent *not* being conned into doing (in Kahoona's words) "stupid things." The crucial life skill was to know the difference between what mattered and what did not, and then to follow that knowing to its logical conclusions.

Beyond Malibu and "Monster Houses"

I move toward a close by way of discussions of history and its requirements, of local places that until now have been in no position to claim larger feminist designs, and of two surfing women in particular who were, and continue to be, quite adept at not doing "stupid things"—Rosemary Reimers-Rice and Linda Benson.[67] The girl localisms of these two women (and a few others who figure alongside them) offer telling companion tales to those related-local stories told about the two famed surfers featured in *The Endless Summer*, Robert August and Mike Hynson.

Moonlight Beach, Capistrano Beach, Hermosa—these were but a few of the town breaks south of Malibu where a girl could grow up with the Pacific Ocean as her front yard. Never as glamorous, star-struck, or monied as Malibu, they were relatively more isolated getaway towns, sleepy seaside almost-neighborhoods, where, in the words of the world champion Benson, from Moonlight, "we knew we had something special, unique."[68] Joyce Hoffman (a later world champ) reports: "You could literally step out the front door and be on the [Capistrano] beach."[69] Or, with characteristic nonchalance, Reimers-Rice says, "Of course we were born and raised right on the beach, you know, Hermosa Beach."[70] Such towns may not yet have been chartered or incorporated in the 1950s and 1960s, a fact that made for relatively unruly, undisciplined social geographies.[71] Building codes might have been lax, police oversight infrequent, schools sparse. Suburban respectability did not dominate neighborhood culture here, nor did class and racial homogeneity. Beach towns came with fringe or Beat elements alongside surfers; they were home to bars, late-night music, and ramshackle cottages. Lawrence Lipton's *The Holy Barbarians* of 1959 offers a look at Beat life on Venice Beach during the 1950s.[72] Smaller towns further south provided additional liminal breathing room for the activity occasioned by growing populations inland. The notion that one could buck conformist historical imperatives on these beachscapes seemed palpable, a practical everyday matter. Women who knew from earliest memory nothing but that more flexible social geography had early training in taking advantage of social openings.

As spaces of an emergent girl localism, these were not mapped by established political traditions, sophisticated networks, or organized principals. The everyday worlds forged by the surfer girls of the late 1950s and the 1960s were never particularly preoccupied with the symbolic import of the Miss America pageant, with anybody's civil rights movements, or with capital-*H* history. All of "that," they might have said, happened far away from the blue-green waters of the California Pacific, which from earliest memory centered their deepest desires. Like the male surfers of the period, surfer girls distrusted politics of any persuasion, for "politics" bound and tied them to History, whereas their drive, their originality, their acts of cultural radicalism, came precisely from opposing History's imperatives. The power of History appeared on the side of coercion and control, and surfing, happily, seemed to be on some opposite side of that equation. The decision to surf, to pursue a surfer's life path, had to do with a particular way of challenging what women perceived that history had, or did not have, in store for them. To locate oneself outside History indicated a *reading* of what women understood to be its mandates, of who or what they understood its subjects to be (certainly not themselves), and what they understood the beach geographies of Southern California to provide in the form of daily relief and alternative.

Nonetheless, alongside their feminist peers across the nation, women who surfed in this period pursued life paths at overt odds with those of the female majority; they were risk-takers, not afraid to go it alone, and not deterred by the charge that their behavior was unladylike. Yet unlike their feminist rule-breaking sisters in the urban northeast and elsewhere, surfer girls' breakaway activities took place in the realm of the *non*intellectual, the nonanalytic, and often in the wilderness. Theirs were very embodied and joyous forms of dissent. They had no female Kahoona or Leatherstocking cultural models to explain to themselves or anyone else what it was they were doing, how it pushed hard against the limits of what women could do or be. Surfer girls were about ocean-going physical power and the serious mental game it took to sustain that. They trained not at the university, in leftist organizations, or at public demonstrations, but rather in the coastal outdoors, the set of related-local surf spots the subculture traveled between with its different breaks and challenges and other local people from whom to learn. Their mentors, to the extent that they had any, at first were men. The rules of the playing field varied according to individuals' competitiveness and some were profoundly driven, surfing the globe's biggest breaks. At the same time, surfing was always also fundamentally about fun, about pleasure. These cultural and political structures of feeling remain largely unknown to women's history or to U.S. audiences in general, and to imagine them as emerging political imaginations one must unlearn countless impressions created by *The O.C.*, *Baywatch*, *90210*, or Beach Blanket films. One must also nuance the Malibu-centrism of both *Gidget* and *The Endless Summer*.

While the Malibu girl crowd certainly constitutes a pivot point of girl localism, an identifiable generation of women surfers also came from south of Malibu, where female surf culture was not clubby and girls or women were rarely seen in the water. I have already noted Reimers-Rice (b. 1938) from Hermosa Beach and Benson (b. 1934) from Moonlight Beach. The surfer identities these two women enacted over a lifetime dovetailed with more conventionally male surfer identities: the loners, the hard-core surfers, and the free spirits who put surfing before all else, and, especially in the early days when it was still possible, surfed alone by design. Reimers-Rice, still surfing today in the cold waters of Santa Cruz, is more of a "soul surfer" (fig. 17). The competitive Benson, whose local break today is San Onofre, was considered the best woman surfer in the world in the late 1950s and early 1960s, winning five U.S. championships, and the International Championship at Makaha in 1959, at age fifteen (fig. 18). Benson doubled for Annette Funicello and Deborah Walley in the surfing segments of the *Beach Party* and *Gidget* films of the 1960s. Also from south of Malibu, from Long Beach and San Juan Capistrano, fitting that loner profile are a cohort of individuals such as Marge Calhoun (b. 1929) and her surfing daughters Candy (b. 1945) and Robin (b. 1947), Jericho Poppler (b. 1951), Alice Petersen, Liz Irwin, and Joyce Hoffman (b. 1947). With the exception of the Calhouns, who surfed as a family, these women ran into one another only rarely in the water. They knew of one another, but as a rule they lived and surfed among men.

Reimers-Rice and Benson, more than did the Malibu girl crowd, enacted as women the dream that *The Endless Summer* put in motion. Reimers-Rice and Benson both describe what they take from surfing in quasi-mystical

17.1 Rosemary Reimers-Rice at Twenty-Second Street, Hermosa Beach, 1950s.
Photograph by Leroy Grannis.

17.2 Rosemary Reimers-Rice at Indicator's (Santa Cruz). Film still from Swell (1997).

18.1 Linda Benson, the youngest surfer to win Makaha International, at age fifteen. Photograph by Leroy Grannis.

18.2 Linda Benson, 2006 Roxy Jam at Cardiff Reef, California. Photograph by Elizabeth Pepin.

terms, as a gift from God, as "spiritual" and "peaceful." Benson describes surfing as a form of "artistic expression." "Being in the water, riding the wave, doing what you could with the wave. It was an artistic expression—it was such a deep, um, desire, to express yourself on a wave."[73] Benson does not position herself away from the loner ethos of surfing. She acknowledges that it was not "normal" for a girl to surf.[74] But the world she lived in itself was "unique, very different from the norm," and she shared that world with her male fellow surfers.

Reimers-Rice, as many surfers do, uses the language of "addiction" and "thrill" to describe her first experiences and the desire to return to the water again and again. But Reimers-Rice's story departs from Benson's at the moment at which Reimers-Rice becomes pregnant with her first child in 1958 (and continues to surf six months into her pregnancy). This is a woman who, when she married at eighteen and immediately had two children, got herself a babysitter, packed her surfboard, the sitter, the two children, and a playpen into her Volkswagen bus, and on weekdays when her husband was at work drove the coastline between Malibu and San Onofre to the south and Ventura to the north looking for waves. She did not surf with anyone else. She wonders, given that that area covers some 250 miles and in those days was not linked by freeway, how she did it in a single day. She continued surfing throughout the 1960s, making many trips deep into Mexico (San Blas), sometimes six to eight weeks at a stretch, taking the kids out of school to accompany her and homeschooling them as they went along. And of course there was the annual pilgrimage to Hawaii. For a time (when her husband was stationed there) Reimers-Rice lived in Hawaii. When asked to reflect on her sense of herself as a woman, about whether she felt odd doing this, about whether she felt she was a different kind of mother than others in the 1950s, she answered no: "It was just one of those things. I just never really thought about it. . . . Of course we were born and raised right on the beach, you know. So I don't know if that has anything to do with it or not. . . . Things like that just don't bother me. That's just, you know, if I feel, if I enjoy doing it, I'm going to do it."[75] Reimers-Rice recalls that by the 1980s she noticed one day in Santa Cruz, "God, I'm the only woman out here. . . . I mean there could have been forty people out [in the water] and I was the only one. But before that you know, it was just kind of a sport that I was involved with, which [as] I had said before, I was just locked into it. And I, you know, enjoyed it so much."[76]

The recurrent description of surfing for the women revolves around enjoyment, fun, play, peace, artistic expression, and simplicity—not exactly the terms that spring to mind to describe fifties femininity during the age of consensus. Reimers-Rice recalls being a high school kid in 1954 and 1955, "barbequing horse meat . . . and drinking beer" at night by the Manhattan Beach Pier. She was with her lifelong friend, Johnny Rice, who had taught her to surf and would become a well-known shaper, and who by 1986, became her husband. In the mid-1950s they would walk on the strand from Hermosa to Manhattan Beach: "people walked back and forth at night" and met up with "lots of Hawaiian guys" to have parties. She names Manhattan Beach regular George Kapu, as well as Ron and Bobby Patterson, Hawaiian beach boys who moved from Honolulu to California as teenagers in the 1950s. Rey Patterson, regarded as one of Hawaii's premier ukulele players, would be playing music. A few girls might be there, but they did not surf. "Time was creative," Reimers-Rice remembers, "It just was a real, real free time." After she had children, in 1962, Reimers-Rice surfed on Dewey Weber's surf team, the first woman ever to surf on a team. This improved her skills enormously because she took more risks and did not have to be as cautious about damaging equipment. By the late 1960s she had relocated to Santa Cruz to escape the sex-drugs-and-rock-and-roll scene of surfing that, in her words, "captured" so many people. She says, "I had to start a life of my own." She divorced her first husband, got a job, bought a house at the beach for $13,000, and raised her children by herself. In these years she surfed less, focusing on her children. But she did take up competitive running. When she got married to Johnny Rice in 1986 and her children were older, she resumed serious surfing. Johnny made boards for her again, and they have surfed together (as they did when teenagers) ever since.

Like Reimers-Rice, Benson carved out a path for herself as an independent young woman, and to do so she avoided the more conventional paths of female advancement, such as going to college. Neither she nor Reimers-Rice was officially "educated," so intent were they on pursuing a different kind of knowledge. Benson never married or had any children. Her early successes as a competitor brought her as close to being a pro surfer as one could be in the years before the professional tour. She was the only woman to appear in what would be the premier issue of *Surfer* magazine. Benson made her athletic abilities pay, and she recalls feeling "rich" from the movie money she earned when surfing as a stunt double. But since a career in female surfing was not yet possible, Benson instead became a flight attendant and recently retired, having worked for more than thirty years for United Airlines. The freedom that job afforded her to travel the world and control her time remained its principal fringe benefit. For years she kept a surfboard in a beach lockup in Honolulu.[77] Benson, too, survived the subculture's rock-and-roll period and reported in 2000 that she had been sober for nearly twenty years.[78] Still living in the girl localist tradition, Benson resides on a farm in northeastern San Diego County, growing avocados and commercial flowers with a female business partner. They hope to retire together on the income they produce: Benson's house is now paid off, and, she says, she doesn't need much—beyond waves, that is—to be happy.

The life courses pursued by Reimers-Rice and Benson offer some insight into the impact of subcultural membership on women's performance of fifties female gender roles. Benson did not marry, and if she took something of the path of a "career woman," such a description warrants qualification since the surf ethos motivated her. A story about Benson's "most memorable day" surfing proves revealing and illustrates the overlap between gender, Southern California military installations, surfers, and Cold War surf breaks. Although it is not dated, I'm guessing that the incident took place in the early 1960s. The location is the famed Trestles, a break so named because the beach sits below train trestles. The break forms part of a U.S. Marine base near Oceanside. "It was one of those beautiful, glassy days, with a slight, warm Santa Ana wind. The waves were five and six feet, perfect. I paddled out and watched Dewey [Weber] a while. He was so hot. I started surfing and it was *so* good. Soon, the Marines rolled up in their tanks and started practice-firing on the beach—not at us, of course, but it was the usual warning to clear out. Everyone else went in but me and Dewey. I figured, 'I'll go in when he goes in.' The Marines were on the beach, and he and I had a super day of surfing. At the end of the day, we were escorted off the beach by tanks."[79]

What I find striking in this story is the word *usual* in the "usual warning to clear out." It's the casualness of such episodes, their almost unremarkable regularity, that speaks to a deeply ingrained way of rebellious being, one that laughs off sneaking into the most humorless of social spaces and then being chased out of them by the ultimate authority figures: uniformed men with tanks. Benson recalls it all in a voice that is about her own purpose, her own story, pleasure, and life vision. Trestles belonged to *her*. Because Trestles recently became a site of environmental contest and victory, as we will see in chapter 4, this early example of girl localism proves all the more striking.

Why else would women take risks of the kinds I have described in this chapter—with the institution of motherhood, with men, with their parents, with economic security, with feminine respectability, with the military-industrial complex, or with waves big enough to kill—but for the promises held out by a subcultural world of meaningful play? What kind of woman would even *like* a Kahoona figure except an "alternative" woman? One who herself may not be the marrying kind, not a type to partner with men so they will take care of and provide for her. To return to Ehrenreich's *Hearts of Men* and her final claim about the consequences for *women* of male non-conformity, it definitely matters that, given the larger workforce structure which paid men the family wage, men's journey toward freedoms often came on the backs of women who were left holding the bag, economically vulnerable and unpaid in the labor of raising children. Subcultural surfing women were less invested in curtailing this flight from commitment, I believe, because they did not want to enact its companion role: the virtuous mother deserving of economic protection. Indeed, the majority of the surfing women ultimately did not live out some kind of fifties marriage plot. All of them were or remain self-supporting. With the exception of Benson who stayed single, all were married, all divorced at least once, and only a few (like Reimers-Rice) have remarried and stayed so. As does Gidget in all but the last novel, these women seem relieved at tale's end to be left to their own designs, sometimes pinned but always at the practical level single and thus free to surf, travel, ski, and work.

I would like to close by suggesting that these women's life histories reflect an expanded set of origins tales for the birth of the women's liberation movement: one engaged not in intellectual projects or the writing of feminist history but instead in physical exertion, stretching the limits of female fear in wilderness contexts, the ability, over a lifetime, as Reimers-Rice puts it, "to carry your own surfboards." Their stories narrate an increasing sense of themselves, not children or husbands, as the subjects of their own lives. Nearly every one of these early rule-breaking women has taken on a leadership role in surfing communities as she has gotten older. Of course a larger social shift, an increasing freedom for women in the post-war period, has underwritten these women's life histories. Yet the particular way in which they have gone about evidencing female freedom has for decades been tied to girl localism. Like surfing men, women found in the subculture's critique of gray-suit professionalism, upward mobility, and the postwar consumer lifestyle an alternative vision lived out in rhythms tied to particular coastal locales. If surfers valued living by the tides, swells, and storms, if the men among them defied normative masculinity by refusing the marketplace's clock, women ultimately faced a different set of social expectations. In their negotiation of them—practicing new kinds of motherhood, enacting new forms of female agency through an athletic female body, scripting alternative public spheres with a feminist presence—the male bohemianism of surf culture had unexpected and politicizing effects.

I want to make a final point about this generation's pursuit of "simpler" lives because it suggests a political economy of girl localism that opposed the consumer drive of fifties femininity and simultaneously critiques contemporary norms of feminist professionalism and outsourcing consumption practices geared toward female demographics. Both Reimers-Rice and Benson explicitly talk about the simplicity of their lives and about their ability to control their lives as women because of that simplicity. "I have lived very simply all my life . . . I don't know any other way," Reimers-Rice says. She is glad not to have been "caught up in monster houses . . . I'll tell you one thing. If I catch a good wave, I'm paddling out, saying, thank you God. You know, I mean, because he's allowing me to be able to take the time, to have the time and not be married to house payments and car payments and all that kind of stuff, that I have the freedom to go out in the water and really enjoy it." Though Reimers-Rice mentions God, she is quick to say she is not religious. Both she and Benson have paid off their houses and do not need to generate income to pay mortgages. Reimers-Rice says, "I kept [my life] that way just in case anything happened." She worries about younger women, she says, who have big mortgages to support, as well as children to raise. "I feel real fortunate, where a lot of the gals nowadays don't have that, you know," meaning that California real-estate beach markets are substantially more challenging than they were in 1970, when Reimers-Rice bought her place. "I just hope a lot of these other young ladies will have that opportunity" to go out and really enjoy life.

Reimers-Rice registers one of the generational fault lines that younger women must navigate if they wish the freedom to play and the time and everyday life practices it requires. Reimers-Rice suggests younger women will have to not "get caught up in . . . monster houses and all that kind of stuff." We might well read this as a cautionary tale for feminist profession- alism of the present. However much I engage in documenting this current phenomenon, archiving photos, gathering interviews, and so forth, the key to fathoming it remains in the realm of desire, or play, in open-air coastal climes. For why else would women take risks of the kind described here, except to realize the freedoms play articulates? In the late 1940s, before she began to surf, Flaxman recalls that her brother would get their father to drive along the coastline in search of waves. She was frustrated at being left out of the things that were the most fun. "Play. I was in love with the ocean and loved playing in it."[80] Rest, play, *jouissance*. There's something more extravagantly creative and risky here than many of us know how to understand.

Two

Wanting to Be Lisa

The Surfer Girl Comes of Age

If you let me play / I will like myself more / I will have more
self-confidence / I will suffer less depression / I will be 60
percent less likely to get breast cancer / I will be more likely to
leave a man who beats me / I will be less likely to get pregnant
before I want to / I will learn what it means to be strong / If
you let me play sports.
—Nike ad campaign targeting young female consumers, 1996

Go to one of those Roxy contests at San Onofre: hundreds of
little girls ripping on all different kinds of boards, and all of
them just so stoked to be a part of the beach lifestyle. This is
way beyond a fad. It's a movement.—Lisa Andersen, four-time
world surfing champion, 1999

On a windblown wintery day in 1999, twenty-four-year-old Sarah
Gerhardt braved the monumental surf at Northern California's
infamous Mavericks, becoming the first woman ever to ride its
twenty-five-foot-plus faces (fig. 19). That's a *minimum* of twenty-
five feet; Mavericks doesn't break on lesser swells. Recognized
instantly as a historical feat by her male fellow surfers on site
who, as she put it, "gave her a lot of high-fives all around," news
of Gerhardt's accomplishment quickly made its way through the
multimedia networks linking today's international surfing communities.[1] If Gerhardt's showing at Mavericks signaled a personal
best for her as an elite female athlete in the most demanding of
extreme-sports contexts (Mavericks credentials the men of the
men), it also dramatized a new arrival for women—the shatter-
ing of a twenty-first-century glass ceiling in the world of high-
performance surfing. Though clearly in a class of her own, Gerhardt nonetheless represents one of a new generation of surfer

19 Sarah Gerhardt at Mavericks in Half Moon Bay, 1999. Photograph by Pete Burnight.

girls whose power approach to surfing, womanhood, relations with men, and international public life differs markedly from that of the "Gidgets" of the 1950s and 1960s. It also differs from the route taken by the less popularly celebrated but very accomplished women surfers of the 1970s and 1980s whose female community-building successes partly account for the emergence of Gerhardt herself.

How do girls grow up strong? Where does courage come from? How does girls' ability to play sports and to win improve their life chances to flourish and thrive? Such questions, opening the book *Nike Is a Goddess: The History of Women in Sports*, frame the concerns of this chapter.[2] Indeed, as the introduction suggested, they also inform a vast recent literature and worried public discourse in Western societies on the topic of young women, consumer culture, the female body, and self-esteem. One answer to these questions in recent U.S. public debate is female athleticism.[3] In the context of the moral panics of the 1990s about self-loathing "Ophelias," hypercompetitive "queen bees," and destructive "mean girls"—panics about U.S. female youth born between 1980 and 2000, or Generation Y—sports has recurrently figured as a safeguard of female psychological stability and confidence.[4] The popularization of brave, brash, and strong female athletes who can *win* (the hoopla following the Women's Cup soccer final in 1999 watched live by a crowd of nearly one hundred thousand in the Rose Bowl comes to mind) offered examples of relatively new solutions to familiar social problems experienced particularly by women: passivity, fearfulness, a preoccupation with body and appearance, and putting oneself second to others' needs, hopes, thinking, and if not doing so, then feeling guilty and selfish.[5]

This chapter puts the popular claim about sport as healthy practice for young women into conversation with surfing as a sport conducted in particular local outdoor settings. As suggested by the epigraph and opening gestures of this chapter surfing is not done just *anywhere*. Unlike soccer, football, basketball, baseball, tennis, or running, surfing cannot be moved indoors to accommodate weather. Neither can one go to a twenty-four-hour gym to catch a few waves. Surfing has more in common with rock climbing, skiing, and river running. The places where surfing happens—the points, piers, beach breaks, jetties, offshore sites, river mouths, reefs—are not mobile. The surfer must go to *them*. Getting to them is often inconvenient and once arrived, what one should do, how best to paddle out and then launch, has to be determined according to real-time conditions. But even though they are immobile, surf spots can change. Petrochemical or agricultural industry runoff after storms can negatively affect water quality. Local development policy (onshore or offshore) will impact coastlines and their underwater worlds, as will processes like erosion or the growth or decline of coral reefs. To learn to surf is therefore to become a girl who knows something about oceanography and global weather patterns, especially as they relate to the breaks where one surfs as a local. In California particularly, where pressures are intense to capitalize coastlines and profit from their ever-denser development, to be a surfer girl is to be a girl who bumps up against well-resourced plans for local places that typically destroy surf spots.

If in the above contexts of best or fair land use of beaches and breaks one can see how a discourse of female sports empowerment merges with environmentalist politics to produce one kind of girl localism, other contexts exist that produce localisms with decidedly vague modes of agency. As we shall see momentarily from my discussion of boardshorts (a lucrative clothing product), everybody in the world of surfing these days has some investment in the new girl localism. Predictably, if the local proliferates alongside the global, if youth industries co-opt as commodities the newest styles and activities of young people, we must necessarily understand girl

localism, in one of its incarnations, as a market niche, a consumer demographic. In chapter 1 girl localism appeared as a relatively simple geography
or gender designation by which to suggest the political outlook, life history, and character of a small group of 1950s girls whose youthful rebellions
turned into lifetimes spent creating alternative feminist public spheres.
In light of surfer girls' active involvement in the film industry, it would
be naive to underestimate the degree to which their girl localisms were
formulated in regard to popular media. Still, the scale of media intrusion
into the global public sphere and its importance in subject formation at
mid-century remained more constrained. By contrast, an explosion of girl
localisms exists today—produced via the global surf industry, the fashion
industry, female-owned independent surf retailers, professional surf organizations for women, popular how-to literatures, subcultural videos, and
via local girls in specific communities. Throughout this book I will track
many of these instances of girl localism from the perspective of how they
"land," that is, looking to their social and political effects.

This chapter emphasizes the crucial elements of story or narrative in producing among girl consumers and subcultural members what ultimately
became (and are still becoming) the new terms of girl localist legitimacy.
I identify the prevailing mythologies about female athleticism that have
circulated in recent surf culture, especially those that girls have told themselves and each other to keep coming back to the water time and again.
They show, I argue, a distinctive Generation X (b. 1960–80) attitude about
girls' interface with authority, the female body, and sport. In particular I
make a case for the importance of the genre of biography and its coming-
of-age formal structure. Biographical narrative offers special insight into
how surf culture answers the challenge of fostering strength, courage, and
female life possibilities. As narrative and representational strategy, biography seems to young women to bridge the gap between the actual and
the fictive and therefore offers a relatively reliable source of support for addressing everyday gender dilemmas. The story of Lisa Andersen—the most
profiled female champion in surf media—begins this discussion. It then
opens onto the ways in which more sophisticated biographical conventions underwrite the critically acclaimed surf Bildungsroman *The Tribes of
Palos Verdes* (1997) and the Hollywood blockbuster film *Blue Crush* (2002).[6]

Toward the chapter's end I distinguish a Generation X imagination from
an emerging Generation Y profile of young womanhood in popular surf

media. To do so, I take up a fashion industry–commissioned series of young adult novels for Generation Y girls which debuted in October 2003 under the name *Luna Bay: A Roxy Girl* series.[7] As far as advertising campaigns go, it was a relatively lengthy phenomenon at eighteen months, during which time half a dozen novels were distributed while several others went to press but did not see circulation. What perhaps was most remarkable about the series was its multilayered marketing outreach program, which linked girls' fashion to online book clubs, chat rooms, instructional surf camps, modeling possibilities, the chance to meet or surf with female champions, and finally, with environmental activist causes. Such outreach efforts suggested to buyers that female empowerment, self-esteem, and activist engagement could all be had in sporting consumer culture.

That is, if consumer culture exploits the insecurity associated with female issues like body image, intelligence level, physical strength and ability, or future work aspirations, the same consumer culture can also be mined for solutions to those problems. Here we have a nexus of the complicated contradictions of the contemporary period which, in terms of degree and saturation, young women (and men) face more than any generation before them. Many of the contradictions of young women's lives might be effectively indexed via the term *sexism*, though the term rarely appears in popular literatures that worry over young women's futures. Sexism in public discourse is once again becoming a political problem with no social name. The girl localisms we see in this chapter put the celebratory discourse about girls and sport into more skeptical dialogue with the challenges posed by everyday sexism in girls' lives.

Girl Power and the Manufacture of the Brand

Boardshorts. The story told in *Forbes* magazine goes that Robert McKnight, the CEO of Quiksilver, was sitting on a Hawaiian beach having a postmortem powwow with one of his chief designers.[8] The company had lost a third of its volume in the United States in 1992, sales dropping to $60 million. Generation X youth were reportedly put off by the loud neon of late 1980s surf apparel. Snowboarding and "the pallid look" were in.[9] Generation X was saying (in Kurt Cobain style) "nevermind" to surf culture, and without youth buy-in, surfing as marker and market for subcultural

20   Boardshort advertisement in *Surfer*, 1999.

cool was tanking. "And [then] this girl walked by wearing one of our boardshorts [for men], pulled down low over her hips, over a bikini." McKnight
recalls, "It was real. It was sexy. We turned to each other and went, 'Ah-
ha!'"[10] Shortly thereafter Quiksilver launched a line of women's surf apparel, under the new label Roxy, featuring women's boardshorts as the
benchmark product. Boardshorts sold well both "in Kansas," as surf industry people say, as well as in California. Very quickly, boardshorts were
hailed as a potential rescue product, resuscitating surf-industry sales and
expanding its target markets in novel, female directions. Indeed boardshorts—the ad featuring Rochelle Ballard shown here as example—have
become *the* signature product of the new world of fast and hard surfing
for girls (fig. 20). More important perhaps than that, girls' boardshorts not
only made actual surfing more comfortable and free (no wedgies or worries
about losing bikini bottoms in rough-and-tumble conditions), boardshorts
changed the way surfing girls looked at *themselves*.[11]

Of course, boardshorts meant nothing outside their association with
a larger and explicitly politicized U.S. girl power movement of the early
1990s. As an artifact of a politics that suggests girls' power and rebellion
against female constraint, the feminist "storying" of boardshorts became

viable only because surf-industry executives accidentally happened onto an emerging movement and managed to exploit its styles and rhetorics toward their own ends. Although the history of this movement is fairly well known in youth cultural studies and studies of popular culture and music, let me recount it here, for it is less well known in the sociology of sport or in cultural studies of global media and globalization.[12]

The idea of girl power emerged from youth music culture in the early 1990s, specifically the punk music scene in Seattle and Olympia, Washington, as well as in Washington, D.C. Although male punk rockers considered themselves radically antiauthoritarian, girls found that in clubs, garage performances, and especially in punk dancing or the mosh pit, girls were expected to play second fiddle to boys' authority. Not about to settle for that double standard, punk girls protested by forming their own bands, converted the fan magazines associated with underground music to specifically girls' zines, and backed other girls as they began to speak out against sexism in the punk underground. In forums similar to those of the 1970s consciousness raising (CR) groups, girls talked among themselves about what it meant to be simultaneously girl and punk. They provided young women a place to speak out about homophobia, girls' lives in the new economy, and sexual abuse. The explosion of girls' zines broadened the local base of these protests until soon girls' media networking via the Internet created communities of like-minded women well beyond Seattle and Washington, D.C., into Canada, Europe, and South America.[13] Some of the more vocal and capable of punk feminist leaders like Kathleen Hanna of Bikini Kill had in fact been schooled in women's studies at Evergreen State College in Olympia and could speak to the history and theory of second-wave feminisms and define themselves as connected to them while also historically and politically distinct.

Unlike the CR participants of the 1970s, a surprising number of these young women also had done sex work or were currently employed in sex industries. They used forums as public spaces for coming out about but also defending their work as strippers or as other kinds of sex workers. They protested the antiporn campaigns of some second-wavers and encouraged more sex-positive feminisms. Among the girl zines, traveling feminist punk band concerts, and other open-mic public forums, the so-called riot girl movement emerged, often adopting the "grrrl" spelling of *girl* as a battle growl of girl power. If familiar features of feminist consciousness resurfaced in the riot girl, the concept also saw a heightened emphasis on popular culture as a site for political protest, on race and multiply situated subjectivity, as well as a more emphatic politics of gender-bending, queer sexualities (including heterosexualities), and the body as site of political action and transformation. For many of the third-wave feminists, whether or not they considered themselves "riot grrls" (and many did not), a political opening seemed to emerge. The important thing was the new context of thought and resistance centering around *them*—around the actual lives of young women, complete with their problems and their everyday opportunities for protest.

By 1993–94, the term *grrrl power* saw a wider cultural circulation. Traveling through and kept in play by consumer culture at large—for example, campy products like butterfly hair clips, Hello Kitty products, Strawberry Shortcake dolls, and later the Spice Girls, the *Powerpuff Girls*, *Titanic* (James Cameron, 1997), boy bands, and eventually boardshorts—grrrl power exploded as a phenomenon outside and distinct from, if nonetheless inspired by, the riot girl movement. In this latter incarnation the political edge and feminist analysis of contemporary culture became more diffused and girl power meant vaguely: girls are good and strong, while also pretty and smart and fighters for justice (warrior princesses like Xena, Mulan, and Buffy seemed to be all of the above). The process of co-optation and its effect on a popular belief in young women's supposed lack of political consciousness has been widely written about. Girl culture ultimately found an unforeseen new home in surfing. The phenomenon of boardshorts—a product that exponentially expanded the market for surf apparel—created the perception (however astonishing to longtime surfers) that surf culture was suddenly "girl aware," even "girl friendly." Moving rapidly into what at the time constituted an edgy new girl market, Quiksilver put its institutional muscle behind the Roxy label, which linked surfing with girl-powered athleticism. The value of the Quiksilver brand skyrocketed and surfing as subculture was on its way to a new image.

Such girl-welcome impressions came at just the moment at which a range of new female-owned surf shops were up and running, and both sensing and creating this new trend, women business owners got on board. Desirous of bringing more women into the ranks of the surfing community, tired of condescending male surf-shop staff and male-oriented product lines, and amenable already to the playfulness of girl culture (one of the

legacies of Gidget), the majority of the new women's surf shops keyed off
on the term of *girl* as they named their new ventures. Starting with Water
Girl, the first women-only shop, founded in 1995 in Encinitas, California, a
host of other shops opened their doors shortly thereafter. They included:
Girl in the Curl (Dana Point, California), Surf Like a Girl and Rip Girl (both
at Hermosa Beach, California), Sea Jane Surf (Redondo Beach, California),
Paradise Surf Shop (Santa Cruz, California), Pink Lava Women's Surf Shop (La
Jolla, California), Honolulu Wahine (*wahine* being the Hawaiian vernacular
for girl), Inner Rhythm Surfer Girl (Vero Beach, Florida), Shirley Can't Surf
(Key West, Florida), Hot Tamales (Wilmington, North Carolina), On Edge
Girl's Board Shop (Huntington Beach, California), Salty Sister (Carlsbad,
California), and s.h.e. Surfs (Satellite Beach, Florida).[14] All these together
created various power centers of global girl localism, the home bases of a
new political economy.

To fully appreciate the revolution in social geography that came with
these new surf shops for women, one needs to understand that, next to
actual surf spots, surf shops constitute the most important social location of the subcultural scene. They serve the role of clubhouse in local surfing communities and provide a physical gathering place, information exchange, equipment maintenance, competition publicity, and the economic
reproduction of the subcultural base. Surf shops might house local museum
archives, screen films, carry their own product lines, and sponsor competitive riders or events. Some do sport clinics, as does s.h.e. (fig. 21). Political
outreach efforts involve surfers in local environmental issues. They might
connect surf camps to local at-risk youth populations or to any number of
social causes.

New female-run surf shops, such as Paradise Surf Shop in Santa Cruz,
self-consciously intended to counter surfing's oppressive female body
ideals. Sally Smith, one of the founding owners of Paradise Surf Shop, reports her own desire as a surfer to see "real body" product lines in swim
suits and wet suits.[15] Specifically she wanted larger women like herself to
find clothing and bathing suits on the racks of local surf stores. Creating
new subcultural visual economies and ways of seeing, Paradise did the unthinkable: it posted a variety of female bodies—across size, age, race—on
its Web site, in catalogues, and in its immediate store environment. It suddenly became possible to go to a surf shop without suffering a sexist and

21 S.H.E. surf clinic, Florida, late 1990s.

soft-pornographic visual assault; one might even see imagery resembling the world girls actually lived in.

At the same time, surf camps and schools and clubs for female surfers began operations and were founded in explicit recognition of the barriers to entry that aggressive all-male surf breaks posed for girls and women novices. New girl localisms sprang up through surf clubs such as Chicks on Sticks (Narragansett, Rhode Island), Ocean Divas (Manasquan, New Jersey), Outer Banks Wahines (Kill Devil Hills, North Carolina), Sisters of the Sea (Neptune Beach, Florida), and Women in Waves (Crescent Head, Australia).[16] Many mission statements and online business biographies of surf camps and schools promised to teach the sport by constructive and supportive training methods as well as to provide female-to-female instruction and girl-gang crews who urged one another on in the water. These new ventures also utilized girl language in their naming practices: Surf Diva was the first in 1996, immediately followed by It's A Girl Thing Surf School (Santa Cruz, California), Saltwater Cowgirl Surf Camp (Jacksonville Beach, Florida), Big Island Girl Surf Camp (Hilo, Hawaii), and, of course, Las Olas, the Mexico- and U.S.-based business in Sayulita that aims to make girls out of women. This list continues to grow and is by no means exhaustive. In 2005 female-only camps existed in Mexico, Costa Rica, Brazil, California,

22 Layne Beachley on a thirty-foot tow-in wave at Backyards (North Shore, Hawaii), 1998.
Photograph by Art Brewer.

Florida, Hawaii, Australia, and Bali. By 2008 Nicaragua had a female surf
school in San Juan del Sur, Peru offered instruction for girls in the north,
central, and Lima regions, and Uruguay advertised girl surfing in Punta del
Este.

The sudden appearance in the late 1990s of surf shops and surf schools
for women became the phenomenon it is because professional women's
surfing has been maturing for twenty years. Former women pros started
and currently own many of these same businesses. By the late 1990s a co-
terie of current professionals of all levels could supply the new market for
girl-identified surf products with a cast of athlete stars and its attendant
star mythology, around which businesses and image producers organized
consumer fan clubs. Not only was Gerhardt busting down the door at Mavericks, but the Australian Layne Beachley also joined the elite corps of male
riders doing tow-in surfing at places like Backyards (fig. 22). A larger context of course frames this development in surf culture. In *Built to Win: The
Female Athlete as Cultural Icon*, Leslie Heywood and Shari Dworkin situate
the female athlete "as institution" within the larger social environment
enabled in the United States by Title IX of the Education Act of 1972.[17] *Built
to Win* fathoms the social imaginations Title IX produced among younger
women and men and links the historical novelty of large demographics of

girls and women doing sport to a related novelty: the creation of female consumer markets now considered large and viable enough to warrant serious industrial courtship. *Built to Win* takes up what it calls "the babe factor" in women's sports—the institutionalization in consumer culture of a new ideal of female athletic strength folded into and set atop that most classic figure of sexist discipline: the female beauty. Surf-industry giants may be among the most intensive producers of the babe factor in sports media today—and women and girls take up this tendency as a problem, as we shall see in the next section.

The narrative glue holding surf subculture together has always come in the form of cultural production, magazines and film and video in particular. The 1990s, however, now brought to the fore female-produced media for women like *Surfer Girl* (United States), *Wahine* (United States), *Surf Life for Women* (United States), *Chick* (Australia), and eventually *sg: the girls' source for surf, snow, skate, lifestyle* (United States), as well as more frequent pieces about women in major subcultural magazines like *Surfer* (United States), *Tracks* (Australia), *Longboard* (United States), *Surfing* (United States), *Surfer's Journal* (United States), *Carve* (United Kingdom), *Surfing World* (Australia), and *Revista Fluir* (Brazil). And there was live-cast ESPN. In magazines, televised competitions, and reams of new video footage, aspiring girl athletes for the first time in history regularly encountered both the images and the coming-of-age surf stories of top-ranked stars like Beachley, Rochelle Ballard, Kate Skarrat, Lisa Andersen, Keala Kennelly, Serena Brooke, Megan Abubo, and Sofia Mulanovich. Their struggle to gain official parity between the structure of the men's and women's tours was widely reported in women's surf media, and when the World Qualifying Series for women was established in the mid-1990s as a kind of feeder system recruiting and funneling elite female surfers into the World Championship Tour (WCT),[18] a new victory seemed achieved. Represented in surf media with the endorsements of heavyweight (male) surf-industry logos like Reef, Billabong, Vans, Quiksilver, Rip Curl, O'Neill, Angel Eyewear, and Swatch, female professionals' increasing stature suggested the possibility of new forms of female institutional legitimacy, backing, power, and respect.

When a young woman today opens a surf magazine or watches the Roxy Pro at Haleiwa on ESPN, she finds a growing number of female icons in whom to invest a dawning sense of athletic possibility: if she can do it, maybe I can do it. From its inception, Roxy was always much more than a fashion label. It quickly came to be *the* global logo associated with the economic and political infrastructure of women's surfing. Roxy underwrites major amateur as well as professional women's surfing events all over the world. Roxy's so-called team riders were and remain none other than the world's best female surfers. Equally important, that young viewer also finds a growing storehouse of narratives that suggest, beyond the *can* I do it, the *how* to do it. The coming-of-age stories of well-known surfers have come to form a kind of practical guide not just to surfing but also to living one's life as a female, especially living it with a sense of no limits.

Lending reality to this image is the historically significant fact that there are simply more women in the water today. While statistics on surfing today appear exaggerated, it is obvious to even casual observers of surf breaks that women's surfing is on the rise.[19] Women and girls are indeed "ripping" more than ever before, surfing fiercely, in part to compete with men, but also to push the limits of what women have been told they can or should do. Things have thus never been better for girls and surfing than they are today, but the gender story such an assertion implies is misleading. While women and girls are certainly active architects of this takeover, they have not been its principal power players and reap a fraction of its profits. Further, the assertion that surfing as a sport and culture is somehow wide open to girls, wholesome enough for even four- and five-year-olds with enough girl attitude, belies not just surfing's unapologetically sexist history but also its very steep learning curve. Generally girls do not just happen to take up surfing. They are raised in surfing families, live near an active surf break with all the attendant community infrastructure, do some related sport like skateboarding or snowboarding, or have friends or boyfriends who initiate them. The visual narrative transmitted about women and surfing by mass culture is often at odds with girl surfers' daily subcultural life. Girls *know it*, talk about it, and long for a more sustained "insider" narrative to explain to themselves how it is they have managed, in relatively large numbers and in short order, to defy the aggressiveness of collective male surf culture and paddle out anyway. Such a combination of larger narratives has begun to surface and circulate. It is to these I now turn.

Biography as History: From Private
Experience to Public Identity

The most widely profiled female coming-of-age story in surf media in the past decade has been that of Lisa Andersen, recent history's favorite female surfer and, I would add, a familiar kind of American character in the history of narratives about rebellious youth. At sixteen, in flight from her parents' stormy marriage, Andersen left Florida for Surf City USA (Huntington Beach), announcing in a runaway note: "I'm leaving to become the world champion of women's surfing."[20] This was 1985, and Andersen remembers that at the time she was not sure that such a title actually existed, but she hoped to impress her mother with ambitious goals. What is interesting about Andersen's tale as a female athlete is that although she won many trophies as an amateur and turned professional at seventeen, becoming a regular on the world tour, she did not step squarely into her four-time world championship reign until seven years later, in 1994, *after* she had a baby. Andersen credits her daughter with motivating her to finally become the best athlete she could be. Before that, she says, "It was really hard for me to see myself winning."[21] After childbirth, however, "the most womanly thing you can ever experience," Andersen felt bolstered by an "enormous amount of strength," which made her "invincible."[22]

While Andersen's is always told as a champion's story—she set the highest goals and achieved them, she took women's surfing to a new level, men and women alike respect her, she gives back to surf subculture and hence embodies the cardinal "Aloha" requirement of surf heroism—it's also told as a story that implicitly maps for readers the pitfalls of female dream seeking as well as strategies for persistence in the face of serious struggle. In Andersen's case, serious struggle begins long before she leaves home. She talks about the years between the ages of fourteen and sixteen as those "that I don't want to remember."[23] Nicknamed "Trouble" because she defied her parents' conviction that surfing was not something "a young lady should be doing," Andersen surfed, sometimes ditching school to do so.[24] In a biography that mirrors many classic American tales of (male) youthful breaking away and struggle, the tension with Andersen's parents over who was in charge of her young female life mounted until her father destroyed one of her surfboards. Her parents later contemplated having their teenage daughter placed under house arrest to prevent school truancy. When she ran away from home to become the world champion, she gained freedom from her parents' conflicts and control but faced new kinds of challenges as a sixteen-year-old girl on her own in rather rough Huntington Beach in the mid-1980s. Sometimes sleeping at night under the Huntington Beach Pier, she was initially homeless. Surfing every morning on borrowed equipment, Andersen took odd jobs waitressing and worked at a local surf shop. Fortunately, she found benevolence in the local surf scene when Ian Cairns (the founder of the Association of Surfing Professionals, ASP) took her under his wing, bending local contest rules to permit her to compete. Winning readily, Andersen quickly made a name for herself on the amateur circuit. Ever precocious, she turned professional at seventeen, but here the bottom fell out of her confidence. In what she terms "nomadic" years on the world tour, she surfed characteristically aggressively, admits to something of an attitude, and was known for "dropping in" on other people's waves, which in surf culture constitutes a gesture of disrespect for which surfers have a long memory. Her way of dealing with other champion surfers like Pam Burridge and Kim Mearig was to "go out and get in their way."[25]

The change came, she thinks, with the responsibility of providing for a child. That responsibility forced her to focus more, and she began thereafter to talk about surfing as a "career."[26] Her split from the child's father, the Brazilian surfer Renato Hickel and a former lead judge on the professional circuit, to whom she was briefly married, has been widely reported, and Andersen muses, "I work better alone. I can't have a husband, boyfriend or anyone telling me what to do."[27] In the years when Andersen was winning sequential world titles, her daughter accompanied her on the tour, and owing to the intense physical demands of that time, her lifelong back problems flared, until a herniated disc and severe sciatica forced a premature retirement in 1997. But the mythology around Andersen grows. While mainstream surf-industry media have featured Andersen during her career, in women's surf media she has emerged as a central figure. Andersen's presence at women's contests and events sparks autograph-seekers and other admirers. She consistently tops the favorite-surfer polls of wannabe surfer girls. Bill Ballard, a surfer and filmmaker, as well as the husband of the female professional surfer Rochelle Ballard, says of both of them, "[they are] true role models. They're people who little girls can dream

23 Girl "Groms" (beginners) with Lisa Andersen, the *Surfer* magazine/Blue Crush All-Girls Giveaway, 1999.

about being. . . . Little girls are opening the magazines and saying, 'I want to be Lisa'" (fig. 23).[28]

For younger Generation Y girls, what it means to "be Lisa" is to be the kind of female who will not settle, who will pursue, in and out of a sport, a no-matter-what philosophy of life. What is important in my formulation is the condition of wanting itself. Younger girls are not trying to best her (be her or be better than her) as much as they locate in her their own desire to go beyond what girls have been told to wish for. Desire for Generation Y girls here means, among other things, embracing other girls and valuing "girl-ness" at the same time as one aims to achieve at the highest level—a balancing act that requires young women to refuse the social pull to become athletic to prove themselves more than or different from being "just a girl."[29] Andersen's narrative offers to younger women a kind of girl hero creation story, an exemplary structure for narrating subjectivity. It actively dialogues with a longer and more complex masculine national cultural tradition and also assumes the possibilities for women achieved by second-wave feminism. Andersen's break from family, her rejection of rules, the struggle she underwent to make a name for herself, her rise from no money to international fame, her ability to have a child and seemingly transcend or escape the female oppressions that come with the institution of mother-

hood: all these features of Andersen's biography establish her as a quintes-
sentially American heroine with twenty-first-century feminist credentials.

Given the superficiality and marketing impulse behind most mass cultural visual images of women and surfing, girls who actually surf readily
take to anything that looks like real information, and Andersen's hardscrabble life story impresses readers as exactly that. The rough edges of
her tale have not been digitally altered to create a predictably pretty picture
of magazine femininity, even as Andersen clearly fits the "babe profile"
(fig. 24). Yet it seems notable that Andersen's is more of an "after" tale, after
she has made it, than a "during" tale. Would she be as attractive a figure if
she had continued as a hard-edged, uncooperative rebel girl and not become a responsible career mother?[30] Would Quiksilver or Roxy tolerate a
product spokesperson who was unrepentantly "bad"? Would Andersen be
as prolifically photographed were she not blonde, blue-eyed, and so classically "babe"? Likely not. Women on the tour have often grumbled about
the politics of conventionally defined beauty, as the former world champion Pauline Menczer noted in the late 1990s: "Women's surfing is . . . Lisa
Andersen. The rest of us might as well not even be here."[31] There is no doubt
that good looks provide a calling card to female subcultural careers. But if
an ambivalence about or criticism of Andersen by Menczer lingers, they
concern less the surfer personally than the sexual politics of the industry.
And these, too, are the lessons of biography.

The genre of female-produced biography operating across different
media has emerged as influential precisely because its generic conventions suit it to the task of suturing the gap between mass culture's commercial motives and what young women regard as everyday subcultural
life. Whether girls read profiles of up-and-coming young surfers in print
media or online, view a film or video that looks in depth at a particular
surfer or group of surfers, visit a Web site for a surf camp or school or surf
contest or surf a reality TV show, or post biographies on Facebook, MySpace,
chat rooms, or YouTube, it is within biographical or life-story genres that
surfer girls most often encounter themselves in organized storied form.
Biographical conventions would indeed be impossible to avoid, since most
material about young women is available right now in this and not other
explicit generic formats.[32] To be sure, surfer girls hear and tell the stories of
their own individual and each other's surfing experiences all the time, for
along the way to celebrating the ultimate ride on a very clean day (surfing's

24.1 Lisa Andersen during her mid-1990s reign as champion and "babe." Photograph by Art Brewer.

24.2 Lisa Andersen at the Roxy Jam, Cardiff Reef, California, 2006. Photograph by Elizabeth Pepin.

trope), surf culture never tires of recounting wipeouts, hold-
the inevitability of being caught inside (trapped in the impact
aking surf). The oral practices and cultures evidenced in girls'
ies on these topics have complex implications.

But it is through written biography that seemingly private, individual, or local oral tales are translated into public and semiofficial ones, forcing a larger reckoning with the character and status of women's surfing, and in the process creating a public female culture capable of operation beyond specific local communities. When girls read biographical profiles, they reposition their own practices of storytelling vis-à-vis the emerging public story of "women's surfing today." As has so often been the case in women's history recovery projects, biography in surf culture functions as a "first wave" genre that documents the fact of women's presence in what otherwise are regarded as masculine cultural geographies. Biographical narratives educate women across the age spectrum about the presence of women in surfing history, the troubles they face with male hostility or the "babe factor," and about their negotiation of the physical and emotional limits imposed on them by other women and girls. Biography provides foundational narrative structure for more elevated forms of cultural production as well, underwriting (in both overt and diffuse ways) novels, films, and short stories.

Before I turn to the other forms of cultural production that will take us to the end of this chapter, it is crucial to note that the breakout moment for contemporary women's surfing starts with the newer generation of young women like Frieda Zamba (b. 1965), Burridge (b. 1966),[33] Andersen (b. 1969),[34] Ballard (b. 1971), Beachley (b. 1972), Menczer (b. 1970), and Gerhardt (b. 1975). A hugely enabling figure like Margo Oberg is on the early cusp.[35] I would identify all these women (including the Australians Burridge, Beachley, and Menczer) as Generation Xers. They grew up in the cultural wake of various First World civil rights movements that produced the benchmark Title IX in the United States. These female athletes narrate their lives through an embrace of sport socially possible for girls only after Title IX. So although they came into young adulthood in an era of political backlash against civil rights gains and of budgetary shrinkage (especially as budgets relate to young people), they constitute the first generation of women to understand themselves from infancy as nonetheless liberated. Their particular opportunities, challenges, self-understandings, relationship choices, and public identities reflect this complicated moment of political transition and set the defining tone for the metabiography about female surf culture traveling the world today.

This particular generational formation certainly underwrote the production, sale, and consumption of the surfing Bildungsroman to which I now turn. The first female-authored surfing novel to date, Joy Nicholson's *The Tribes of Palos Verdes* (1998), provides a clear example of a Generation X athletic profile; at the same time, female surf stories here deepen their reliance on biographical genre conventions, also innovating them to tell new stories.[36] New is the protagonist's upper-class status—most surf stories tell a far more working-class tale. The protagonist, Medina Mason, is daughter to a father who is a heart surgeon to the rich and famous. Her mother is a former model. At the novel's opening the family's emotional center is crumbling. The father chases other women; the mother compulsively eats. The saving grace for Medina is her relationship with her twin brother. Most often compared by marketers to a female version of *Catcher in the Rye*, a direct advertising bid for the lucrative girl market, the story under construction here is that of a young person struggling against powerlessness in society's mainstay adult institutions: the nuclear home, schools, the surveillance systems of local neighborhoods. But if the *Catcher in the Rye* tag sells, suggesting that girl culture today constitutes as important a public topic as did boy culture in the 1950s, as critical analogue it only goes so far. The antiauthoritarianism of an upper-class female Generation X surfer from a coastal town in Southern California is worlds away from that of a preppy New York young man in the immediate postwar years. Of all the differences, I want to highlight the role of sport in this young woman's opposition to authoritarian power hierarchies, since it is sport that enables her to oppose the class-inflected gender roles installed on the women and girls of Palos Verdes. By surfing, Medina refuses the principal dictate of upper-class femininity: to maintain a "tasteful" and "feminine" appearance by any method necessary.

The protagonist explicitly claims the four-time world champion surfer Zamba (fictionalized as Frieda "Zane") as her own female athletic role model, which is to say that the novel establishes its insider subcultural status by gesturing to biographic and historical realism. Illustrating the surfer girl fan club culture to which I alluded earlier, Medina learns of Zane's life story from a magazine article. The magazine photo of Zane in Hawaiian surf hanging above Medina's bed enables her to articulate a sense of ultimate female possibility. It is thus no wonder that Nicholson explicitly acknowledges both *Surfer* and *Surfing* magazines, and also not so cryptically thanks "F.Z.," whom we can reasonably read as Frieda Zamba.

Because the fictionalized Zane is a world champion, Medina assumes that women can operate at the world-class level. The question for her is *how*. Importantly, Zane forwards not just any athletic philosophy, but a specifically Generation X philosophy. Medina quotes her magazine mentor as saying: "Don't limit yourself to being a lame chick in the water . . . use your mind and your arms."[37] So as not to be a "lame chick," to resist the anxiety that she may forever remain "just a girl," Medina trains hard, cross-trains, surfs every day, and pushes herself into bigger and bigger surf. The mental training perhaps proves hardest, since Medina confides to the reader how difficult it is to ignore that the locals laugh at her beginner's efforts in large measure because she is a girl. To be admitted to the all-male surfing tribe whose home break is in front of her house, Medina has to prove herself twice as much as does her brother (equally a beginner). To do so, Zane's suggestion that she forget she is a girl and surf "like a man, aggressive and fierce" (24), seems to map the only viable direction. Medina grits her teeth, keeps going no matter what, tolerates trash talk about women in the water, and teaches herself to become a "paddling machine" (26). Reminiscent of Andersen, Medina blasts any girl who gets in the way. This take-no-prisoners method constitutes the standard mental and physical plan for young women of this particular generation who are intent to turn themselves from "just girls" into athletes.

If the competitive psychological and physical edge Medina nurtures is designed to support her as she takes on surfing's stiff learning curve, it also protects her from the world of pretty appearances that governs the aspirations of other Palos Verdes mothers and daughters. In a local culture of cosmetic surgery for teenage girls and Bibb lettuce luncheons for their ever-dieting mothers, in a family whose father understands women to be, like landscape painting, connoisseur objects of the cultured male gaze and whose mother can resist this gendered visual ideology only by way of self-destruction, surfing offers the best cultural system through which Medina might hope to value her body alternatively: for what it can do and where that takes her, not for how it looks. For Medina is explicitly *not* "a babe." Readers repeatedly overhear her parents tell Medina that she is not beautiful. For Medina to value her body according to alternative visual and philosophical economies—those of the athlete—is to minister to the places with which she struggles as a thirteen-year-old female born into upper-class contexts. Surfing as everyday practice offsets the oppressive dictates of owning-class girl-ness that surround Medina at home, in school, and in her gated beachfront community.

The text also illustrates many of the defining differences between second- and third-wave feminist cultural norms. In implicit defiance of the second-wave tradition of "women-identified women," consider that Medina's best friend is her brother (indeed, she has not a single girlfriend). Medina reflects casually on surfing as sometimes akin to "religious experience," sometimes "pure domination" (48). No doubt Medina would prefer calling herself not a feminist but, in the tradition of the Generation X television queen Roseanne Arnold, a "killer bitch."[38] But *bitch* is not the hardest self-affirmation for a second-waver to swallow. At a moment when she fears her brother will not go out into the surf with her, she chides him: "Oh Jim, don't be such a pussy, just close your eyes and go in" (15). Third-wavers, one might say, have much stronger stomachs than do their second-wave predecessors.

In her sexual behavior in particular, Medina illustrates the third wave's expansive sense of female sexual agency and its complex relationship (to the dismay of many secondwavers) to sex work. At the beginning of the text Medina makes a deal with a neighborhood boy to lift up her shirt for ten seconds in exchange for a surfboard. She gets enough of what she wants out of that deal that she makes it again, with another neighborhood boy, and proudly takes home—her own version of a trophy—another surfboard, a gift to her *brother* so she now has surfing company. If a second-wave reading of this text might wonder about Medina's status as a victim or object of masculinist sexual discourse, asking whether this is not vaguely a representation of prostitution, a third-wave reading might understand Medina's act as one in which it is not she who has been exploited but the sexual attitudes about girls of the neighborhood boys. Indeed, we might read this moment as a 1990s innovation of the 1960s "feminist zap," for Medina's parents are rich, and at her request would likely have bought her and her brother surfboards. Since much of the text is given to narrating Medina's sexual coming-of-age, and probably only one sexual relationship falls into the category of a "healthy" or mutually respectful relationship, the second-wave reader is again tempted to frame analyses with the word *victimiza-*

tion in mind. But such a frame would have to answer to the claim, implicit in a character like Medina, that the subjective experience of female victimization has undergone a radical revision and that girls like Medina feel less victimized than did or do second-wave women.

Still, a world in which one's mother and twin brother commit suicide is hardly a good one, and in testimony to that fact, the book ends starkly. Medina paddles outside the breaking surf line, bringing along her brother's empty board. In a ritual goodbye to him, she lets the board go, saying, "I'll be surfing in Hawaii soon. After that, Bali, Java, Thailand. I have no itinerary, no plans to return. I'm going to surf until I die" (218). The final departing sentence, five lines later, reads: "No one knows I'm crying" (218). I would note the familiar Generation X trope underwriting this lone conclusion: the feeling, as used to be said in international studies, that the time we live in, instead of being one of the Cold War, is now one of hot peace. No place is safe.

Nicholson chronicles the absolute shock of the post-1989 cultural order. On a personal level, Medina's family has fallen apart. Her father comes and goes, with a new and, of course, beautiful and young girlfriend. In lieu of a family, Medina relies on her "tribe," comprised of the local surfers in Palos Verdes. If one of the reviewers applauds the power of a young girl to save herself, the *necessity* of self-preservation actually makes this tale so stark.[39] In the text's representation of friends as family, and the complete "on one's own" status of children in this particular U.S. family, *Tribes of Palos Verdes* stands in for one of the most frequently told of Generation X tales. As analogues, think of well-known texts like Bret Easton Ellis's *Less Than Zero* (1985) or Douglas Coupland's *Generation X* (1991)—both novels that marketers also tout through a *Catcher in the Rye* comparison.

Let me here turn to a different kind of generational text that illustrates for this chapter the transition in recent years between Generation X and Generation Y philosophies about empowered girlhood—the blockbuster film *Blue Crush*, filmed on location on the North Shore of Oahu. Like Andersen and the fictional Medina Mason, this film's protagonist, Anne Marie Chadwick (Kate Bosworth), knows what trouble is. Viewers immediately learn that for so young a person, she already has something of a history. We learn that Anne Marie has been effectively abandoned by both her mother and her father, leaving her in charge of her younger teenage sister, who is herself heading into risky directions with boys, booze, and drugs.

As do most young people, Anne Marie turns for employment to the service industry, where she works as a hotel maid, though it does not allow her to make ends meet. Yet Anne Marie is anything but a victim. The story of Anne Marie as a hopeful competitive surfer structures the film's sense of female possibility, as does its opening off-screen voice-over taunt between two girlfriends. One of them (an echo of Andersen) says, "I'm gonna be the best surfer in the world," to which the other retorts, "*I'm* gonna be the best surfer in the world." This friendly but serious competitive tension sets up the film's discussion of women's surfing today. If a young Andersen "gets in the way" of other great female surfers, if Medina Mason finds female relationships to be all about competition for men, the map for girls' survival in *Blue Crush* suggests a different female world: all roads lead to figuring out how girls can hang together and fully back each other.

A cinema of girl power underwrites *Blue Crush*, and a discourse of girl cockiness reverberates throughout. Drawing from the critic Mary Celeste Kearney's arguments about some other nonsurfing teen films, I see *Blue Crush* as a film incorporating contemporary feminist themes, particularly those of "the need for girls to develop confidence, assertiveness, and self-respect apart from boys and through same-sex relationships."[40] The impulse to cheer one another on to more difficult goals not only frames the film's opening exchange between Anne Marie and her childhood best friend, Eden (Michelle Rodriguez), but it sets up the authority of Eden as a figure capable of training Anne Marie. That is, Eden is herself substantial enough as an athlete to see Anne Marie through what turns out to be a comeback bid after a near-drowning surf experience. The comeback will be staged at none other than the legendary Pipeline Masters on Hawaii's North Shore—one of the world's most photographed waves.[41] Unambiguously a masculine social geography, Pipeline breaks with enormous force, over a shallow reef, and it shifts—waves are famously hard to read. Like Mavericks, Pipeline has historically credentialed the men of the men. Anne Marie is a wild-card entrant, meaning she is a special local invitee. If Anne Marie can surf this legendary spot skillfully, she has a chance to get her competitive prospects back on track. Nobody seems to have a better handle on this fact than Eden, whose training philosophy mixes the all-out aggressiveness of a Zamba or an Andersen with the power found in female solidarity.

The need for a defiant girl attitude, indeed, why girl power has proven so useful to young women since the early 1990s, is suggested early in the film as viewers are treated to one of surf culture's classic pecking-order scenes: that of the oceanside parking lot, where surfers ready themselves to go out, studying the waves and crowds and sizing up whoever else is present. The majority of such parking lots resemble, to women, outdoor male locker rooms. One becomes very self-conscious of one's female presence. As the *Blue Crush* heroines are getting gear out of the car and readying themselves to go out, up pull a few Pipeline local guys. Male characters in the film repeatedly address these young women (with various kinds of intentions) through the language of girl culture. "Hey howz'it, girls?" is immediately followed by a challenge to Eden, from what turns out to be Anne Marie's ex-boyfriend, JJ: "Does your girl have her head on straight this time?" Eden defends Anne Marie, "You know it," but the guys do not buy it. JJ says to Anne Marie, "What's this I hear, you're going to surf Pipe Masters?" "Why don't you find some girly bowls?," which means gentler surf, finalizes the insult. This challenge to Anne Marie's surf prowess is met by her trainer's rejoinder, "My girl's gonna charge [the Pipe]," "My girl's gonna dominate." Calling what looks to them like a bluff, but also wanting to give their local girl a chance, the guys offer to "block" for Anne Marie so she can get in a good practice session; they will use their locals' clout in the water so that Anne Marie gets more than her fair share of waves. To save girly face, now the trainer and the wild-card entrant must assent to this essentially male dare.

But if Eden's talk about charging and dominating is bold, the girls' actual wave selection is far tamer. Cowed by conditions visualized as extremely fierce, the girls do not follow JJ and his buddies toward Pipe's steepest peaks, where the guys jockey for waves. Instead, they surf off-center, on the shoulder. Only after JJ paddles away from the men and over to the mellower shoulder, asserting, "You're not gonna win the Masters sitting on the sandbar," does Anne Marie actually paddle herself into Pipeline's heart. Here again girl language figures as JJ grandly announces, "Welcome to the arena, girl, let's get you into something big." This, the viewer senses, is a different scene altogether. The lineup for this most elite of world waves is all male — a sea of floating male bodies on surfboards. Anne Marie balks on the first setup, which locals understand as well-nigh criminal, given the monster wave breaks unridden. Outraged, they yell out, "What the hell is she afraid of?" And also, "This ain't a beauty pageant!" The pressure is on Anne Marie to show herself as more than "just a girl," more than a pageant contestant who looks good in a bathing suit. To "get into something big" in *the* arena requires more than Anne Marie can deliver just now, however. When she takes off, trying to measure up to the "I dare you" logic operating here, the viewer senses that this type of motivation will not result in the command of her body and mind that Anne Marie must find to perform at peak. She goes down hard on a huge wave (triple overhead), and in the next shot we see who cleans up the mess: it is her gang waiting onshore, her trainer Eden cutting her no slack, commenting: "It's all up here in your head . . . if you would have just committed [to riding that wave] . . . but you didn't have the balls to really charge it."

Fear stands between this young woman and the life she is close to realizing as a competitive surfer. The antidote to fear is commitment, committing to the wave, to her ability to ride all out, without hesitation, "charging it" fully. She must put into action the no-matter-what ethos with which I began. To have the life she wants, both in the water and onshore, Anne Marie needs to go for broke, to risk everything. She needs to summon the post–Title IX subjectivity that underlay the life logic of Andersen, Zamba and Medina Mason. This embodied subjectivity insists that women take up public space in new ways: with edge, swagger, entitlement. It oozes "masculine" confidence and refuses anything suggesting "victimized" or "just girl" femininity. The film asks the viewer to make this no-matter-what pact with Anne Marie, to get behind the idea not only that she *can* do it but that she *must*. Her integrity and her livelihood as a young woman depend on it, as do those of her gang.

For their lives are at stake too. Since Anne Marie's parents have deserted her and her teenage sister, the "family unit" keeping Anne Marie and her sister financially afloat consists of this crew of surfer girls. They work as maids and live and surf together, and by pooling wages, they make rent. But future prospects for none of these young women are promising unless they can make surfing pay. The Pipeline Masters is Anne Marie's ticket to somewhere, as close to a career audition as she is going to get. As Eden tells the viewer, "Every single sponsor" is in town, and "it's just you and one other girl out there [in the contest lineup]." Spying that other girl at a local gas station—the big-wave surfer Keala Kennelly (a current professional)—Eden declares enviously, "She never opens her wallet," meaning that sponsors foot all her bills. When a few moments later the girls count pennies to

pay for their breakfast and still come up short, the viewer begins to appre-
hend the economic predicament these young women face.

Keeping the class dimensions of this tale front and center, we begin to
imagine what is riding on Anne Marie's ability to perform at Pipeline. *Blue
Crush* advances a working-class narrative in which a single protagonist is
the principal symbolic hope of her renovated all-female family; their for-
tunes will rise and fall with hers. Anne Marie's emotional scars from the
near-drowning episode threaten not just her own well-being but also that
of others who depend on her, whose futures are also on the line. As evidence of Anne Marie's working-class concerns, consider the conversation
between her and her love interest in the film. He asks her what she wants
from life. She answers that she wants her sister to go to college; that she
wishes for a female on the cover of *Surfer* magazine; that she longs for a
month in which she has money enough to pay the electric and the phone
bills at the same time. This discussion—mapping working-class female
desire for the film—speaks to Anne Marie's sense of living not as an indi-
vidualistic or middle-class subject, but as one whose deepest affinities are
tied to group-identified emotional networks and hopes. So the fear shadow-
ing Anne Marie in big surf is that if she drowns, the whole family will go
down with her. She must succeed because she is everybody's ticket out. To
do so, she will have to overcome not personal fears but the fears layered on
classed and female populations that they cannot truly do what it takes to
overcome all that society gives them in terms of obstacles and challenges.

The film puts forward a twofold rescuing philosophy to meet this challenge: first, one has to charge big surf and, by implication, any of life's most
daunting obstacles. The particular language used in the film to articulate
this program I have linked to a Generation X formation since, to advance
female risk taking and boundary busting, to survive various social and personal abandonments, it makes use of what are typically understood as masculine strengths and strategies for survival ("balls"). But to charge big surf
according to masculinist logics alone, to denounce the feminine to push
hard for whatever goal one desires, is a recipe for female failure because
it leaves unchallenged the lingering sense of inferiority associated with
being female (she's good "for a girl"). Hence, the second part of the film's
rescuing strategy consists of combining a philosophy of charging with one
that explicitly values a fierce defense of connections between girls. So the
political vision under construction in the film suggests that only by com-

bining Generation Y "girlishness," girl-gang solidarity, and fem
with Generation X's ferocity, courage, and willfulness are female:
connect with one another and to back each other fully. Only when
refuse to denounce femininity or to compete with each other for 1
proval or masculinist social rewards will they free themselves from sexist
oppression and succeed on their own terms.

Some points about the relationship among girl culture, women's professional surfing, and the world of everyday girls need to be made here. First,
the film dramatizes all the elements of the late-1990s surf scene. Some of
the world's best female surfers—Skarrat, Beachley, and Ballard—appear
in cameo during the contest sequences and provide the film's spectacu-
lar female surf footage. Organized amateur youth surfing like the National
Scholastic Surfing Association (NSSA) gets a mention, since Anne Marie is
reported to dominate the junior NSSA. Surf logos, especially Roxy and Billabong, get plenty of visual air time. The existence of the world of surf camps,
schools, and lessons, run by *young women*, is taken for granted, and the film
shows how much of an economic carrot or subcultural career surfing can
offer young women like Anne Marie and Eden. Their surf lessons earn each
of them a whopping (and exaggerated) $150 an hour. Tow-in surfing and
elite performance training, with Eden driving the Jet Ski, visualize female
presence in extreme sports in which 99.9 percent of the participants are
men. *Blue Crush* marks a new level of popular exposure for women's surfing, all the while suggesting that the subculture's infrastructure is open to
rank-and-file girls with enough capability, attitude, and girl solidarity.

Blue Crush takes full circle surf culture's tendency to narrativize the
life stories of everyday girls through and alongside those of surf stars. The
screenplay of *Blue Crush* is borrowed from a magazine story, "The Maui
Surfer Girls" by Susan Orlean, first published in *Women Outside* in 1998.
In terms of genre, "The Maui Surfer Girls" falls between short fiction and
working-class group biography, and like the film, it is focused on a gang of
everyday, hardscrabble girls. They actually make their homes at Hana, not
on the North Shore. Although screen credits do not name it, the film also
likely draws inspiration for its title from the well-known surf video *Blue
Crush* (1998)—a familiar romp through interviews with surf pros alongside
some great international footage, but a real first in surf videos to feature
the decidedly "girl power" sensibility of its all-female cast (fig. 25).[42]

The private stories of everyday girls like those on which Orlean bases

25.1 *Blue Crush*, 1998.

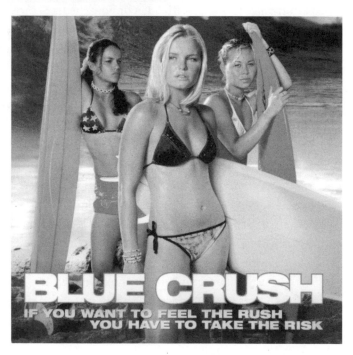

25.2 *Blue Crush*, 2002.

her story are also being rewritten as girls see the subculture itself reconstituted into a more public female culture within mass media. Most interesting to me is the film's final take on competition between women. During the contest heats Anne Marie watches a perfect wave approaching. But she has been balking all day, not charging 100 percent. It is the real-world big-wave professional surfer Skarrat—in cameo as Anne Marie's fictional competition—who tells Anne Marie she has to commit all out, reinforcing everything Eden has urged. With this kind of in-water solidarity between women, Anne Marie demonstrates a personal-best performance, even as Skarrat wins the heat and the contest. If Anne Marie's win is not one that brings home a first-place trophy, her great final showing ensures that she will now be sponsored and therefore have a future in professional surfing. She has accomplished the comeback. Alongside this win is another, namely, on the terrain of women's relationships with one another. The ability of females to stand as a group against social wrongs, to take a no-matter-what direction in the face of any suggestion that girls do not rate, is the core challenge girl power mounts. By sticking together, by not letting destructive competition come between them, girls' collective (as well as individual) power grows.

Toward a Generation Y Global Girl

In 2003 Quiksilver began to promote its label Roxy Girl through corporate-hired *literature*. Since surfing has typically had a bad-boy image and the parents of teenage girls flee from anything predatory when it comes to their daughters, Quiksilver reasoned it could expand its market share by revising the surfer girl image so it might suggest something like "nice sporty girls who read." Quiksilver struck a deal with the writer and surfer Frances Lantz of Santa Barbara to pen a series of novels for girls.[43] It debuted the first novel under the name *Luna Bay #1: Pier Pressure* with the Roxy pro rider Veronica Kay (the quintessential "babe") shown surfing on the novel's cover (see fig. 26). During the next year and half's advertising season, four additional novels saw circulation, all of them aimed at the nine-to-twelve age group. During the months of the active ad campaign one could find a book club online at the Roxy Web site. Site visitors could join, discuss books, chat with one another, and a Roxy editor responded to girls' comments. Discussions always noted the girls' hometowns, which

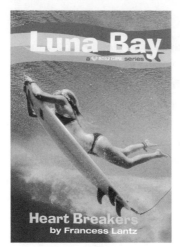

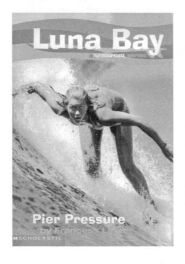

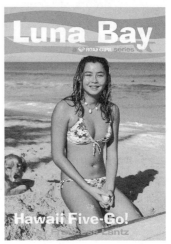

26.1 *Luna Bay* books.

showed a telling internationalism: Australia, Puerto Rico, England, Fiji, South Africa, Japan, as well as obvious parts of the United States (California, Florida) but also those less predictable (Midwest, New Jersey). Marketing ploy or not, these global addresses are not random. The international women's surfing professional tour, sponsored in part by Roxy, stops in surfing communities in all of these places except England, the Midwest, and New Jersey.

The novels' story lines take up the newest surfing adventures and the freshest romances in the lives of five best girlfriends who also are competitive surfers. They live in a fictional beachside town in Southern California, somewhere between Los Angeles and San Diego. The friends represent classic types of surfers well known to subculturalists: hard-core shortboard "shredders," big-wave surfers, longboarders, soul surfers, and one, the protagonist, who combines these types and can do everything. Importantly, the social base of their friendships is a small business—a surf shop run by the protagonist's parents. Readers' introductions to the everyday structures of surfers' lives come as much through "stoked" water scenes and teenage romance as they do through representations of the microeconomy of the subculture, particularly the local surf shop where the girls work as camp counselors for summer surf camps. Through the economic networks of contemporary surf culture—its competitive amateur circuit, high school surf teams, product-endorsement opportunities, modeling work for competitive surfers, and opportunities for surfers to market their original products and inventions (the protagonist designs T-shirts)—readers come to make sense of the girls' relationship to surfing, to one another, to boys, to adult authority and institutions, to the surrounding coastal hills that influence water quality, and, since the culture of surfing in this series travels, to globalization.

The series features a three-time world champion as the mother of the protagonist, a kind of second-wave graying blonde feminist role model for the young women in her social orbit. Her daughter, with much anxiety, tries to walk in her footsteps. The mother, whose name recognition frequently opens doors for the girls, is the controlling (if not exclusive) authority on surfing as sport, traveling culture, and everyday life. Most of the adult women and mothers in the series vaguely register as liberated WASP second-wavers. One of them "insists" (as her daughter puts it) on changing her own car tire when she has a flat. Another is a capable businesswoman and single mom. Another fights with her husband until they separate because he wants her to follow him and his job to a new town, a move that would jeopardize her work as a horsewoman and trail guide. The exception, and I will return to this point, is the Mexican American mother of Isobel, who seems more "traditional."

In contrast to these second-wave moms (and at least one equality-supporting dad), the girls of this series are unmistakably Generation Y and in terms of gender philosophies fall broadly under a third-wave feminist umbrella. Perhaps the signature evidence of the girls' Generation Y location is the use of the language of "hotties" to describe attractive young men, and young men's bodies often serve as objects of a female gaze. This gaze remarks in detail on boys' musculature, narrow hips, facial structure, and hair. But if this certainly drives a heteronormative plot, the real emphasis has less to do with "boys" and everything to do with female self-respect and respect for bonds between women. These are not youth versions of the romance genre. Girls speak a language fully conversant with popular psychological discourse about what makes and what does not make an emotionally healthy girlhood. No self-deprecating Ophelias or destructive "mean girls" here. When one such "queen bee," Vanessa, appears in the series, the group of friends disallows her to poison their relations. These fictional "Roxy Girls" evidence stable mental health guaranteed by sports activities and supportive friendships, but also by (generally) benevolent adult authority. The girls back one another when the going gets tough, and they bring each other back to sisterly sanity when anyone gets too distracted by boys. While they sometimes enjoy the encouragement of male peers in the water, these girls are independent enough to "rip" (surf aggressively) even without it, cheered on by girlfriends and effective adult female leadership. For them, no surf spot is too heavy, no hard-core male locals scene too hostile. In several scenes of sexist intimidation and hazing, the girls keep their heads, speak up, and keep surfing strongly. All the while they respect femininity; they insist it be valued, taken seriously. These are no tomboys, wishing secretly to have been born boys, but they are also not "just girls," or surfers who are "pretty good for girls." What is youthfully feminist about these tales is the bravado and self-celebration that animates girl culture, its ability to identify and resist overt sexism and to show girl-gang loyalty in the face of destructive pressures for young women to compete with one another over social status, physical difference, or boys.

If the third-wave leanings of these girls show in their ability to fight with boys when necessary, they also show in girls' ambivalent relationship to a feminist ideal that is all work or achievement and no play. Indeed, official feminism in this series is most often figured through independent mothers whose life examples seem implicitly to demand of daughters that they work, work, work, prove, prove, prove. Compete. One ongoing drama of the texts concerns each girl's efforts to be sponsored by surf companies so she can travel and perhaps go pro. This dream requires entering the world of competitive surfing with its contests, scores, rankings, and press. How competitive to be and what constitutes "good" versus "excessive" competitive behavior figure as ethical and personal dilemmas. Each girl has a competitive personality to some degree. The second-wave champion surfer and mother, who herself loved to compete and win, advises all the girls on this topic, especially her daughter, Luna, the best all-around surfer and the one for whom the series is named. Luna fears she cannot measure up to her mother's example. Her doubts stage the opening drama of the series in the first text, which ultimately resolves by Luna forgoing a wave that would potentially bring her first place in a contest.[44] She would have had to choose the wave over her best friend, who is also competing, and Luna just does not want the wave, or the win, as much as does her friend. The first book ends with Luna embracing her ambivalence about whether she wishes to follow her mother's brand of feminism. Both her competitive mother and her laid-back father support her in her efforts to figure it out. There are no second-wave lectures about betraying the cause.

One also sees an implicit dialogue with third-wave feminist consciousness in the texts' work with body issues. These girls are very aware of conventional ideals of femininity and their straitjacketing effects. The girls navigate the constant presence of beauty culture or the babe factor in surf culture, fully aware of doing so. Girls are fit, strong, and feel good about their strength and about what it permits them to do in the water. At the same time the cultural imperative to be athletically heterosexy keeps them ever anxious that their shoulders, stomachs, chests, legs, and hair will mark them as too athletic, as too this or not enough that. Some of the earliest discussions focus on the girls' envies of one another: whether it is the ability to eat anything without weight gain, comparisons of hair, comments on a lack of freckles, one's willowy legs, beautiful skin, and so forth.

The final book in the series tells the story of the girls as surfers and models on a women's surf magazine photo shoot to Hawaii.[45] Like the representations of competition, this modeling sequence tells a tale of ambivalence and a search for balance between the opportunity such modeling occasions afford and their unforeseen complications. The social perks available to girls willing to embody this role come with a downside: not just the considerable unglamorous hours spent fixing hair and doing makeup but also exposure to other exploitive aspects of the microeconomy. The photo shoot story is linked to a related one about the displacement of native Hawaiian surfers on local waves by the influx of traveling California mainland surfers. If the girls do not stand up to the magazine editor in charge of this particular photo shoot, they will become complicit agents in the popularization of yet one more secret surf spot. Local boys make clear to the girls the history of U.S. colonial takeover of the Hawaiian islands, putting the photo shoot opportunity into a longer political context. The girls finally side with the boys in a gesture of critical localism that ousts the editor from her job while the shoot proceeds without revealing the location of this locals-only surf break.

Such side-taking locates this series in the mainstream of Generation Y visual and ethical economies related to race, bodies, and notions of cultural sensitivity. These tales represent multicultural bonds between young women. The protagonist of the series is blonde and through blondeness readers understand she is white. Her name, Luna, is given by her parents for its Spanish meaning ("moon") and to link her to the place they live, Luna Bay. Two other members of the crew also are white, Rae and Cricket. Their racial types are gleaned through discussions of their bodies—strawberry blonde hair, freckles, skinniness, and flat chests. Kanani, another girl, is of mixed race, Hawaiian and white. Yet she is adopted, and her adoptive parents are white. Kanani is explicitly identified as a mixed-race person. She is the group's ecoactivist, a girl passionate about "saving the planet." Her body has curves and she is beautiful, everyone agrees. At the same time, Kanani is shown to be exoticized, which her friends understand as a burden. Another of the girls, Isobel, has flawless "toffee skin," is dark-haired and muscular, toned in some places and soft in others. She is not talked about as a racialized person. Rather, her Mexican American ethnicity comes through a representation of a culture of family and through her Spanish-English bilingualism.

Difference is topical in this series at the same time that there is not a sense that multiculturalism or race would destructively divide these friends. Insofar as diversity is the norm of most youth Generation Y story lines, and cross-cultural respect is the constant narrative informing diversity, we might say that notions of racial tolerance have been aggressively incorporated into youth media and markets. White-nonwhite relations do not figure as tensions between these girls, even as a tale with a surprisingly anticolonial impulse is told about the Hawaiian locals. Or at least tensions do not figure for long. In a conversation between Kanani and one of her white friends, Cricket, about the local boys' desire to keep their surf spot a secret, Cricket offers the opinion that more tourist dollars and exposure can only create jobs and more opportunity for local Hawaiians. Kanani disagrees and makes a case about who profits most from the tourist industry, as well as pointing to the ecological cost of the tourist industry to locals. One of the resorts is running a new pipe that dumps sewage into an area in front of one of the locals' homes, which means that his family can no longer swim or surf there without falling ill. Such an uneven distribution of environmental burdens infuriates Cricket, and ultimately both girls decide to use local media to publicize this wrong and get it righted. Cricket, by book's end, is a white girl with a new consciousness about the history of colonialism as it applies both to Hawaii and to herself as a white Californian surfer who needs to show respect to local native surfers.

A critical white racial formation seems to be under construction in this literary advertising campaign, and its racial logic has to do with border crossing and education. Histories of racialized conquest are presented for young readers and the intended message is that white people need to overcome white racism. California as a homebase region seems a "natural" site for the demographics (whites, Mexicans, Asians, Pacific Islanders) generating such structures of cooperative raciality. A border-crossing sub-regional identity then travels to Hawaii, where it can respect locals' rights. Nonetheless, the fact is that the blonde people of the text own the surf shop and center the economic structure of the tales. The bodies of those white people, particularly of Luna and her mother, occupy the role that most closely resembles an idealized type—even while the logic of that type is always under scrutiny as the girls actively critique the ideal and support one another in not falling prey to it. Moreover, the fact is that Luna herself is not represented as worrying over her body to the same degree as do the other girls.

A number of coming-of-age narratives underlie this series—that of sec-
ond- and third-wave feminism, of Generation Y American girls, and of girl-
friendly surf culture as a liberalized or updated version of masculinist surf
history. I would locate these contemporary coming-of-age stories in the
context of a formal convention, that of the Bildungsroman of the late eighteenth century and the early nineteenth that historically represented and
narrativized a nascent capitalist modernity. Franco Moretti argues that
such a task was accomplished by inventing "youth" as a modern social
location capable of articulating tensions between more traditional social
contracts and the individualism that modernity occasioned.[46] These tensions of course are historically, if not exclusively, biased toward men and
are Eurocentric: the social contract has always constrained women's individual liberties far more than it has men's, and maturity in the colonial era
often meant coming-of-age into philosophies of the self and of community purpose identified with Western progress.[47] In terms of the gender life
cycle, the apprenticeship or Bildungsroman plot traditionally assumes its
protagonists' ultimate claims on a skill or trade, especially a modern, Western, "public" social location in excess of "private" marriage and/or parenthood. Travel abroad, to the colonies perhaps, and sexual initiation historically aided the maturation journey for men. Women's unchaperoned travel
or sexual experience by contrast compromised the successful Bildungsroman resolution since the major life "choice" of the female narrative is
that of a partner and motherhood.

Clearly the women's liberation movement in the United States has
altered all these foregone conclusions, and the biographies and coming-
of-age stories of contemporary surfers suggest that the formerly male life-
cycle options of the classic Bildungsroman might now be open to women.
Such is the implicit claim made by the Roxy Girl series. We have in surf
culture a credible support network for female coming-of-age: a three-time
world champion female mentor, a group of accomplished and motivating
peers, injunction to travel and to gain (with definite constraints) sexual
and romantic knowledge, as well as a larger context of transnational surf
culture approving of female efforts. As an advertising campaign, *Luna Bay*
books make a bid for the serious benefits of surfing to girls. It gives girls
novel opportunities for careers, travel, healthful living, and the education
that comes from exposure to new people and places. With that travel comes
responsibility to the local places one visits and an awareness of the ecofoot-

print and cultural intrusions one's travels potentially create. The Roxy Girl series advertises surfing as a form of youth citizenship. Surfing for these teenage friends involves political ecocommitments that in turn create social consciousness and a sense of global ethics.

While clearly possibilities for female development have opened, it is important to note that the series simultaneously reads as a contemporary version of the older tradition of the conduct book. It is clear what "good girls" ought to do as they negotiate this demanding moment in global history: they should compete, achieve, support one another in similar goals, take care with their appearance (but not somehow too much or the wrong kind of care), and eventually join their fate to that of a single boy. They should enact "cultural sensitivity" since many people will be racially mixed. Where there are differences based on race and culture, girls should strive toward awareness and tolerance. In other words, the conduct required for contemporary girlhood is implicitly gender-liberated and racially and culturally tolerant. Girls will not merely hope for female public accomplishment in addition to fulfilling the roles of wives in family life; rather, these public roles constitute new social mandates. They are *requirements*. Surely this is one reason why the series echoes with so much ambivalence, especially for the "privileged" protagonist Luna. For how "liberating" can a discourse of women's liberation be if it is already known and also required?

As Nancy Armstrong has shown, courtesy literature, along with the novel, is implicated in the feminization of culture beginning in the late eighteenth century and coincident with the making of the middle class.[48] Echoes of this history operate now with the formation of a new global space of girlhood. If in the nineteenth century bourgeois "civilized" womankind was under intense construction, in the present moment consumerist American girlhood is under construction. The terms of a successful girlhood are prescriptively professionalist and it is understood that competitive professionalism, not some dialogue with politicized feminism, facilitates liberated femininity. The factors that are to underwrite tolerance are unclear—beyond the fact that blurred boundaries between "us" and "them" have made supposedly pure racial categories increasingly obsolete. The Roxy Girl texts, like surfer-girl discourse more generally, form part of an attempt to manage this new icon of global girlhood. To the forces who can manage "her" will go considerable spoils, particularly the better she performs in nondomestic markets.

American Western heroes and heroines have traveled the world for two centuries, producing profit and various knowledges about the American, the real, the masculine, the beautiful, the bohemian, the edge. "California girls," for at least the past fifty years, are heir to a similar international reputation. As I noted before, the new Generation Y surfer girl represents big bucks. Her visualization and emotional profile is currently exported as one highly desirable figure of normative young American femininity—a significant new player in a global marketplace selling liberated gender identities and ideals. As one ideal of dominant visual economies, this figure will discipline women whose bodies and social values do not fit the norms signaled through her. As a figure for the world's women to emulate and the world's men to desire, she should not be dismissed as a form of "culture lite" because that is exactly how the politics operating through her will fail to attract and sustain critical scrutiny and practical intervention.

Part II. Globalization from Below

Three

The Politics of Play

Tourism, Ecofeminism, and Surfari in Mexico

Something about an impending major hurricane levels a lot of playing fields—for a little while anyway. During the storm, and then when it is over but before daily life resumes, all the social seams show and people are obliged to go about habitual roles differently. Such anyway was the case for us, the collection of campers and surf staff who made up the Las Olas surf camp session when Hurricane Kenna came ashore in 2002 and sent a section of the Mexican Pacific coastline into crisis.

We arrived on a late October afternoon. I came in from Houston, fifteen women came from northern California, and six total from Florida, New York, and Colorado. The category-five alert had not yet been issued—but there were indications. Heavy bumps during my own flight and long bands of black thunderheads outside the window suggested alarming weather. Even the Texas regulars—practiced in the two-and-a-half-hour flight from the Gulf Coast to second homes in Puerto Vallarta—got off the plane rattled. Few of us living in hurricane-aware Houston would have boarded a plane knowing so powerful a storm was out there.

Once on the ground, however, the quaintness of Vallarta's airport took over. Notwithstanding its international bustle and hustling taxi drivers, the pace of the everyday instantly decelerates. In this part of Mexico, one does not need products "to go." This is one of the famed regions of Mexican hospitality—*a sus ordenes, señora*—offering that healing affective balm for world-weary tourists. So it became possible to imagine an anxious flight had been more a function of First World nerves in need of downtime than of a major weather event in the making. Besides, the airlines would not have flown passengers directly into the eye of a tempest, would they?

And then the other balm, the enormous energy of the Las Olas surf instructors who greeted each camper. Two of them with heavy Australian accents, one a native Hawaiian, two from Northern California—women in their mid-twenties to early thirties, our official tour guides, and if initial impressions held, playmates of the first order. Already the carefree spirit of teenage girls in a group infected us and made even the wait in the airport for transport to Sayulita full of laughter. What were we laughing at? Anything, the smallest thing, all of us women in a group, with the power of a group to be loud and take up public space without worrying (as women worry) about giving offense, stepping on someone's toes.

Introductions between campers were made. Two mothers came together from Boulder; two young friends from Florida; a number of women, most of them young, had ventured alone, as had I; a mother and daughter; a group of ten friends had come from the Bay Area to honor one friend's fiftieth birthday. This latter group called itself, loudly and proudly, the Hot Flashes. Now that was something to laugh about. The reverse finishing school mission of Las Olas, to make "girls out of women," seemed to require nothing more than social permission, a decision to relax the responsible role of mature female identity.

We exited the airport into a humid, seventy-five-degree afternoon and piled noisily into vans for the forty-five-minute drive up the coast to Sayulita, the village headquarters of Las Olas. The road cuts through heavy jungle and returns to a visible coastline only once you have arrived. With no view of offshore activity, we talked little of the storm systems witnessed in the air. Either way, most of the campers were Californians, and to get their attention one would have had to say "earthquake" or "fire"; hurricanes do not figure in the California regional vernacular.

At 2 a.m. we got the knock on the villa door: "Here are some trash bags. Hurry, put some stuff in them, we are evacuating to Puerto Vallarta." Despite forewarning during the group's first dinner, most of us had gone to bed convinced that nothing would happen. For one, we had the loveliness of our treehouse accommodations to distract worries—Villa Amor lulled us into a beautiful dream (fig. 27). At a deserted beachside restaurant, the owner of Las Olas, Bev Sanders, had joined us for the evening meal and offered her customary first-night welcome. But this time around she had

27.1 Treehouse accommo-
dations. Photograph
by Elizabeth Pepin.

27.2 Outlook on the local break
at Sayulita. Photograph
by Elizabeth Pepin.

focused less on our learning to surf than she did on the weather situation. At dusk indicators showed a category-five hurricane watch in effect for the state of Nayarit. Bev informed us that her husband had happened to make the trip with her from their home in Benicia, California. While as a founding principal of this female-only surf camp he typically remained out of sight for group activities, during the hurricane watch he became more visible as he made the rounds in town to consult the coast guard and the four or five people who had computers. Since most of the staff, including Bev, spoke little Spanish, his language proficiency was a blessing.

The campers took these announcements in remarkable stride given that we looked out, from our restaurant table, onto what seemed to me an ominous offshore scene of nearly black cloud cover. Or perhaps it was just a spirit of adventure in waiting—the "surfari" already delivering its requisite promise of danger? Before Sayulita drew tourist dollars into its local economy, livelihoods were rooted in a village fishing industry. A clus-ter of twenty or thirty humble wooden boats continues to populate the northern end of the town's beachfront. The men who owned these boats had pulled them well up into the footpath and away from shore and their regular nighttime moorings. A modest insurance against a potential storm surge, but one took the precautions available. As we walked home from dinner along the unlit dirt road, we stepped around, over, and inside the open-bowed boats as best we could, dim flashlights affording little aid. I remarked to one of the women from Boulder that, were we to come back over them in the dead of night and in driving rain, these *pongas*, as they are called, would seem less picturesque and make more of an obstacle course— some of them with slippery surfaces from the day's fish catch (fig. 28). The wind by now was picking up. Her response, more an impatient exhale than a direct rebuttal, went something like, "You think too much, relax." In this view of me, she had company.

But over the boats we came, at 2 a.m., in blowing rain, encumbered by trash bags stuffed in a hurry, tearing holes as we rushed, slipping on fish slime and then trailing a smell behind us. Soaked by the mile trek from Villa Amor into town, we arrived at the Las Olas headquarters in a confusion of forgotten passports and increasingly convinced of emergency. At last there was group attention for information. Was it true that an approaching hur-ricane sounded like an oncoming train? How reliable was the prediction of landfall in the actual area where we, with our trash bags, sat shivering and

28 Local fisherman at Sayulita.
Photograph by Elizabeth Pepin.

wet? What did people *do* here, without computers, without information? What were *we* to do? In their hurry to leave Villa Amor, some were not sure they had locked their doors behind them. And who spoke Spanish, besides Bev's husband, me, or the Mexican American member of the Hot Flashes? Who would navigate hard information? The husband was in and out of the headquarters building, conferring with other men, I noticed. My own offer to join them met with an unspoken no. After the flurry of initial questions and with no oncoming-train sounding, a general sense of festivity eventually took over. Hey, one of the Hot Flashes said, won't this make for a great story later? That tone then dominated. No matter that surf lessons had not yet begun, the surfari was already in full swing.

At around three or four in the morning a middle-aged man announced that he had located a bus and a driver to move our group to a hotel in Puerto Vallarta. We waited. Eventually up pulled a bus, its young driver (nineteen maybe) smoking a cigarette while talking on a cell phone. He was laughing into the phone, oblivious to us as we heavily boarded. He shut the doors abruptly, ground the gears into forward, and then split his talk between whoever was on the phone and the middle-aged man, our apparent companion for the trip to Puerto Vallarta, now tall in the bus stairwell. It was no time for complaints. Holed up in Las Olas for the last dark hours, we had found the storm stronger once we walked, against the wind, the few blocks along the street to where the bus waited. Hair blowing wildly, papery trash scooting along the ground in the rush of sandy air pushing hard onshore, now would be the time to go! On otherwise bare and dark streets, one small *tienda* was lit. We stopped in front of it long enough for our driver to open the door, his companion to jump out, spirited greetings from inside to drift back onto the bus, then a victorious return with two Cokes. Grinding back into motion, we retraced the jungled route south to Puerto Vallarta, rain sheeting down at times, the companion watching the right side closely for branches and downed trees and twice getting off the bus to move aside, in the shine of our headlights, huge tree limbs. The man was strong. Many people nodded off as we sped along; there was a quiet settling in. But the hairpin turns, rain-spattered windows, and the urgency of escape—all while the driver smoked, nursed his Coke, chatted, and laughed—offered me too little security for sleep. I thought of my sons, my worried husband (a Gulf Coast native) who would be watching the global weather news, and my own reservoir of adventure memories—they belonged to another lifetime, another person.

At last the hotel came into view. After the check-in, after walking the echoing tiled hallways to a separate room and dropping the plastic bag on the floor, I turned down the bed, listening to palm fronds scratch the windows and to the low howl of wind. I had what seemed like good information from local police outside the hotel (were they actually standing guard?): the storm had been downgraded as it neared shore to a category three.

The morning after: banana palm fronds heavy with thorns scattered across the hotel lawns; blossoms torn from flowering bushes and floating in the hotel pools; air heavy still with storm moisture; tourists wandering about in strange dress. But from the breakfast scene in the central courtyard, who knew? Massive food service, waiters blending margaritas and brewing coffee, and was that somebody skinny-dipping in the pool? Everything suggested a big party. The Las Olas crew breakfasted around multiple tables. One of the Hot Flashes was recruiting water ballerinas, as she called them, for a performance she wanted to stage in the next couple of hours. I had already been to the front desk, asking about the weather, and rumors had it that the storm was recycling offshore and we were in for a second round. I delivered this news to the group, which received it without comment. We stared at two women—what were these women about? They wore black fishnets and what looked to be Playboy Bunny suits, but in black, with black ears. In the lobby I had already seen the women and overheard their story at a desk set up for people evacuated here from the beachfront hotels. It had been in the wee hours, all of them in costume at a party in somebody's suite, when they had learned of a surge wave, not huge at ten feet, but big enough to take out the first floor of the Puerto Vallarta Hilton, which had held even with its first-floor guts removed. They had high-tailed it, winding up here. Their rooms were all bones now, no flesh; their passports and underwear mingled somewhere at sea. When I recounted this information to our group, at last I seemed to offer something relevant.

At about midday, having realized that, indeed, guards were posted and keeping watch at the threshold of the hotel doors, I left our sheltered enclave for post-hurricane chaos. All I could think of was the film *The Year of Living Dangerously*: what I saw suggested the same meltdown minus the overt political intrigue.[1] Perhaps two hundred weary English-speaking tourists—matronly women in muumuus, newlywed couples, mothers holding children by the hand—lined up on the hotel's sidewalk and used it as a kind of lean to protected "home" for now. They awaited buses to take them somewhere, and had been waiting for a dozen hours. The lucky ones sat on suitcases. Across and down the street toward a commercial strip I could see flooding—cars and furniture floating in a parking lot and people wading, trying to run through standing water that in places was hip-deep. As I got closer I understood that I was witnessing lootings, and I stood there for a moment staring dumbly. Local people of all ages, including children, rushed around, packing clothes, small appliances, and linens, some hefting big chairs or TVs over their heads to avoid them soaking. A tourist with a toddler in her arms stood next to me, a dumb witness too. We realized at the same moment that looting was not a spectator event and mumbled something about her getting out of there with her little one. I asked had she heard where the storm currently tracked and if it was recycling and coming ashore again? She knew nothing. I then moved on too, sticking to the straightaway streets where the occasional police cruiser drove by.

Colorful hotel couches floated in the ponds that now encircled the Hilton. In the small mom-and-pop shops that front these hotels, old women and men swept water out of their stalls with long bristled brooms. They were in no hurry, and we traded earnest greetings. By late afternoon local police informed me the storm was officially spent. It had made landfall at San Blas, destroying the town but resulting in few deaths. Damage to Mexican property was reported at $100 million.[2]

At the evening meal I mentioned to the Las Olas group the weirdness of being inside a guarded compound for drinking pool-frolickers while the immediate vicinity underwent a meltdown. One woman was knitting. I did not use the words *privileged* or *First* and *Third World* or *global unevenness*. Still, these were not conversations to be had. Later Bev called a group meeting to report we would return to Sayulita in the morning. All afternoon Bev had wrestled with whether or not to cancel the surfari and refund our money, but air travel would likely be suspended for another day or two, and we needed to return to Sayulita anyway to retrieve our things. She took pains to explain her reservations about returning to the village and whooping it up, having fun surfing, when the storm had likely created hardships for local people. She resolved the dilemma by asking the group whether it wished to become a workforce for the town of Sayulita in whatever recovery efforts it was making. The request had barely left her mouth when it met with the group's jubilant and total approval. Everyone wished to give something, to do whatever we could do. If this was not a crowd with whom *The Year of Living Dangerously* had traction, it was also not one that doubted that there *was* something to be done. Not temperamentally given to discouragement or political agonizing, the Las Olas crew hopefully talked up our group intentions.

The next day we worked in small clusters to clear the beach at Sayulita of big pieces of wood, tree parts, trash, and blown-off roofing fronds. Local fishermen—their boats not much damaged and now returned to daytime launch positions at the shore break—treated our efforts as endearing oddities. Simple talk passed between us in Spanish: Where were you during the hurricane? Their response, always: "In the hills." Such modest social openings hung in the air easily for a couple of days. What turned out to be true is that Sayulita fairly easily returned to normal. It is not a high-maintenance place, and, in a category-five hurricane, that fact would have left it leveled, like nearby San Blas. Palm fronds make up the *palapa* roofs of most beachside restaurants. They are plentiful, cheap, and rethatching roofs makes for an afternoon job. Businesses and homes have floors made of stone, hard dirt, polished concrete, marble, or tile. Unlike carpet, it gets wet, dries, and sweeps or mops clean. Windows often are open-air passageways; there is nothing to shatter or replace.

But if our group created a conspicuous ecopresence on the beach in the post-hurricane days, the real help our presence signaled was the promise of a resumed tourist economy. Local merchants stepped up efforts to ready their places for business. On our first night back, with electricity not yet restored, we entered a restaurant as its only customers and looked down a line of fifty white candles enchantingly lighting the table. "Hospitality" was returning, transitioning from crisis to noncrisis modes. The food was cold, the beer warm, and conversations between restaurant workers and us resembled those with the fishermen: How did you pass the hurricane? Not the conversation of service-industry roles. But as the night wore on, the roles returned. I remember a distinct feeling of shame when some of the women drank too much and, given the half-functioning status of things, asked for too much. The shame of privilege, too, indicated a transition back to normal.

I returned many times to Sayulita after that first visit in 2002, gathering more material not just from the surfers who come through on holiday or make semi-permanent homes but also from the local Mexican towns-people on whom the new economy relies for various kinds of labor, economic cooperation, and broad cultural consent. I came to think of my hurricane introduction to this place as a metaphor of sorts for the tempest of changes that globalization has occasioned. My time in Sayulita brought into sharp relief the expanding transnational character of girl localism. I began by being a participant observer in the Las Olas camp, evacuating with everyone to Puerto Vallarta, eventually attending class, going surfing, frequenting bars (fig. 29).[3] But beyond Las Olas and its English-speaking clientele, on that first trip I initiated a series of other conversations with workers in service industry jobs, local real-estate people, Sayulitan women of many ages including surfing girls, nonlocal Mexicans who travel to Sayulita for work, and Americans relocated permanently and now making a living from tourism.[4]

These other conversations took on an unforeseen dynamism because of the massive promotional press Sayulita began to receive around that

29 Presurfing class at La Casita. Photograph by Elizabeth Pepin.

time in U.S travel literatures in particular. Articles about new real estate and getaway opportunities for Americans appeared in *The New York Times*, *The Seattle Times*, and *The Dallas Morning News*.[5] Upscale English-language magazines like *Travel and Leisure* marketed Sayulita as "La Nueva Rivera," a place for destination weddings and yoga retreats.[6] And at least one book targeting retirees was published, *Gringos in Paradise: An American Couple Builds Their Retirement Dream House in a Seaside Village in Mexico*, by Barry Golson.[7] By 2008, on my most recent trip to Sayulita, the effects of such promotion were everywhere—in the enormous expansion of the town, its changing transnational complexion, its new chic feel, its booming construction industry.[8] The relocation of many in-town barrios to outlying areas has made way for this gentrification. Surf-related businesses have exploded and now offer lessons, rental equipment, coastline tours, lodging, boutiques, clothes, surf food, even surf folk art—like the surfer girl *calavera* (a skeleton doll-like collectible). Mexicans now run half of the surf businesses; when I first visited they ran none.

In what follows I report on these conversations, which have emerged and matured in very short order. I begin with those of the Las Olas tourist women on the topics of surfing or sport, its relation to the world of work (paid and unpaid) for U.S. women, and what I call "the politics of play." The premise is that the Las Olas camp culture and business philosophy aim to "globalize from below," and to do so explicitly with attention to women and the leisure industries as a response to the overworked lives of First World middle-class women. I try to think through the role of play in the recent history of U.S. women's liberation, arguing that certain forms of intense play or sport, like surfing, implicitly politicize and alter consciousness in ultimately feminist directions. Since second-wave feminism inherited from both WASP and U.S. leftist cultures an aversion to frivolity, and since *younger* women's tendencies toward play and leisure are often bitterly renounced by second-wave public figures as politically escapist, I am interested in making sense of groups of women for whom female liberation means something about the female body's ability to play hard, play rough, and play for keeps, as though one's life depended on it.

As a female-focused camp with a self-consciously gendered mission statement, Las Olas aims to politicize women's and girls' identities and caretaking roles so that they care not just for others but for themselves, the environment, and a larger world. Surfers' global play has created millions of new environmentalists, and what is happening in Sayulita works in tandem with this larger impulse. But the specific issues raised by global surf play cannot be anticipated in advance. To think about less expected outcomes, I will work in a moment with one scene of ethnographic encounter in particular, a case of spontaneous intergenerational female solidarity. That scene came to function for me as a feminist parable about the generational distances between second-wave feminists like me as stand-ins for university feminism at large, "nonpolitical" boomers like the Hot Flashes, and younger Generation X women who have grown up in a world bettered by contemporary feminism. These women do not call themselves feminist even while traveling the world as liberated women.

Of course this play takes place in Mexico, in a market niche that explicitly *sells* hospitality, even social privileges—again, *a sus ordenes, señora*— and these latter accrue, after NAFTA, disproportionately to Americans who can pay for them. Such a social context makes for countless complications in an argument forwarding glimpses into intergenerational feminist solidarities. One wants to know between which generations, between which national constituencies? To the extent I eventually offer a critical reading of touristic privilege, it comes from the perspective of local Sayulitans whose conversations with me centered on the impact of travelers on their town before and after what they call *libre comercio*, free trade. How are things in the new Sayulita for women and girls, I asked repeatedly, what has changed about everyday life? The responses to these questions are deeply conditioned by Mexico's debt crisis, its declaration of bankruptcy in 1982, and the lean years that characterized local economic life until NAFTA produced new sectors here for revenue generation.[9] As do women from the United States when they talk about their work lives in the new economy and the need for respite or holidays, Mexican women are attempting to wrestle with globalization and its opportunities, new productivities, and new gender and generational relations. Not surprisingly, Sayulitan women differently evidence globalization's discontents, complications, and poignancies, expressing deep anxiety about the seeming out-of-control-ness, lack of a driver of this hurricane vehicle speeding down twenty-first century paths to prosperity.

Girl Power, the Environment, and Intergenerational Play

One of the more socially interesting facets of the girl power phenomenon is its availability to females who are no longer girls—that is, to mature women like baby boomers. If the resurgence during the 1990s of *The Endless Summer* allowed boomer men to return to the scene of their coming-of-age and take stock of all that has transpired since, a similar phenomenon has been unleashed as boomer women witness the coming-of-age of girl power—a narrative about powerful and respected young womanhood that not even remotely characterized their own adolescences. Baby boomer women have observed younger women's unprecedented opportunities and cultural presence and might be forgiven if they find themselves wistful for a girlhood they themselves did not experience. When the surfers of the 1950s are interviewed today about contemporary surf girl culture and its relative opportunity, they indicate something of this wistfulness when they remark that they were just born at the wrong moment in history.

The Las Olas mission statement to "make girls out of women" falls into this larger context. Las Olas has been in operation since 1997, and middle-aged women between thirty-five and forty-five comprise the majority of its clients. The typical camper will be a white mother, often hailing from California, will arrive with friends, and is in the paid labor force. Always she is middle- to upper-middle-class. Such demographics mean that she likely is "doing it all"—kids, paid job, community work. She is simultaneously more liberated and exhausted than was her own mother, with no identifiable target to blame (other than herself) when she senses something wrong with the picture. Her central motive for making the surfari trek is the promise of a particular kind of rigorous yet girlish play undertaken in an all-female environment advertised as generous and nurturing (fig. 30). She is up for a personal challenge and assumes that she will walk away from the experience somehow physically and emotionally empowered. Women who do Las Olas characterize themselves and one another as risk takers. Given that Las Olas now operates not just this flagship surf business but has expanded to offer "golf safaris" and "creative artistic safaris," all of which claim the same "make girls out of women" mission, it is clear that the reverse finishing school process appeals. I have not interviewed Sanders about the ecological implications of the golf offerings, though this newer aspect of her portfolio raises questions about the compatibility of business and activism. But why the appeal of the reverse finishing school? What are its political claims and effects?

Among international surf camps, Las Olas is more the norm than the exception in its overall philosophy of surfing and its understanding of gender relations. To the degree that these surf camps overtly theorize the status of women, and the women's camps and businesses often do, they do so in classic ecofeminist terms. Women are "instinctive caretakers," the mission statement of Las Olas asserts; "empower us and the whole world benefits."[10] Although university feminism has renounced these versions rigorously for their essentialisms, such ecophilosophies appeal because they speak to and value the enormous caretaking and nourishing work these mothers and community members already do and which cannot readily be left behind. The strategy or path to empowerment these days is not so much the "women's culture" link between femaleness and moral superiority, as it was in the 1970s and 1980s, but new links between girlhood, play, and power: "Our strength can be discovered by the little girl inside who just loves to play in the waves."[11] Girl consciousness, suggesting the ideal of unencumbered female possibility, opens a sense of freedom, of political agency. By leading women to play in the ocean, to develop a "friendship

30   Intergenerational play. Photographs by Elizabeth Pepin.

with the ocean," Las Olas hopes to facilitate a new connection to the waves and to foster a sense of the ocean as "a living breathing thing" that allows women in an "uncertain world" to remember what is "truly important."[12]

Taking her lead from a recurrent visitor to Las Olas, the third-wave eco-feminist Julia Butterfly Hill (the activist whose yearlong residence in a Washington State redwood tree brought public scrutiny to logging-industry practices of cutting down old-growth forests), Sanders sees human connection to the natural world as a precursor to environmentalist activism. That relationship, Sanders believes, "enables women to speak up for what we believe in, the rights of our families and communities, or on behalf of an abused ocean or forest."[13] Her ecofeminist successes in her hometown of Benicia, north of San Francisco, suggest the political sincerity of her mission statement. In 1997 she and other women organized a successful campaign to block the building of a coke (a polluting byproduct of oil) facility on her town's waterfront.[14] In 2001, after staging a protest with a group of women against the cutting of local old-growth trees that the local press slammed as "too emotional," Sanders hosted an alternative event that emphasized *fun* (jumpy tents, games, attractions for kids and their parents). Butterfly Hill showed up to speak on behalf of the green oasis. Sanders's positive style swayed the community and the trees remain standing.

The footprint Sanders and her business leave in Mexico is a more complicated matter, however, and no one knows this better than does Sanders herself. Las Olas orientation sessions for new arrivals last, over two days, about six to eight hours, and much of the instruction, before one ever gets into the water, concerns local culture, customs, and appropriate behavior while in Sayulita. "Please cover up when you leave the beach," campers are instructed. Mexican women do not walk down the street in bikinis, and if Americans do, it creates bad transnational blood between women. And if you request takeout from local restaurants, bring a container or otherwise your food will be packaged in Styrofoam. Every week the group engages in beach cleanup efforts, and the townspeople who watch it nod approvingly. Although Las Olas manufactures souvenir T-shirts and provides rash guards and other items to campers with its own logo, Las Olas does not sell them in Mexico. As Sanders sees it, once you have women trying on T-shirts and choosing colors, they start looking in the mirror, comparing bodies, and commenting on their own deficiencies. This scenario, even though it would make her money, would undercut Sanders's insistence on a no-pressure, noncompetitive atmosphere. Although Sanders has been a businesswoman all her life, beginning in the snowboard industry, her economic philosophy is not driven solely by bottom-line concerns. She talks about how Americans confuse wants with needs, a confusion underlying personal unhappiness and political injustice. However paradoxical it may seem, her business ethos critiques consumerism, critiques the solutions offered by that same consumer culture to chronic female overwork, and critiques the profit makers' willingness to produce and then exploit female insecurity to make money.

But of course she cannot even begin to control all the variables that her ten to fifteen camps per year, meaning three hundred to four hundred tourists annually, potentially occasion. And here serious complications arise for an enterprise professing grassroots globalization. Las Olas caters to upper-middle-class U.S. touristic tastes, the price of the camp starts at about $1,800, excluding airfare, and there is only so much "roughing it," at this price, that the already exhausted women want. Sanders puts up guests at the architecturally sublime Villa Amor, owned by the American couple Rod and Mary Ingram, who live permanently in Sayulita and have built not only the three-story villa but also an art-piece of a condominium next door. One of Villa Amor's entrances, in a nod to the new economies created by NAFTA, actually flies the triple flags of the United States, Mexico, and Canada. The Ingrams' real-estate firm, Playa Mita Realty, connects the Sayulita luxury real-estate scene to that emerging in nearby Punta Mita—where a Jack Nicklaus golf course, a Four Seasons hotel, and all the ancillary development have begun, in barely a decade, to re-landscape that formerly sleepy village and surf spot. More is coming. Fonatur (the Mexican National Trust Fund for Tourism Development) has slated Punta Mita to be a three-state mega-destination by 2018. There is no doubt that the principal flow of money in the Las Olas financial circuit goes from U.S. tourist to U.S. surf camp owner doing business in Mexico to U.S. hotel proprietor doing business in this and nearby developing areas in Mexico, with not very costly stops along the circuit to pay Mexican hotel staff, bus drivers, maids, restaurateurs, and roving beach vendors who hawk silver, local indigenous (Huichol) beadwork, and blankets.

To put into even sharper focus the broader political economy into which Las Olas falls, but also to make clear that small businesses like Las Olas should be understood as definitely different and certainly opposed to the other development ventures currently sprawling, let me detail the mega-destination construction efforts now underway at Punta Mita. They fall into a larger recent trend of the Mexican production of touristic "green zones" (at Cancún in 1967, Iztapa in 1968, and Huatulco in 1984) developed in conjunction with the World Bank, the Inter-American Development Bank, and Fonatur. The one at Punta Mita has emerged from a partnership between Fonatur and U.S. and Mexican developers and venture capital. It is

> oriented to high-end tourism . . . vacation living, sun, beaches, sailing and water sports, ecotourism and golf. . . . Plans call for low environmental impact with but 12 rooms per 2.5 acres . . . 11,000 rooms by 2018 . . . 150 boat capacity marina, three golf courses, a marine theme park, beach clubs, shopping centers, 34,000 homes and condos, airport. Forecast goals, for 2018, 1.025 million visiting tourists, an investment in hotels of US $12.85 billion and US$860 million in foreign exchange receipts. . . . Fonatur owns some land in the project area, and in place of expropriation it is currently negotiating the acquisition of additional properties with area landowners. . . . Fonatur will sell appropriately zoned properties to private developers and entrepreneurs. . . . 2006 goal is 240 hotel rooms . . . that will necessitate an investment of US $26 million. Estimates are that those will . . . serve 23,700 additional visitors, with foreigners alone spending US $14 million. . . . 780 new jobs will be created.[15]

The enormity of this financial undertaking—especially if one previously surfed the modest point at Punta Mita and ate a simple fish-and-fries dinner in the town's *palapa*-roofed restaurants—takes one's breath away in the manner of a chokehold. The ecotourist rhetorics of such a project remain without substance; they are public relations sound bites for conscience-pricked American travel markets rather than credible efforts to meet any kind of guidelines for responsible tourism.[16] In Mexico "ecotourism" presently seems to indicate any business near "nature," and it also implicitly includes ethno-tourism. Moreover, as a former Las Olas surf instructor reported, some local Punta Mita landowners have indeed effectively had their lands expropriated as whole communities have been strong-armed into the relocation process.[17] The interim outcome of this wholesale transformation of a natural landscape has been a meager 780 jobs, developments that offend and outrage the Las Olas crew and its typical clientele. Indeed, they represent the intractable power operations that a business like Las Olas, by

founding itself in rural Mexico and not coastal California, had hoped to ob-
viate. And that Las Olas stands to profit (at least in financial terms) from
such radical transformations is all the more confounding. In late 2009, the
Four Seasons Resort at Punta Mita opened, offering both Bahia and Paci-
fico golf courses. The latter situates one of its eighteen holes directly on
the beach so that golfers can overlook what the resort website promotes as
Punta Mita's "famed El Faro surf spot."[18]

Surf culture has repeatedly encountered such contradictions during the
past half century as it has circulated the globe in search not just of the
perfect wave but also of new forms of sociality capable of intervening in
Protestant work ethic disciplines, gender expectations, and cross-racial and
cross-national human relations. In chapter 1 I made the case that surfari
as a desire invented by surfing men provided them an alternative subcultural pathway through which to imagine lives not prescriptively devoted
to the family wage. Chapter 2 pulled this way of understanding the politics
of rebel play into more contemporary contexts wherein sports constitutes
an ideal of new global femininities. This chapter expands that claim by
addressing the fact that, since the 1990s, surfari is now able to go female.
Long-standing hopes of the U.S. subculture—that surf travel will produce
new masculine gender identities and cross-racial alliances—are now
staged explicitly with U.S. female gendered dilemmas in mind. One of them
is the desire for rest and reprieve from the expanded workload of caring,
including the responsibility for children, aging parents, and local community organizations that falls overwhelmingly on midlife women now that
the welfare state has collapsed and neoliberal domestic policy and its ever
more individualist ideals of freedom govern daily life. The rhetorics of girlhood recall a time of lesser caretaking responsibility.

But there is another and related gendered dilemma to which "girlish
play" responds: that which goes broadly under the banner of "sexuality"
and that I will emphasize as age-inflected pressure. That is, the play I am
tracking responds to new and more aggressive forms of sexism created by
neoliberal openings—especially intensified demands for women, from pre-
teen girls to sixty-five-year-old baby boomers, to appear hip and heterosexy. Never before has the aging process seemed so changeable or socially
stigmatized, especially for women. To explore these claims, I turn to my
ethnographic work.

I focus on a set of scenes that occurred on the last night of my first trip to

Sayulita in 2002. These encounters undoubtedly display many of the privileges available to U.S. tourists with money in Mexico. But for now I am less interested in the endgame of the critique of touristic privilege than I am in trying to understand and communicate to readers what I saw as a remarkable First World conversation underway. That night has stayed in my mind because it revealed not just the gaps in connections and understanding between generations of American women but also spontaneous strategies to bridge them. It alerted me to my own distances (and these could be traced directly to the insularity of academic feminism) from "normal" nonfeminist and nonintellectual women and girls. I recalled the "A New Girl Order," conference I had attended in London in 2001, when the keynote speaker Angela McRobbie asked a mixed-age audience about the "bad girls" so many of us boomer feminists used to be, the women whose outrageous behaviors and out-of-the-box thinking made the very staging ground for what became a feminist presence in the university. Where are those women, she wondered. Are they us? And if we answer yes to that question, can we also answer yes to the question, are we them? We "career feminists"?

So let me begin here with a night of festivities engineered by the Hot Flashes. Their delightful group name functions as an umbrella term to identify about thirty or forty women who come together in various larger Bay Area sports leagues to play soccer, basketball, and softball. Off the field they throw parties. But if they are united by forms of adult sport and play, they are also united by their culture of mutual parenting support, for most of these women are divorced single mothers. While the Hot Flashes made up less than half of our group of twenty campers during our six-day surfari, these baby boomer women and beginning surfers unquestionably dominated all the camp's group events and outings.

Early in our camp time together, one of the leaders of this wild pack, Polly, a junior high school sports coach and divorced mother of two teenage sons, informed the group that she had gotten away on vacation by telling her school that she was obligated to a family wedding in Mexico. Since Polly is up for everything that makes life "interesting," she thought why not stage a wedding in a Mexican restaurant and photograph it? With photographs she could document that a wedding had in fact taken place. Moreover, the Hot Flashes "just happened" to have along some nun habits, and we had already been treated on a previous evening to singing and surfing nuns (why not, had not Sally Fields also played Gidget?). The habits seemed aching for a more public audience. On the final night, something special, something additional, was required. It was time to put these nun habits to new uses, to sacred marital uses, and what could be better fun than to stage a lesbian nun wedding in a respectable family Mexican restaurant, a few miles outside Sayulita proper, in San Pancho?

To enact this fun, two Hot Flashes recruited the surfing instructor staff as bride and bride, complete with attendant flower-bearing best women. Polly, as is her talent, officiated, regaling us with marital vows penned for the occasion: do you take this woman through high tide and low tide, in any kind of weather? Since the memories of Hurricane Kenna were still fresh, as was the image of the Hilton's grand piano floating out to sea, the line about "any weather" found a ready audience. At some point in the hilarity one of the Hot Flashes' shirt sleeves caught on fire. But only briefly, someone later noticed, and with no real consequence. How was it, somebody demanded, that table candles in restaurants did not more often catch people's clothes on fire anyhow?

For those of us with less bravado or margarita on board, this was but one in a series of public events that took many of us well beyond the limit of what could be called a good time. Had many of us non–Hot Flashes not had our sense of public decorum pushed hard for a week already, had we not endured the hurricane together and come, against better judgment sometimes, to fall into line with the extreme antics of these women, many of us would not have continued to show up for group events. I was a conspicuous weak link, and many of the Hot Flashes worked hard, as one of them put it, to "loosen Ivy League up." Since I was writing a book on surfing, how could I object to entering a sedate local restaurant singing, screaming, actually, the Beach Boys' "Surfer Girl"? It was material, was it not? A lesbian nun wedding in a Catholic country, what more could I ask for?

The second incident followed immediately. It took place back in town at Don Pedro's, one of Sayulita's best-known beachfront establishments. Like many local places it has open-air windows, and onlookers can witness, from the nonpaying outside, what is going on inside. Fifteen of us campers entered the bar, and so large a group of women made a palpable stir. Several twenty-something white men were already there. They looked to be surfers, but none of the surf staff knew them. Sayulita is a small break, and regulars know other regulars, even if one is not a permanent Mexican resident. But perhaps they were new arrivals in town, men just passing through. A few of the Las Olas surf instructors began dancing, but one of the Australians, one of the Californians, and the Hawaiian stayed seated next to me. These women in their mid-twenties to early thirties all evidence the babe factor in surfer girl visual economies—short skirts, belly tops and form-fitting sweatshirts, sun-kissed skin and sun-streaked hair, and Polynesian "grace." Our eyes adjusted to the darkness. The surfer men already on the dance floor sang to the music very suggestively. I thought to myself, "Ugh . . . I'm too old for a sweaty scene of spring break fever." The guys in particular were over the top—their hips gyrating, mouthing songs with pouty, hypersexual suggestion. The surf staff kept dancing. Though there were more women, the guys clearly owned the floor. I shook my head in disgust.

Then suddenly the Hot Flashes joined in, meaning they took over, since their intentionally goofy behavior disrupted the steamy heterosexual logic of this seaside bar. They danced so parodically, doing faux pirouettes and exaggerated sexual moves, that the hot-and-heavy cues and hetero-impulses that had governed the space could not continue. All at once, as if in answer to the Hot Flashes' challenge, a tall white blonde man arrested the group's attention by pulling up his shirt and motioning to everyone to line up so he could parade himself, half disrobing. In what appeared very practiced male-stripper motions, he danced down the line amid much ado. I wondered if he might be a sex worker, though this thought, I realized later, marks me as a not-young person, since his brand of heavily sexualized performance, I have since come to understand, is common. His male friend made a big show out of sliding a long-necked bottle of beer very slowly in and out of his mouth. That same male friend then, again in stripper style, rubbed his crotch against one of the bar's poles, at which point most of the younger women exited stage, both put off and fascinated.

I had never entered the dance floor and was now triply relieved to have stayed on the sidelines at a quiet table. Before I had been annoyed that nobody wanted to go home and thus I was condemned to wait in the bar for somebody to get tired enough to accompany me down the unlit beach to Villa Amor. The memory of the Mexican mothers looking confusedly over at the lesbian nun wedding sufficed for one night. I could not think about their school-aged children, their ironed clothes and slicked-down hair. No longer just annoyed, I was now furious to be watching this "I've got a hard-on" performance, this twenty-five-year-old men's sexual *whatever* on display while younger women were push-pulled into the most clichéd of dramas. If they wanted a judgmental second-wave feminist, they had one. That it was "material," who cared?

But then Polly, who declares about oncoming surf that will clearly take her under, "I'm not going to let it get the better of me!," turned out to be unwilling to concede center stage to these stripper guys. She sidled up to one of them, dancing with extreme suggestion that was also half parody. She waved for her closest friend Judith to get on the other side of the guy, so the two of them could have him in the middle. But Judith, for the first time, declined a challenge. Polly persisted, and the whole bar—including the Mexican townsmen who had been drinking beer and smoking in the dark outdoor circle surrounding the place—looked on. The collective trans-national male gaze weighed heavily. The surf staff pulled up chairs next to me at the table in the corner, cowering but spellbound.

The young man, seeing the surf staff at our table, changed course and in a kind of ritual slow motion presented himself to us. His shirt was already unbuttoned and open. He very deliberately removed, one at a time, the salt shaker, the pepper shaker, and then the napkin holder, setting them on the floor. Then with controlled balance he jumped onto the small cocktail table, landing evenly on both feet, and began to dance, shoving his crotch in the surf staff's faces. One of the Australian staffers shone the flashlights we needed to get home at night up onto his undulating body, staring. I could see the day's sun in her cheeks, the blue in her eyes. She was the youngest of the crew, not quite twenty-five. And she was intent, interested. The guy went on, finally jumped down to much male hooting, and it seemed that the Las Olas staff, shrinking but wide-eyed, was left immobilized by his action. Trumped.

Before any of us could make a next move, Polly jumped up on the table herself. She is a compact, not really large but muscular woman. But there we had it—the legacy of the female gym teacher, short butchy hair, ready for game time. Now she pumped, grinded, shook her butt, letting loose with whatever she had. She stayed atop the table—dancing, commanding public attention. It seemed to me that the collective male gaze could not quite file this visual scene into any established system. At some point there was spontaneous female consensus that Polly's answer to the young man had evened the playing field, neutralized his seduction/aggression, and all us

Las Olas "girls" (now including me) were cheering. Just elated. After that, the heterosexual power struggle between these young adult men and the Las Olas group was effectively settled and the tension depressurized. What had changed the temperature and intervened in the young adult sexist dynamics of this very hetero bar scene was the Hot Flashes, with midlife, androgynous Polly coming forward as a leader when it counted most.

The next morning when I interviewed Polly, she told me that the dancing "wasn't anything sexual . . . that's very private for me, and not many people get in there."[19] This statement, alongside many others, confirmed for me that the Hot Flashes' "play" had less to do with desire in sexual terms than with insisting on a female presence in public space and, hence, with female power: power as menopausal midlife women, power as women banded into a collective unit, power as women raising children in a female village, power as women pleased with themselves and their bodies no matter what popular culture suggests is a "nice" female body (for most of these women are large), power as women who do sport. These constituted generally unselfconscious or unspoken group values, but they took as givens what contemporary girl power and girl culture also do: that females matter, that they deserve to take up public space and not worry about it.

Such powers, while certainly enacted (to whatever degrees) in the everyday lives of these women in the Bay Area, found a new edge or border during their trip to Mexico to learn to surf. A renewal of group energies was happening alongside the spontaneous discovery of new areas against which to test themselves, of new occasions for expanding female power. In this case, an unexpected situation arose in which the Hot Flashes managed to give a hand to the younger women of the group when they did not know how to stop a form of public behavior from their male peers that crossed the line from flirtation into sexual and sexist intimidation. The instructors' excited reminiscences about the "battle dance" the next morning over coffee made clear their pleasure about the intervention.

One of the more telling pieces of this story as a feminist parable was that, as the "official feminist" of the Las Olas group, as the single person there who claimed the label "feminist," I had had no immediate strategy to offer the younger women in their struggle and no stomach for that kind of fight. I did not understand its terms, nor did I want to understand because they were too infuriating. In my adult life, I no longer had to fight that kind of battle—those were the fights of young women; I had fought them and never wanted to have to do it again. As a consequence, I could not think about what it took to get in there, today, and do feminist business. What did it mean that both the Hot Flashes and the surf instructors saw in me (correctly) someone ready to bail out of a situation such as that in the bar rather than battle-dance to settle the score? How had someone like me—no stranger to hard-core party scenes and a person whose everyday feminisms in the years before university would have made the Hot Flashes proud— how had she/I come to very much need the Hot Flashes for lessons in new feminist practices that could push hard against the constraints of midlife responsibility? How to reawaken the "bad girl" willing to take risks not only with ideas but with out-of-the-box performances? Such new skills, I came to believe, would be required for "official feminism" to offer political backing and *thinking* (versus impatience) to this younger group of women in the real-time struggles they faced with their male peers. And more: midlife women needed this, I came to think, for their own liberation. The restaging of one's self and one's midlife body, the unsettling of midlife "responsible femininity," count among the political effects of surf play to which I earlier alluded. That such a restaging partly takes place in tourist circuits designed for middle-class leisure of course implicates all these newer political subjectivities in globalization and its many contradictions.

But to what degree are such struggles particular to U.S women and history? Do generational differences meaningfully characterize Mexican women's lives since *libre comercio* or the series of gradual changes following the debt crisis that today gets talked about as "the change"?

Sayulita: Mexican Girl Localisms

The first time I visited Sayulita in 2002 I passed on foot through a little barrio on the backside, the hilly jungle side, of Villa Amor. Winding away from the hotel and its front on the beach is a narrow dusty road that takes its name, Playa de los Muertos, from a hillside cemetery tended by Virgins of Guadalupe, fresh flowers in rusting cans, and wreaths of crepe-paper ornaments under protective plastic covering. Walking along this single-lane road that dips down onto the jungle floor and then climbs for a short distance until the vista comes clear, I found ahead of me, in 2002, a barrio of neat, small homes made of brick. Women sat in plastic chairs on simple front porches of packed dirt, watching passersby and sometimes offering for sale *refrescos* (refreshments) or a Mexican hard candy called *dulce duro*. The adventurous or Spanish-speaking tourist bought such fare, but just as likely the women provided them to one another.

No such houses now remain. The running children, loose chickens, and wood fires are gone, moved elsewhere, along with the women. In their place clusters of colorful, multilevel vacation homes sit nestled in the shallow hillside, architectural fantasies realized with names like Casa Pájaro (the Bird House) where, as I walk down the street in 2008 marveling at these changes, a huge parrot could be glimpsed through an open blind. Pared down bougainvillea, meandering wisteria, banana and date palms, and fifty varieties of flowering bushes lushly bring to life this controlled jungle, overflowingly ripe and miraculously shrunken into enclosed, manageable yards. A few local teenagers are watering yards, but I do not notice a lot of other activity. It is difficult to argue with these new, quietly empty places in terms of aesthetics; they are beyond beautiful.

Eventually, at the corner of Niños Heroes and Primavera, I make out three women sitting on backless plastic stools in front of an older-style brick house.[20] I say "older style," but until recently these actually were the new homes of relatively privileged landholders, having replaced the stick homes more indigenous to the region in one of the central government's campaigns to promote cement and concrete. Eight or ten flat roofed single-story homes in a row make for a kind of holdout section at this corner, a dam against the recent flood of construction. I stop. Most pedestrians on this street are local Sayulitans, although a few tourists also amble by. A small, black handwritten "Ceviche" on the house's face, as well as a large Sprite sign, suggest that this is one of those combined homes/little stores I recall from before. Through the open-air block windows I see a boy of around nine playing intently at a few standing video game machines. The three women sit outside, chatting and calling out to the people who walk by. One wears a large wooden crucifix. Two of the three women are younger, about the age of the Las Olas surf staff, though they appear older. They are not performing themselves as childless or heterosexy. The other woman is maybe fifty.

I tell them I am writing a book on surfing that has a chapter about Sayulita, before and after "the change." May I ask a few questions? I am a *profesora*, not a tourist, a business owner, or a journalist who will publish what they say in an English-speaking magazine for the local Americans to read.

They don't say no.

What happened to all those little houses that used to be up there, on the Playa de los Muertos road? You know, the ones with all those women sitting in front of them? Is my memory wrong, or is a whole area just gone?

I have asked a right question. They have gone, I am told, into the hills. They got paid a lot of money.

I wait, let it sink in. I repeat, may I ask a few things? I am curious to learn what it is like, for you, with the women gone and all the changes. (One nods and gestures her hand up toward the hillside, "Si, aquí es puro Americano.") Are things different for you, for your daughters and sisters?

And now the young woman wearing the cross offers me a stool. She introduces herself as Sofia.

The issues ultimately raised by a series of conversations I had with various groups of Mexican women in Sayulita concern the footprint globalization tracks on the local environment and on the politics of local mobility—who lives or moves where, and by what larger transnational policy mechanisms property changes hands. Like the physical landscape, the economic landscape in Sayulita is undergoing radical transformation. New configurations of work, including formal and informal labor sectors loosely associated with the entrepreneurship of play, are remaking the structure and experience of everyday femininity. If globalization rekindles familiar tensions (between Americans and Mexicans in particular), it creates newer ones too as trans-border strangers are brought into ever more intimate contact. I here explore the rules of engagement—that is, situational resolutions and ethics—that arise to accommodate these new relations. Clearly, the players in this global drama are not equally empowered. Yet less advantaged people often show the most insight into the making of this new Sayulita, even if they do not have the greatest agency because of it. This local/global intelligence is not lost on the next Mexican generation.

Sayulitans are a very generous people; they forgive one's linguistic imperfections and appreciate efforts to reach toward them. They tell me a great deal. What has changed since globalization came to town—for women *and* men—is that there is more work. I learn this from the women on the corner, from manicurists, hotel maids, waitresses, store clerks, and, eventually, from the local *surfistas* (Mexican surfer girls) who have begun over the past few years to show up as regulars in Sayulita's reef break. Before the change, there was little work or money. Men fished or traveled to Puerto Vallarta for jobs. Women worked in their homes. For medical or educational resources, one went elsewhere. For much of the 1980s, the years during which most of these respondents grew up, Mexico struggled to recover from the prolonged recession of the 1970s. But now women go out to work, they go into the stores, they clean American women's vacation homes. They do not sit and talk so much as they used to—the day I find the women on the corner talking is a Sunday, and they are at leisure, having come from early Mass. Many women have now also moved to the newer neighborhoods outside town—Colonia de Escuela Secondaria, Los Avestruses, Mangal, or Tamarindad. Or they have permanently gone. Popular anecdote suggests the depopulation of locals since the change came to town.

The twentieth-century history of Sayulita could be outlined through its ejido families—Ruiz, Cruz, Placiencia—to whom the Mexican government deeded out parcels of land in the decades following the Mexican Revolution.[21] As economic entities, these extended ejido family networks have long-standing claims in real estate (Ruiz), local food markets (Cruz), and the fishing industry (Placiencia). Still, to draft Sayulita history and its political economy through notions of large holdings is misleading, since it remains a small town (the local population consists of about five thousand, and nonresidents form the majority) without a hospital, gas station, police force, or local governing body. Although the law requires ejidos to have a governing body, in Sayulita, recent growth has made local governance structures less visible. But Sayulita's smallness is fading. The economic and real-estate ownership profile has thoroughly shifted in the past twenty years, especially in the past ten, by the appearance of tourists and tourist dollars, both coming mainly from the United States. To the extent there is any real money in Sayulita today, it does not come from family fishing economies but from two new, NAFTA-related revenue streams: tourism and the local land boom. Surfing constitutes the principal tourist attraction, and Sayulita's break supports beginners, the current cash cow of the surf industry. But tourism (with surfers as curiosity and spectacle) has become an excuse of sorts for a more consequential economic story: that of the land rush underway, along with all the outcomes that this rush sets into motion.

One outcome, say the women at the corner of Niños Heroes and Primavera, is the loss of local cultural and religious tradition. "Many traditions our people are forgetting," reports Sofia, the woman wearing the cross. And there are new traditions now, say the other two women, an adult niece and her older aunt, that many local women do not like. They do not like the Americans' Día de las Brujas (Halloween); it celebrates Satan, in their view, and they do not like it when the tradition rubs off on Mexican children who come to trick-or-treat wearing devil masks. At the same time, the still largely Catholic village unites less for its own historic festivals, especially La Posada and El Doce de Diciembre (December 12), the celebration of the Virgin of Guadalupe. There used to be more Masses, pilgrimages, first communions, baptisms, singing. These events are much harder to organize now. They mean less. The community has diffused: some have gone or are working long hours, others seem distracted by a new secular culture of cash, things to buy, and the buzz of change.

I ask them if there might ever come a time when too many Americans live in Sayulita, but it takes a few hours to warm up to this question. A daughter rides her bike in and out of our circle of conversation, falling down, and, wailing with aggravation, is chided to get up again and ride. One of Sofia's boys, flicking a lighter, burns Styrofoam to-go packaging as the women shake their heads, scolding "careful, careful." A neighbor comes over requesting ceviche, and out of Sofia's kitchen eventually comes a platter of stacked, freshly deep-fried tortilla bottoms, shrimp and pico de gallo on top. While she is inside making it, one of the younger women is joined by an older sister. She tells me that her mother-in-law raises chickens about five houses down and that the American woman who currently lives next door throws little rocks at them when they cross into her yard. Why? She shrugs her shoulders, "Es delicada!" (She is fussy!). One of the woman's sons likes to boogie-board, and at some point he exits the house with the board under his arm, heading the few blocks to the beach. That same woman spies one of the barrio's old men walking toward us slowly with a cane in each hand and calls, "Come here, old man, meet the professor." As an aside she tells me, "I like my old people," and they all make a fuss over him as he lowers himself slowly into a chair. He is very stylish: cowboy boots, sharp hat, shirt pressed and tucked in, a tooled belt finishing off what look to be new jeans. His skin is very light; one of his eyes is white, the other milky. I cannot understand a word of his Spanish. After a while he moves on from a sense, we speculate, that this is a woman's circle, women's talk.

You do not have to worry about offending me, I tell them. They need permission to say what is in their faces. Will there ever come a time when too many Americans are in Mexico, maybe even in Sayulita? The answer as it unfolds begins with a statement about work. I have asked why there are no Sayulitan women working at Villa Amor. One of Villa Amor's maids, Laura Beatriz, a Huichol Indian from a ranch in Jalisco who cleans my own room, taught me first what more research bears out: that nearly all of Villa Amor's employees hail from *el otro lado*, meaning broadly the other side of the jungled hills, including Bucerias, Puerto Vallarta, Acapulco, but also as far as Tijuana. The women on the corner claim that the work environment at Villa Amor is not good. Plus it is not well paid. "You have to respect yourself and what you should be paid," I am told, and the pay was bad for a lot of work, carrying heavy linens up and down the hillside, for ten or more hours at a time. This attitude is something new, I sense, and Laura Beatriz does not yet herself have it. While Laura wishes for a better job because this one is ruining her back, she has a child to support and extended family on the ranch who need her cash income. These locals, by contrast, are landowners, and they have discovered that they have some options. We can work for the American women, they tell me, "it's a much better environment." Sometimes the Americans are very nice, and it is not like working for a business. It is private work, a single boss, in someone's home, only four or five hours a day.

Eventually, we get to the nitty-gritty of things. I ask around on safer topics like Sayulimpia, the new local garbage removal business and clean-beach campaign widely welcomed as good for the town. This discussion prompts the aunt, a midlife woman from nearby Chacala, to note that Americans also have bought land in her hometown. But they have built a library in Chacala where courses are offered in both Spanish and English. They also have helped with the Chacala school. Those efforts are not yet visible in Sayulita, and with all the money Americans are making, these women want to see more. Yes, someone volunteers, some of the Americans in Sayulita are good, but some are "despotas, groseras, racistas" (despotic, crude, racist). The father-in-law of one of the sisters sold his house, on this very street, because he felt himself to be "surrounded" by all the new construction. He left town swearing, "los pinche gringos!" This is the same woman who now mentions that she has told the American neighbor who throws rocks at her mother-in-law's chickens, "If you kill one of them . . . you'll be sorry." I raise my eyebrows at this threat, and she gives a hearty, satisfied laugh.

I have detailed these particular conversations about the local impact of globalized tourism because the women on the corner of Niños Heroes and Primavera expressed what I found to be representative concerns of Sayulitans; at the same time none of them wished to discontinue the changes or turn back the clock. In terms of options, these are the best and only ones on the horizon, and the era of Mexico's debt crisis constitutes the unspoken negative backdrop against which these changes are measured.[22] Today Sayulitans believe themselves better off, with lucrative jobs and larger and better-appointed houses, even if they have had to relocate to the outskirts of town. As the *taxista* Miguel Guerrero Avce tells me, his own children will go to high school in Sayulita, something he could not do because fifteen years ago the town had no high school.

Both boys and girls will have better opportunities in the new Sayulita; the latter will study more and envision futures for themselves beyond mothering. Miguel's own wife works with the licensing division of a local private business and earns a good income that helps pay for their new home. He has high hopes for his daughter too (now age three). But it is not a perfect world. The women at the corner of Niños Heroes and Primavera tell me they would wish for Americans to come out to the festivals, to understand why they sing to the Virgin of Guadalupe. Sofia in particular muses that she could write down information in Spanish and get someone to translate it. Then she could post it around the barrio so that people might learn. But she speaks with a certain fatalism, indicating little confidence in the power of local people to effect changes or to find willing Americans. One of the sisters has a sixteen-year-old daughter currently going to school in La Peñita (a neighboring town) who plans to work in a bank. But the girl dislikes that to do so she must learn English. "It's an obligation, not a choice," her mother tells me. I repeat this statement to the *taxista*, Miguel, who laughs in embarrassed agreement. He and I are having this conversation in Spanish, but we could be having it in English. As a *taxista*, his prosperity depends on his translational abilities and willingness to live part of his life not in his first or preferred language.

To date, there is no organized effort afoot to regulate building or any other change in Sayulita. Were such regulation to come, it would also require a mechanism for its enforcement. Since no official body oversees development, grievances air by way of locally circulated petitions that do the work of formulating community opinion and organizing dissent. But the petition process cannot be juridically enforced. No labor or environmental policies exist, and the most serious petition effort to date—generated by Americans and Sayulitans to curtail the condo project at Villa Amor until environmental impact could be established—did not succeed.[23] Lots of townspeople declined to sign on and agreed with Rod Ingram, the owner of Villa Amor, that building projects bring jobs. Perhaps few locals anticipated that Villa Amor would rely exclusively on non-Sayulitan service workers. In any event, there does not seem to be the political acumen or cohesiveness that sustained the successful "golf club war" of 1985 in Tepoztlán, where the population resisted a proposed Jack Nicklaus golf course and business complex. When one drives up into the highest points on Gringo Hill via narrow roads steeper than the steepest in San Francisco, one can only wonder about the consequences of such profound earth moving and heavy equipment traffic on what otherwise remains undeveloped hillside. Given that many of these homes come with million-dollar price tags, one assumes that such buyers can afford this kind of financial risk. Yet to be sure, it is not only Sayulitans to whom a conversation about risk applies.

The purchase of property by non-nationals in Sayulita, simple in comparison to the pre-NAFTA period, nonetheless comes with hurdles.[24] In the wake of the Mexican Revolution the ejido system established a wealth redistribution program granting individuals personal-use parcels that they could deed in perpetuity to offspring. The system also granted communal lands for group use. The title to especially valuable real estate (border and coastal seaside areas) was understood to require further protection given the economic might of Mexico's northern neighbor and its history of military incursion. Mexico's Constitution (Article 27) specifies "restricted zones" within fifty kilometers of the water in which only Mexican nationals can hold real-estate titles. Much of Sayulita was, and remains, just such protected ejido land, making for the hurdles to which I alluded above. Yet in 1992, then-president Carlos Salinas reformed Article 27. Ejido holdings became eligible for a qualified privatization, meaning that titles can now be mortgaged or transferred. The easing of historic restrictions opened up new markets to foreign investment. Foreigners today can buy via bank trusts held in the name of Mexican nationals (names are not hard to come by). The process is complicated and not without risk, and lending practices require more cash and formal and informal fee payments than do typical U.S. real-estate markets. Real-estate agents sometimes warn American buyers not to put all their nest eggs there, thus acknowledging a risk. Still, the bottom line is a local culture of intense transfer, deal making, and the legal safeguarding of foreign investment. While title to property is not held outright and must be renewed in fifty-year increments, it is hard to imagine a world in which the Mexican political context would change so much as to enable the seizure and reappropriation of foreigners' lands.

For now Sayulitans generally take a let's-see attitude to the situation. What better choices do they have? Globalization's effects positively register a growing economy, an expanded social infrastructure (schools, sanitation facilities, medical clinics), new possibilities for women, and a sense of hope for the future among younger people. Some women's vacation play creates work opportunities for other women, and the transnational relationships growing from this work-play economic nexus spin off in countless directions. The women at the corner of Niños Heroes and Primavera earnestly hope for mutuality with the transnational visitors and neighbors in their midst, even as their conversations, so far, mainly concern business. They negotiate with American women about work, hours, and pay. Or they decline to negotiate real-estate transactions. These conversations principally concern terms: the terms of ongoing contact. The daughters and nieces of these mothers seem headed in similar directions. What is to be done about the clear downsides of this kind of uncontrolled growth, such as environmental degradation and cultural dilution, they do not know. Not knowing alarms them, and they look for whatever writing might be on the wall.

Surfistas

For Mexican women and girl surfers, or *surfistas*, meanwhile, globalization is arriving through (among other avenues) forms of surfing play made possible by girl-promoting global leisure and tourist industries. These industries create networks of shared interests, political commitments, employment opportunities, and the possibility of deeper transnational contact and friendship. These, too, make for conversations about the terms of transnational relations. Someone like the surfer Sofia Silva Sánchez, a thirty-four-year-old native of Mexico City, embraces the opportunity for more head-on negotiation of the terms of relations, as do the American women who become friends with her.[25] I became interested in Sofia initially because of the novelty of *any* Mexican women surfing in the local breaks at Sayulita—hence the question about the *kind* of woman who could buck so many social disincentives to surf seemed foundational. What became clear was the degree to which Sofia's involvement in surf culture signaled a particular way of relating to, and a special purchase on, the process of globalization itself. Sofia offers one example of a popular intellectual and activist whose politicization process is both informed by and actively informing surf culture's efforts to globalize from below—to impose her own needs and political interests on the process of globalization. The range of issues Sofia fights for—Mexican female dignity and freedom, the cultural integrity of Huichol Indian peoples, environmental development policy—all get addressed through surf culture and her multifaceted relation to it.

Not a single Mexican woman yet owns or manages a surf business—and this in spite of the fact that the business of surfing and women's surfing in Sayulita is booming. Weekend tourists drive or are bussed in from Puerto Vallarta, so many, in fact, that they can support Tigre's Surf School, the Duende Surf School, Patricia's Surf Lessons, Nacho's Tours, Surf Lessons por Captain Santiago, and Simien. Except for Patricia Southworth, who was born and raised on the U.S. northwest coast but is now a permanent Mexican resident, lesson givers are Mexican young men with English-language skills. Three of them have emerged as world-class competitive surfers.[26] These young men and their crew members come in and out of the surf all day long, give lessons, and make their way between beachside businesses and eateries with a jaunty sense of local celebrity. Rows of umbrellas and little restaurant tables line the beachfront, and everyone fixes their gaze on the water. The Mexican young men hot-dog it up, riding out this moment in history for whatever it is worth.

As recently as 2004, no Mexican women or girls surfed the local break. But this is changing. One of the first Mexican women to surf Sayulita regularly was Sofia Sánchez, mentioned above (fig. 31). These are the directions to Sofia's apartment: "Find the Fish Taco Restaurant on the plaza. A Virgen de Guadalupe image is on your left, and you will see a little hidden aisle there. Take it, pass the spiral staircase, and you will see a turquoise door. That's me." She tells me this via cell phone in colloquially perfect English. I arrive down the aisle past several surfboards standing on end, step over the turquoise threshold and into the pleasant studio home of a woman

31   Sofia Silva Sánchez. Photograph by Elizabeth Pepin.

who likes her things just so. Something smells very good on the stove. Sofia interviews me before consenting to being interviewed. What is my project? What am I doing with surfing? Why do I care about her as an informant?

Sofia has the air of a worldly woman, urban, sophisticated. She wears fitted, black stretch yoga pants and two tank tops, one skirting out underneath the other at hip line. Her hair is down, wavy, dark. Obviously fit and (I surmise) single, Sofia is the same approximate age as the women at the corner of Niños Heroes and Primavera and the Las Olas surf instructors. But there would be no wooden crucifixes around her neck, no front-yard Sunday chats or fussing over *viejos*. Sofia has pursued very different life goals. A surf calendar is up on the wall; cooking magazines fan out on a coffee table. She looks me over not as the *profesora* but as a peer calling on her limited time. She hands me a card: personal chef, massage, fluent in English. She begins by telling me that she "ran away to San Blas [a beach town forty miles up the coast] with a boyfriend," where, in the late 1990s, she founded a nonprofit organization to educate people about the Huichol Indians of the Sierra Madre mountains. Sofia describes San Blas as similar to Sayulita, with the blessing of too many mosquitoes sheltering the town from over-development.

Like so many women who learn to surf as adults, Sofia reports that surfing changed her life, "helping me overcome my fears." She began in 1999, on a trip to Sayulita to give seminars about Huichol mythology and history to Las Olas camp-goers. As an English speaker and a woman on her own in a transnational world, Sofia was quickly claimed by the surf instructors as a kindred spirit. In their off time they taught her to surf, and she became one of the crew. She reports, "hey, if you can handle those big waves" or "go on a surf trip through Central America alone, hey, you're OK." To be sure, Sofia already was a woman not held in check by gender proprieties. But surfing opened up new ways to pursue a powerful female life. She entered the Mexican competitive circuit in 2004–5, traveling to a contest at San Miguel in Ensenada. Sponsored by Squalo Surf Company, an underwriter of the Mexican Surfing Association, she did very well. But a new wrinkle in surfing as gender-liberation discourse emerged as Sofia began to see who gets noticed by media and who does not—blonder and lighter-skinned Mexican women got first and top billing even if, eventually, she too garnered attention. This was not a battle, Sofia tells me, that she wanted to fight. Already in her thirties, she did not deem it an ideal time to begin a competitive surfing career anyway.

Sofia represents herself as above the fray of the politics of blondeness— she has a perspective on it, and it does not damage her sense of racial or female self. She is not only proud to be Mexican but "I have it clear who I am as a Mexican, and I don't keep my mouth shut [about it]." Part of that Mexicanness for Sofia has to do with what we might call "mestizo indigeneity."[27] She herself is part Huichol Indian, and her work to chronicle and preserve Huichol culture nurtures her own Indian heritage. Sofia worries that the cultural dilution effected by globalization, what she calls a "Westernizing influence," will "suck up the Huichol Indian culture." She muses, "the communities live far up in the [Sierra Madre] mountains [in Jalisco and Nayarit]. When they come down to do other things, they separate from the mountain, get sucked up into Western ways, and lose the traditional path of beadwork so basic to identity and livelihood. I don't want them to lose it." She and I do not have all the necessary conversations that might address the questions—about race, cultural purity, and so on—that such a statement raises.

Sofia points out her enmeshment in a host of other contradictions, which she takes up directly as ethical and political challenges. "I have to deal with the fact I make my living from tourism," she points out. To whom other than Americans does she give massages? And who buys her Thai curries or special-occasion desserts? She recalls asking a local friend who sells property to Americans, "How do you feel? YOU? Selling to them, when you can't afford to buy this house for yourself, or your own kids?" The friend told her, "I feel bad, it's happening right under my nose, but what can I do? It's my chance." Both of these women confront the fact that they contribute to and benefit from the very cultural dilution or structural reorganization they oppose. Sofia tells a related story about going on a surf trip to Nextel, a surf spot further south, with an American friend. They arrived late and tired and decided, atypically, to stay at cabins not owned by Mexicans. The American proprietor complained to her how little there was to do in Nextel, how he lived in Europe for half the year, drinking wine in the cafés, here the other half, but it was so boring. He wanted to build a swimming pool, he told Sofia and her American friend, and bring in more people, some tourists, for company. "And he's doing this [development] because he is bored!," Sofia rails. Still, as she knows well, these are the doors opened by large-scale tourist economies, and she is one of its rank-and-file entrepreneurs of play.

But she is not "them" either. Her own business and those of surfers should not be confused with the mega-destination developments like that at Punta Mita. In fact, she actively works against those developments. She insists, "There needs to be a way for the Mexican government to stop it [overdevelopment], not let it go so far." Punta Mita has already blocked large sections of formerly public beach access; she personally knows people from neighborhoods who were forced to relocate. "Certain [natural] areas need protection, no matter how exploitable or profitable they might be." She recoils from recent events at another previously remote surf spot, Platanitos, a turtle nesting ground that, until recently, saw very little traffic besides surfers. Platanitos is being turned into a small-scale ecopreserve resort. "Why not just let it be?," she demands. "Why not just respect nature?"

The ways in which Sofia expresses the environmentally degrading effects of globalization are familiar to scholars working with contemporary antiglobalization actors. Organized responses to these effects, if not easily implemented, have been frequently imagined, especially through critical localist movements focused on the environment and development.

These genres of political imagination are under construction in Sayulita, and surf companies, as well as the global environmental organization Surf-rider, play current and likely future roles in ecopolitical organizing. But another effect of globalization begs to be dealt with locally, one concerning the global surf industry's penchant for blondes, which reinforces and adds another complicating layer to Mexico's own history of racial hierarchies (on popular display, for instance, in the blonde stars of *telenovelas*, soap operas). Sofia's battles as a woman who is not blonde suggest the necessity of critical localisms able to identify the wounding effects of racialized and gendered local and global visual economies, as well as to politicize and mobilize people toward new ways of seeing. If women generally report an increase in female opportunity via the new economy, its preferred female figure—the global California girl—arrives with disciplining effects for non-Cali girls and with privileges for those who fit the bill. This fact of a "blonde divide" has yet to register *as* an effect, and hence it must be noticed and explored.

Sofia represents herself as secure about her Mexicanness, as above the fray of the politics of blondeness. But yet she, too, must negotiate the challenge. Because she surfs, the majority of her friends are Californians and West Coast Canadians. The previous day I saw them all go out, Sofia the only dark woman amid (mostly) blondes headed into the water. She finds it curious that some of the local Mexican guys drop in on her waves, for no reason, just to be jerks. As would any surfer anywhere, she takes this (as she should) as an insult. I ask if the guys drop in on the American women surfers, especially on the blonde women? No, they do not. I have heard from some of the current Las Olas surf instructors (mainly blondes) that the local Mexican women feel competitive with them about Mexican men.[28] The Las Olas women pronounce this fact with puzzlement, even a sense of hurt. Sofia disclaims such competitive feelings. She will not take up with the kinds of guys who drop in on her waves, she has nothing to feel competitive about, and therefore she mentions their insults to her American women friends.

Men in Mexico, she says, do not support women surfing as men would in other contexts. There is more encouragement for surfer girls in the United States and in Australia. Girl power, she ventures, has not yet come to Mexico. Many women Sofia knows, the wives or partners of surfers, would love to surf, but they are watching the kids. The Mexican surf industry is not as encouraging either, though there are signs of change here, stories in surf magazines like *Olas*, and women's photos on the Web sites of the big company teams (again, Squalo comes to mind). So there is a form of girl power spreading, one that has opened Sofia's own life possibilities as a woman. It started with Las Olas. Her work as a former surf instructor and as a provider of services to those who surf (among others), definitely locates her in the orbit of surf subcultural career microeconomies.

Still, girl power has spread unevenly. That Sofia speaks perfect English makes possible her current relationships, since none of the women I saw with her the day before—Las Olas instructors and a surf photographer—speaks Spanish. And it seems reasonable to imagine that some form of wounding occurs when Mexican surfers befriend and treat blonde American women better than they treat her or other Mexican women. One of our final conversations dwelled on a friend, Tikkla, a well-known Mexican woman surfer from Nayarit State who, as Sofia puts it, "rips, she just rips as a surfer." Still, Tikkla does not look a certain way; she is understood to be "ugly." In years past she got no media coverage, which tanked what should have been a great surfing career. The last Sofia heard, Tikkla was still surfing, however. Maybe in Pasquales. Very definitely, Tikkla was surfing.

This chapter's previous section has argued that the contemporary work-play economic nexus operating in Sayulita has occasioned a range of new transnational conversations and relations among women. The terms of the new relations are under discussion for all of them—whether women from Sayulita's ejido families who vow never to sell homesteads, or migrants from Mexico City like the surfer Sofia whose livelihood and social networks grow from girl-powered leisure industries. Additionally I have opened, through a discussion of the politics of blondeness, new sites for thinking through globalization's effects. Turning finally to the youngest *surfistas* of Sayulita requires some adjustments to this previous section's frame. It is clear that girls' rules of engagement, their terms of contact, already begin from more mobile versions of the local, the Mexican, the American, or the gender-normative. For these youngest surfers of Sayulita's beach scene, globalization has indeed produced much flux in categories previously assumed stable.

There are some seven or eight regulars in the local girls' surf crew. Of them, I was able to talk with Izta (fourteen), Lola (nine), María (fourteen), and Chacha (twelve).[29] Jimena (thirteen) always stayed in the water. The most sustained conversation was a giggling, give-and-take interview conducted standing up in a sandy beachfront *taquería* where María's family has friends. Lola danced through it all. I in fact marveled that I had managed any connection, because for some seven previous hours, one whole workday, I got the runaround from María. It had taken me several long, dense hours to realize it. Initially I had observed her on the beach, a petite, dark-haired girl with a brooding or perhaps just shy face. The manager of Duende's Surf Shop (Davíd, from Puerto Vallarta) had pointed her out to me, and I instantly imposed on him to introduce us. I had heard that local girls now surfed the break, but I had not yet had the luck of being there when they did so. María was walking with two male friends, no board. Later I understood that she was on her way to smoke some pot. We had a general conversation, and I noticed that she was not in school on a Monday morning. She is in the second year of secondary school, the equivalent of the U.S. eighth grade. School does not interest her, she let me know, and she hopes to get a job related to surfing. She and I agreed to talk in an hour or so, and she would get her girlfriend Jimena to join us. I expressed my gratitude for this, since I was flying out the next day. I waited at a distance, keeping her in my peripheral vision. But the first lesson I learned from María: she knew well how to evade adult surveillance.

I pursued her throughout the day, joking with one of the local surfer guys, who was helping "the professor" track her, that I was an intellectual stalker. He told me she lived a few doors up the block in the back of a small, prospering *tienda*, so I went there to inquire. Through many promises of "in a minute," María said she would come outside to talk. I resumed my post on the beach, waiting at a safe distance from what I now understood as the local pot-smoking social geography. I saw María come up into this space, noticing the other local guys who hung out there greet her with familiarity. She belonged. Not wanting to compromise her, I got somebody to ask her to come and sit with me, and again, she said she would be right over. About ninety minutes later she had again vanished from the scene, and a second later I saw her on the other side of the tide line running into the surf with her board. I began to despair.

I watched her through the binoculars. She was probably the best of her crew: hard cuts, fast. Eventually I noticed for the umpteenth time that I could spot her no longer. She had eluded me yet again and exited the lineup. I never would have gotten a chance to talk to her or her crew had not the very different *surfista*, Izta, then emerged from the water. Sunset was coming on. I ran toward this young woman on the beach, calling out, casting the ethnographer's studied nonchalance to the wind. She stopped. Her face was very clear from the surf session: dark eyes, dark hair with blonde streaks showing through, a curvy body in a bikini, a thin macramé choker. Yes, she said, of course she knew María, as well as all the other girls. Sure, why not answer some questions about surfing? Her voice was easy, excited. The wind was kicking up and I wondered if she was hungry or cold or was expected at home? She had been in the water a couple of hours at least, since coming home from school. But no, Izta was not cold and did not have to go home. She lived very close, it was no problem. Did I want her to go over to María's and bring her along too? Well, I allowed, if she wouldn't *mind*.

That was the second lesson: María and her crew march down very different paths of everyday surfing femininity. Before I had a chance to worry that Izta would not return, there they came in a tight cluster of three: Lola, Chacha, Izta. They nodded over to the restaurant, where María was hunched over, nursing a cut to her foot, which she had bandaged. Sayulita's reef has two main downsides: sea urchins with their puncturing spines and coral-like rocks. One learns not to set foot on the ground, but occasionally, well, María's foot had found a rock. She also now had reason to be off to the side, happily not part of the conversation—how elegantly she found the edge of a group and stayed there! A rebel girl who knows how not to talk to authority. So it would be the three girls and me. We stood in the middle of much restaurant activity, waiters squeezing by, people staring at our animations, the girls not noticing the commotion, and me trying to hear over plates and laughter.

The *surfistas* are eager to talk, pleased someone wants to know what they think, but they're also shy, laughing. Lola's arms move in wide arcs. Chacha covers her mouth with her hand, and I realize she has braces—the only person I have seen in Sayulita with braces. I ask ages, birthplaces, how long people have been surfing. Izta and María, both fourteen, were born in Sayulita and come from ejido families. Chacha is twelve, very tall, and was born in California. I ask her where in California, and she says she does not know. You don't know your birthplace?, I ask. Izta speaks up for her, saying, Santa Barbara, but Chacha says, no, actually, she's not sure. But you live here now, I clarify, and she says, yes, for most of the year, but I travel a lot. Lola, the youngest at nine, was born in Paris, but now lives here permanently. All of them have been surfing a year or two except for María, who has been surfing for four years. Again, with the exception of María, all have surfing siblings and/or parents.

Do you feel that as surfers, I ask, you are different from other local girls your own age? This gets an emphatic, yes! How, I want to know. I am fishing: With boys? Your parents? Tell me, what? Yes, again. All of them talk at once, creating a group statement to the effect that they are less interested in looking good or being cute or spending time in front of the mirror and more interested in nature, in what is going on in the world outside Sayulita, and also in *contaminación*. This last gesture toward environmental consciousness gets energetic support, especially from Lola, who nods vigorously. Whenever they see trash on the beach they clean it up. And anything in the water, like bottles, they swim over and get it, and then come out and throw it in the trash bins.

What about Sayulita, what are your opinions about tourism in Sayulita, and all the changes the town is going through? Might there ever be a time when there are too many Americans? In a single voice they venture that there already are too many tourists. Izta, the apparent spokesperson for the group, points out the constant new construction. And the jungle is being cut down to make way. They think more jobs a good thing for Sayulita, but some of the Americans (and they use this word) are racists. They treat people badly because they have a lot of money.

But, in spite of it all, yes, in recent times, they believe women and girls have more opportunities. I am trying to track the path through which young female aspiration travels—is it the media, education, economic mobility, surf culture? None of them has heard of the term or the concept *girl power*. I explain it and they are interested, but they do not comprehend the commercial aspect. Mexican media do not target youth demographics aggressively, and the girls are not exposed to U.S. youth programming and its promotion of girl groups, strength, and buying power. No Powerpuff Girls or Buffy or Hannah Montana. Only Izta's home in fact has a television. Of course media is not entirely absent. These girls love music and listen to a lot of it—reggae, reggaeton, hip hop—and here Lola and Izta dance together as proof. In terms of their studies, Izta is in seventh grade, while Lola and Chacha are homeschooled, Chacha by a friend who is a teacher. Remembering the distance María takes from school contexts, I try to get a sense of their faith in the importance of studies or education. To the extent I get any beat on this, they seem hopeful, cooperative, without reasons to rebel.

What plans do you have for yourselves as girls, I follow up, what dreams? Lola laughs, shrugs her shoulders, dances, but Izta, a teenager, offers a response in a serious tone: "See the world, surf." Chacha shakes her head and shrinks a bit, but I press her, saying, oh, come on, there's something on your mind I bet, what is it? And she offers, "Draw."

Darkness is falling, and I wonder again if they need to go home, if anyone will wonder where they are. It's no worry, I am told. So I move to the trickiest part of the conversation, about relations between Americans and Mexicans. Are they close? Do they lead separate lives in Sayulita? It seems to me, I tell them, that the older women in town remain pretty separate. Do they think girls are separate? Izta and Lola do not want to say *separate*; they want to say *different*. Well, OK, different, I mirror, but how? Do the three of you, for example, have American friends? Yes, yes, they say easily. And how are those friendships? Izta declares that she has a very close friend at school, a boy, who calls himself a Mexican, but to her he is an American. It turns out she is referring to Travis Southworth, whose U.S.-born parents own a local restaurant and a sport fishing and surf equipment rental business. "Patricia's Surf Lessons," as they are called, are given by Travis's mom, Patty. Travis has lived in Sayulita since the age of two or three; he is now fourteen. On an early trip here in 2002, I remember well several days of conversation with Patty, and the topic of Travis calling himself a Mexican came up more than once, and she did not know how to feel about it. Moreover, one of my own sons accompanied me on one trip and they became fast if short-term friends (in English). Travis's older brother Dylan, who is seventeen, currently ranks as one of Mexico's national surf champions (he does not tour as an American national). He is a local star, and a handwritten sign in front of Captain Pablo's, the family business, announces a recent first-place finish in Argentina.

But Izta is not persuaded by either of the brothers' claims on Mexican nationality. When I offhandedly comment that Travis speaks English with a heavy Spanish accent, whereas his Spanish sounds "native," she is startled and takes this in as new information. But clearly tensions exist, and I wonder about the larger family histories implicated in these young people's relationships. The Southworths, like the Ingrams at Villa Amor, have their local and very public enemies, and I do not know how that might influence Izta, since, like María, she hails from an ejido family and they may be economic competitors.[30] As this conversation goes on, Lola's brother passes by on the street. Anybody watching the local boys hot-dog has noticed him in the surf. He is small like his sister, with white-blond hair, and one might easily place him as a Californian. He calls out something to his sister, a passing greeting from the street to the restaurant, and she answers him: both in French. The girls take this as a matter of course.

Chacha seizes on this apparent opening as an occasion to say more about herself. The whole animated time we have talked together in Spanish, she has stayed quieter than the others. Now she turns to me and without transition, confidingly talks in everyday adolescent English. My jaw drops. She is keeping quiet, she apologizes, because she thinks of herself as also American. When we talk about Americans, she feels she should listen and not speak. She travels so much, "everywhere" she says with flat affect, that she does not call any place home. But she has been in Sayulita now off and on for five years, a long time, though she visits her photographer father in Santa Barbara a lot. I fathom, again, a girl traveled enough to wear braces but also so traveled that she does not know her birthplace. And who imagined a girl from Santa Barbara could know nothing of girl-powered youth media? The next day at Puerto Vallarta's airport, I appreciate just how much she travels. There she is, Chacha, with her two brothers. Her mother, an Argentinean, to judge by the accent, is putting them all on the plane for Santa Barbara. Then the mother will return to Sayulita. Introductions are made; the conversations with me are now in English. Chacha and her surf-doggish brothers could easily be perceived as American tourists returning home from holiday. Granted, they look scruffier: the boys are long-haired, and I imagine their father meeting them at the Santa Barbara airport, thinking that they look as if they have come from "elsewhere," from far away, the nonsuburbs. Their Spanish is "local." But that healthy California blond glow of the popular imagination is on them unmistakably as they rush off, Chacha waving, toward boarding announcements and other lives, families, friends, and surf breaks.

Who are the "locals" of the *surfistas* at Sayulita? Who are the Mexicans? The Americans? The many others? In this ethnographic context it may be easier to answer the question when it concerns adults. It is much harder to do the math with young people like Travis, who moved from Seattle at age two; or like Chacha, who moves continually; or like Lola, living permanently now in Mexico while maintaining ties to Paris. And what about the brand of girlhood these *surfistas* live out? Were the *Luna Bay* series I show-

cased in chapter 2 still in production, Izta might well have provided the out-
line of a new character. Hopeful, eco-aware, a girl with a global conscience
and consciousness, Izta is among the most Roxy Girl of recent surfer girls
I have encountered. And she has never heard of Roxy Girls. She does not
know the Las Olas staff, since most of them speak English only. Obviously
many forces, well beyond surf culture, have produced this moment of contact between girls from different parts of the world. At the same time we
cannot overestimate the power of girl-friendly global surf culture to produce the kinds of transnational formations of girlhood seen here in a small
village where, only five years earlier, no such presence existed. Las Olas, too,
by bringing thousands of sporting women to Sayulita, has created a local
climate in which a group of local-transnational surfer girls, without any
ties to Las Olas, now surfs.

Girls story this surfing activity; they narrate the meaning of it by reference to various kinds of feminist and antiracist critical localisms. They do
what critical localist projects usually do: in this case, take the health of the
local beach and jungle seriously, as well as put its plight and their own inside economic North-South development power struggles. But they are also
thinking about their own girls' culture as linked to and made meaningful by these struggles. They are friends with each other, but friends joined
in a shared purpose. Surfing condenses and expresses that purpose, and
there is more to their play than "fun." In their examples critical localism
becomes about female well-being and life hopes, not only about place or
nonhuman habitat. The word *racism* forms part of the everyday vocabulary
the girls use to speak about their town's troubles, and young Chacha per-
ceives enough about her own complex privilege that she does not, during
our conversations anyway, displace Izta's leadership and authority. In so
doing, new bonds of transnational girlhood seem (again at least for now)
affirmed.

Coming back to Houston after the most recent visit to Sayulita, my
thoughts remained with the youngest *surfistas*. I had begun imagining
the production of such transnational girlhood formations before Lola was
even born. To find them today as real-time presences in a place in the world
where, only five years earlier, they had not existed, was, first of all, amazing. Rarely do humanities scholars see large abstract theoretical claims (in
this case about surf discourse as a model of global femininity) translated
so tangibly into embodied subjectivities. Beyond amazement, what seems

clear is that long-term work must be done to follow up these new formations. I wonder about young Chacha, her life in Santa Barbara, her schooling outside institutionalized educational contexts, her relations with Mexicans (should I say "other Mexicans"?) in California. I wonder about María, a
young woman already in some kind of trouble, I sense, but one armed with
the strength to resist authority. How will she fare? She sees her future as
crucially tied to the opportunities surf culture offers in Sayulita. As a more
morena or darker surfer than her peers, how will she navigate the politics
of blondeness? Perhaps the girl localisms her crew is formulating will challenge the surf industry's sexist racism in new, effective ways.

Finally, I wonder about all of them, but about Izta in particular, that
poster child of aware globalist femininity. What long-term reckoning will
she or any of them make with deep friendships and childhood bonds that
they, growing older, may come to understand in ever more complicated
ways? In the United States, when given the chance, children will play
together across race and class, often for very long periods of their childhood
and adolescence, before they find their lives and relationships cement-
ing into the heartbreak of constituency-defined socialities. What might it
mean for someone like Chacha to live out an intensely transnational life, or
for someone like Izta to have a best girlfriend like her? These are questions
of the future, and these are girls whose hearts, at present, are open.

Four

Countercultural Places

Surf Shops and the Transfer of Girl Localist Knowledge

> Paradise has definitely been a place where young women can come and learn about the sport of surfing. The events I have promoted over the years . . . have left impressions upon the younger generation that you must give back to your community and your environment in order to live a life of right human relations. —Sally Smith, cofounder of Paradise Surf Shop in Santa Cruz, 2008

> We grew up with punk, not boomers burning bras. With Madonna, the Queen of Capitalism, our idol. Talk about a feminist icon. Or Latifah and other rappers, and Gwen [Stefani]—all of them preaching empowerment, and all of them with their own lines of shoes, clothing, bags.
> —Izzy Tihanyi, cofounder of Surf Diva, San Diego, 2008

In November 2004 the surfer and community activist Donna Frye shocked Southern California's conservative political circles by staging a successful write-in campaign for the mayorship of San Diego. Launching a grassroots bid barely a month before election day, Frye exposed to public scrutiny the local culture of political secrecy and corruption she had confronted since becoming a city councilwoman for District Six in 2001.[1] In response to widening city financial crises that the then current incumbent mayor Dick Murphy, an ultraconservative, refused to disclose (earning his administration the dubious tag "Enron by the Sea"), Frye's campaign emphasized telling the truth, doing the public's business in public, and caring about one's local environment, including its coastal waters.[2] This platform of public honesty (which her Web site calls "Open Government"), alongside a commitment to local people and the health of their public spaces ("Quality of Life"), had the additional benefit of spotlighting that three of the city's nine sitting council members were awaiting trial for bribery. In a city well known for its conservative electorate, Frye won the popular vote, appealing across party lines as an independent populist with integrity who was interested more in local people's well-being than in backroom dealing.

At the end of the day, unfortunately, the popular vote did not carry. On a technicality, Murphy remained in office: some five thousand voters had misspelled Frye's name (Fry, they had written); or they had not filled in the bubble next to her name. The mayor called the disputed votes "illegal" and state election law supported him. Frye sued, arguing, "[Voting] is not a literacy test . . . it's an expression of the intent of the voter. . . . A lot of people have been disenfranchised on a technicality."[3] In the weeks of judicial wrangling that followed, the city's financial and legal problems came home to roost, forcing Murphy to resign in disgrace. In the runoff election to replace him, Frye placed well ahead of ten opponents (the closest opponent receiving 29 percent of the vote to her 47 percent), but the law requires an outright majority victory. In a subsequent head-to-head contest between Frye and her closest competitor, Jerry Sanders, the former police chief, Sanders won the majority vote.

But if Frye is not yet the mayor of San Diego, her reputation as a maverick "surfer chick" leader is growing (fig. 32). The lingering memory of the political charade (some charged fraud) that followed the popular upset vote has earned her considerable public goodwill.[4] She retains the friendship of the many progressive organizations who endorsed her legal challenges — San Diego labor groups, women's groups, teachers' unions, the Sierra Club, the Chicano Democratic Association of San Diego, the Martin Luther King Democratic Club, *El Sol de San Diego* (a newspaper), Wheelchair Access, the San Diego Coastal Alliance, Indian Voices, San Diego Democrats for Disability Rights, and the University of California, San Diego, *Guardian*. Beyond San Diego proper, she has earned statewide recognition too. In 2004 Senator Christine Kehoe honored Frye in Sacramento as the "woman of the year." In 2005 she was named "legislator of the year" by the San Diego River Park Foundation and received the San Diego Environmental Champion Award from the San Diego League of Conservation Voters.

Recently Frye played a supporting role in what likely will become one of the most momentous David over Goliath victories in California state history: the grassroots campaign to protect the beloved surf spot Trestles

164

Jack Smith for The New York Times

32 Councilwoman Donna Frye, 2004.

and its undeveloped surrounding ecosystem from a proposed extension of the Highway 241 toll road.[5] This multiyear, megamillion-dollar project forwarded by the California Transportation Corridor Agency (TCA) would have paved over parts of the popular San Onofre State Park to ease traffic congestion on Interstate 5. On 7 February 2008 the California Coastal Commission (CCC) voted eight to two to deny the TCA toll road, deciding it would "violate provisions of the Coastal Act related to endangered species, wetlands, public access, recreation, surfing, Indian sites and greenhouse gas emissions."[6] One can see from the CCC decision just how many constituencies can be concerned in campaigns that center around (but exceed) surf spot advocacy. San Onofre State Park is not only home to Trestles, a world-class surf spot and one of only ten choice stops on the world professional circuit. The park also is home to the San Mateo Creek Watershed, the least developed and cleanest coastal watershed and wild habitat remaining in Southern California, as well as to Panhe, the sacred ancestral site of the Juaneño

Band of Mission Indians. In the Save Trestles campaign Frye introduced a resolution to the City Council in 2006 that would have San Diego join a host of other coastal cities in opposing the toll road. She was outvoted four to three, members citing ignorance for their no votes (they claimed not to have had enough time in the three months to read the package).[7] The no vote caused so much public embarrassment that, a year later, a second resolution came again before the council, this time passing six to two.[8] With its passage San Diego joined some dozen other coastal cities who had opposed pouring tons of concrete into Onofre State Park.[9]

As expected, the secretary of commerce appealed the momentous decision to block construction of the toll road, and grassroots organizing efforts to defeat this TCA appeal were redoubled.[10] The coalition of groups and city governments who came together for the campaign (Surfrider Foundation the umbrella organizational voice) held tight to the sense of possibility that immediately followed the victory. For surfers, rolled into the victory is much more than their ability to continue to surf along the wilderness coastal beach at San Onofre, or even the ability of the surf industry to continue to stage its annual world-class competition there. A feeling of social movement and large-scale solidarity is building, a vindication of surf culture's sense of ocean stewardship and its vision of public coastal lands as legacies for future generations. Many of those "future" generations indeed knocked on doors, went out for marches, held signs in parades, and turned out finally at the Del Mar Fairgrounds, where the ccc ultimately held its hearing. Young people responded to pings, e-mail blasts, instant messages, and prerecorded voice mails from celebrity surfers like Sal Masekela, or Surfrider's director, Jim Moriarty, seeming to indicate political dividends reflective of the massive educational outreach Surfrider has done in K-12 school systems over the past decade.[11]

By all accounts the nearly three thousand protestors (the vast majority of whom were related to surfing) at the fairgrounds shattered any previous attendance record at a ccc meeting. Not just young people but also surfing celebrity figures came out: photos of Frye alongside her husband, Skip, showed up on Surfrider's Web site the day after the victory. Shaun Tomson, Mickey Munoz, Taylor Knox, the Hobgood brothers, Greg Long, and the Gudauaka brothers also showed support, some taking the public stage. All the major surf industry brands were out in full force. Busses with Billabong, Etnies, Vans, Reef, and GFH Surfboards logos transported some of the protestors to the Fairgrounds from prearranged beach pick-up locations. A week later, the staff of Surfrider, in the Web pages of *Surfer* magazine, walked its readers again through the day's glorious events. They confessed continuing post-victory amazement, finally explaining it by referencing a quote: "First they ignore you. . . . Then they mock you. . . . Then they fight you. . . . Then you win. Gandhi."[12] That amazement at a victory exponentially grew when, a year later, the U.S. Department of Commerce denied the toll road, and the powerful TCA suffered its biggest political defeat to date.[13]

What politicized Frye? How is her identity or life history as a female surfer linked to the political programs she forwards as a city councilwoman? These questions open onto the present chapter's largest arguments concerning California's girl localist regional knowledges and their current transfer between generations of women both inside and outside surf subculture. If the previous chapter offered an ethnographic case study in the impact of global girl-powered surf culture and businesses on a recent "home" to female surfing in Sayulita, Mexico, this chapter shifts the angle of approach by charting that same topic by way of the social and geographical place claims that Californian women surfers have articulated in the past decade on behalf of areas they have long lived in and surfed. Formal political activity has typically been spurred by the experience of water pollution in local surf breaks—Frye's own political career as an elected official grew out of her successes as a grassroots organizer to clean up the sewage in San Diego Bay that was making her surfing family and friends sick. "Other people would be out surfing," Frye remembers, "but I would crawl up a cliff to look for a storm drain. I knew one was up there, making people sick. I would find it, map it, report it, publicize it, figure out a way to solve it."[14]

If the most obvious institutional site seeming to underwrite the politicization of someone like Frye are green groups such as the nonprofit Surfrider Foundation, other histories of challenging the status quo also figure. Some of those histories consist of straightforward political advocacy. Frye, for example, has agitated on behalf of women's causes her whole life, starting in junior high school (supporting girls in math and science), continuing into college (addressing equal rights issues, the plight of divorced older women reentering college, the formation of women's political caucuses), and beyond (participating in the National Organization for Women, the ratification of the Equal Rights Amendment, and the Geraldine Ferraro campaign; fighting for abortion rights and against workplace discrimination).[15] But other histories—messier, more ambivalent, not so easily or frequently told—have produced other significant political educations. These have to do with two generations of women who came of age in various experimental West Coast countercultures (hippie boomers and punk members of Generation X) and who formulated, by way of them, knowledges about individual female and regional communal health and well-being. Not only do such knowledges remain underground because they are difficult to speak about when women gained them by applying countercultural values to survive sexist violence, illegal abortions, illegal drug or excess alcohol use, and sexual experimentation. They are also diffuse and deeply individual—slippery terrains of scholarly evaluation. Existing scholarship on the topic of hippie countercultures in particular is generally skeptical that they added up to more than another form of consumerism.[16]

There is no analogue to the Surfrider Foundation through which I might chart women's reckoning with countercultural epistemologies. Still, institutional sites of their production exist. One such site, I claim in this chapter, can be found in the handful of for-profit small businesses owned and operated by women surfers up and down the coast of California. Locally owned surf shops, in particular, have in the past decade played the role of subcultural feminist clubhouse and served as local communal meeting places. Frye herself previously managed her husband's surfboard shaping business (Skip Frye's "fish" and "egg" boards are world renowned). The process of going public with alternative visions of and ethics about specific places and about how to live in them—and the Save Trestles campaign was a study in exactly this kind of multi-sited critical localism—has brought to the fore feminist knowledges about female well-being, health, family, and community, as well as strategies for navigating the dense urbanism and charged multiracialism of most of the California coastline. These localist epistemologies speak to the everyday aches and pains, and also to the feminist resources, that come with city life and that surfing as *urban* subculture and practice addresses. Such knowledges are finding their way to new generations of girls and young women through campaigns like those of Frye and also through the female-owned surf shops of local communities.

In this chapter I focus in particular on two businesses doing what small businesses very often do: to putting their constituency's weight behind political issues (if not typically politically progressive issues).[17] One is the only girl-focused Northern California venture currently in existence, Paradise Surf Shop of Santa Cruz, with which I have been ethnographically engaged for a decade.[18] Paradise Surf Shop sits on the East Side of town and is centered around the breaks at Pleasure Point; the West Side is home to Steamer's Lane, the premier big-wave spot in Santa Cruz. The other shop, Surf Diva in La Jolla (in the northern city limits of San Diego), is the best known among a few girl-focused businesses in Southern California.[19] Given the more diffuse nature of La Jolla women's surf communities relative to that of Santa Cruz, my ethnographic work with Surf Diva has been aided greatly by its penchant for self-representation in global media.[20]

I am interested in the missions, political philosophies, and outreach projects of Paradise Surf Shop and Surf Diva and in how these interface with Northern and Southern California female surf cultures. At stake are generational issues and their impact on strategies for social change. Sally Smith, Paradise's owner, exudes the natural style and simple-life politics of the Northern California boomer hippie, whereas the Southern Californian Izzy Tihanyi of Surf Diva, as noted in the chapter's epigraph, claims the Generation X "material girl" Madonna. But these geographical and generational distinctions are not hard and fast, as we will see. Southern California feminist surf history can be just as insistently feminist as that associated popularly with the Northern California scene. And both businesses have created new politicized constituencies of both girls and midlife women surfers and linked them to their own local/global political outreach projects, as well as to one another across the northern-southern divide. The result is an unfolding feminist political imagination invested in generational bridge building and female self-respect, conversant in local/global ecoissues of the twenty-first century. This feminist imagination can be found in girl localist sites up and down the coast well beyond Paradise Surf Shop and Surf Diva.

Northern California Female Surf Culture

Paradise Surf Shop opened its doors in 1997 to much hopeful fanfare, combined with a sense of "it's about time!"(fig. 33). If any city in the surfing world could support the mission of a woman-identified surf shop—bathroom sticker art at Paradise proclaimed such lines as "Just because some designer cranked it out doesn't mean you have to wear it!"—Santa Cruz would have seemed to be the one.[21] Part organic hippie town and hotbed of progressive activism, part affluent resort where old and new (high-tech)

33 Paradise Surf Shop
at Pleasure Point in
Santa Cruz (1999).

money mingles, Santa Cruz has come to be home to a mix of feminists since the civil rights movements of the 1960s: counterculturalists, out lesbians, socialists, punk rockers, witchy earth mothers, organic farmers, alternative health and lifestyle seekers.[22] The bar of my own youthful Southern California feminist consciousness was routinely raised in Santa Cruz—it was the only place I encountered in late 1970s California where a barely twenty-year-old female like me was respectfully referred to as a "young woman." These varied women work as stockbrokers, self-employed entrepreneurs, computer scientists, massage therapists, yoga instructors, secretaries, nurses, teachers, and in the unpaid labor force as mothers and school and community volunteers. Many surf and have taught their children to do the same; some work in the area's extensive surf microeconomy.

Reflecting the feminist character of life in town, local surf culture in Santa Cruz has a reputation, as Steve Hawk nervously joked in a 1999 *Surfer* issue showcasing women's surfing, for the "most finely tuned sexism detector in California."[23] Reporting more women in the water than any other place in the world (15–20 percent), Santa Cruz has nurtured multiple generations of iconic figures revered for their "hard-core" abilities to brave icy water and hold their own in the thick, pounding surf of the Northern California scene. Setting a kind of inspirational gold standard for the rest of California women's surfing are Jane MacKenzie (Jane at the Lane), Robin "Zeuf" Janiszeufski, the former professional surfer Brenda Scott Rodgers, and the former champion surfer Anne Bayley.[24] Younger women, too, are invested with larger communal hopes for female strength and courage: Michaela Eastman or Miranda Pitts (who lost her older sister Beth to a surfing drowning accident at Steamer's Lane in 1999).[25] That hard-core presence in the water has made itself felt over the years in the most influential organizations identified with female surfing, especially the Women's International Surfing Association (WISA), Women's Professional Surfing (WPS), the Association of Women Surfers (AWS, headquartered in Santa Cruz and founded by the owners of Paradise), and, most recently, NorCal Women's Surf Club. More about these clubs later.

From the beginning, Paradise Surf Shop conceived its mission to be as much about bolstering the women's surfing community as it was about for-profit business. Begun by a group of four female friends, all active members in both the AWS and the Surfrider Foundation, Paradise sought to provide its women founders with a livelihood as well as provide local surfing women with something akin to an environmentally activist women's center.[26] It also imagined bridging a West Side/East Side subcultural rivalry by bringing women from Steamer's Lane to Pleasure Point for public events, visits, and equipment purchase. Paradise patrons and community members talk about the shop as "a place for girls to come hang out," as a "safe space," and as "home base," claiming, "everybody is so nice it's almost like therapy."[27] The store is "not just a shop, but a place to be with my friends, a haven."[28] Or in the words of one mother, "I can hang out in between whatever errands I'm doing during the day."[29] Another tells a familiar story about the intimidations of going into a typical surf shop, "with a young guy behind the counter, who looks at you like you don't belong. . . . You don't want to ask him questions about boards or suits or things you don't know."[30] By contrast, Paradise is a setting in which women surfers can talk to each other, ask questions, learn, and decompress after a bad day or a bad surf session. Paradise even provides phone lists of girls and women available to surf, so one can go out with a friend.

A favorite story, reminiscent again of 1970s emergent feminist communities but with an important 1990s twist, has to do with a day, during the winter holiday season, when the two owners were hanging holiday lights and having problems with their screw drill.[31] They fussed with the drill, trying to figure out why it was not working. On the inside couches of the store—inviting hangout spots for groups of girls and women to talk, read, or relax—a few young women were sitting around knitting. In walks a local young surfer guy, who takes the measure of this new kind of surf shop scene: the women with the drill, now working, other women knitting and joking around, all against the backdrop of colorful surfboards and women's clothing and female surfing images on the wall. The story goes that the young man just broke into a broad, approving smile, nodding, "yes, the world is going right here." As a hopeful allegory for the 1990s, indication of all that's transpired in the historical interim, it shows some surfing men, especially younger men, have changed.[32]

Almost instantly, Paradise took its place as a local feminist institution attempting a blend of old-school (1970s) and new-school (1990s) political outreach. In its mission statement Paradise pledged support for women's organizations and health initiatives, as well as for local environment groups.[33] Since then, regular fundraising events like surf contests and local swap meets have donated proceeds to the Women's Crisis Support Center of Santa Cruz County, to Ride-a-Wave Foundation (for kids with disabilities), and to Surfrider Foundation. Group surf trips for Paradise community members promoting healthy living for women and girls came under the outreach umbrella too. If the foregoing might be characterized as old-school causes of second-wave feminism, new-school or third-wave feminist events pivoted around contest promotions. Sponsoring contests in surf culture is perhaps *the* pet project of established shops, the oldest outreach game in town. But in the case of Paradise, contests provided regular occasions to develop a new game: multigenerational networks of women come recently to the sport, alongside the showcasing of Paradise's own "team riders," a crew of cross-age surfers recruited not for elite competitive ability but for their desire to surf and their community-mindedness.

Paradise has emerged as a major organizing force behind Santa Cruz's Women on Waves Surf Fest, a long-running surf contest in California. This event brings together women longboarders of many ages and from various local breaks up and down the coast. The contest's structure depends on age-specific categories ("Menehune," which is ten and under; Juniors;

Women; Senior Women; Masters; Grand Masters), making them very age-aware events. In a clear gesture of rituals related to the life cycle, girls and younger women contestants are celebrated, listened to, and mentored; the best surfers, typically between eighteen and thirty years old, are congratulated, consulted, and admired; older women are appreciated, respected, and depended on for surf counsel, perspective, and local/global knowledge. Such events create cross-generational conversations between girls, their mothers, young adults, surf elders, and pro surfers about female-positive living, everyday trials and hopes, women's and girls' health issues, and the health of the ocean and of regional coastal zones. Through events like Women on Waves, Paradise offers new opportunities for cross-generational contact and connection, and from them has grown an emerging self-conscious public culture of politicized surfing women and girls.

This public culture facilitates a transfer of knowledge, history, and experience between generations of surfing women that far exceeds information about surf equipment or competencies. Feminist consciousness is a key outcome, and I would emphasize its distinctly West Coast feeling, a self-consciousness about the female body in outdoor spaces. The political contours and everyday expression of female surf culture in Northern California have to do with communal gendered subjectivity tied palpably to the natural world. Santa Cruz occupies a borderlands space between the Bay Area and California's Central Coast. The battles and opportunities inherited by virtue of that social and ecological location produce a regionally inflected feminist epistemology. Its principal features include a social premium on everyday outdoor activity and on sustainable human engagement with nonhuman nature; a critical sense of relationship between local and global surf locations and their viability as sustainable places; and a program for everyday *urban* living since Santa Cruz, like most of the major surf spots along California's coast, is a town fully implicated in urban life and subject to all of its tensions.

Let me spell out this Northern California feminist surf consciousness. When admirers (often Southern Californians) say they take inspiration from supposedly hard-core female Santa Cruz locals, they encode in this colloquialism a value system that prizes sound judgment and female bravery in demanding outdoors and wilderness environments. Hierarchies in wave and environment difficulty definitely exist, and places like Steamer's Lane present a more challenging wave than do many surf breaks down south. Those who surf the most difficult breaks earn the most subcultural capital. But judgment or surf skill does not merely concern wave selection or braving heavy conditions; it also concerns coastal use and development, community priorities, the social tone one embodies in the water, and what, as Smith says in the epigraph, makes a "life of right human relations." What footprint is one leaving on one's *community*?

To return to some of the local celebrity figures I mentioned earlier: Mac-Kenzie has for years run the Santa Cruz Longboard Union that oversees annual contests.[34] Indeed, she introduced me to many of the leading surfers in Santa Cruz, which proved instrumental to the successes of this project. Rodgers founded Hotline, specializing in wet suits for women, and through her company provides much popular education about women and sport.[35] Zeuf does breast cancer outreach and acts as the local ambassador of surfing to women who come from outside Santa Cruz. Along with MacKenzie, Zeuf personally took me into the water to celebrate Clean Water Day in 1997, when I was six months pregnant. With us came my three-year-old water-capable son, Benito. Ambassadorial generosity on the part of Mac-Kenzie or Zeuf is a commonplace.[36] While Bayley ran the Surf Like a Girl school, she worked with some of the disaffected younger people at Pleasure Point whose drug of choice, in the late 1990s, was heroin.[37] None of these women would be respected (no matter how well they surfed) if they did not also embody everyday community integrity.

All of them demonstrate "Aloha," meaning community-mindedness and a spirit of public service. Here the most beloved of Santa Cruz women take their lead from the late "Queen of Makaha," the Hawaiian Rell Sunn. A predictor of winds, tides, and swells, a world-class free diver and spear fisher, a paddler of outrigger canoes, and, of course, a big-wave surfer and longboard stylist, Sunn traveled the globe as an accomplished competitor and a founder of the women's professional circuit. She taught hula and effectively promoted surfing among native youth as an antipoverty, antidrug practice. She hosted radio programs, wrote for magazines and newspapers, and, until her premature death at forty-seven after a fifteen-year battle with cancer (she was sprayed with DDT as a child), did breast cancer awareness and environmental health seminars and fundraising. Zeuf's own struggles with breast cancer and eventual public outreach programs drew directly from the example of her friend. While Sunn does not appear to have formally participated in the Hawaiian native sovereignty movement of the

1990s, she became a symbol of it and a vital practitioner of cultural revitalization and indigenous knowledge. Her teachings and personal example spread a message of decolonial pride, and much like the popular singer Israel Kamaka'wow'ole in "Hawai'i 1978," Sunn imagined and inspired others to imagine a righted past and present for Hawaii.[38]

But while Hawaiian culture offered examples of embodying hard-core values, the Northern California scene also piggybacked on and gained momentum from mainland California trends. Gendered subjectivities fostered in outdoor spaces—in which women learn competencies that enable them to think about themselves and the social and natural order from new critical perspectives—owe much to the California countercultural movements of the mid-1960s. As social and cultural geographies, California and the West have famously served as curative climates for the nation's imperial health since the nineteenth century.[39] But in the 1960s that established cultural role took on a new antiestablishment edge as young people drawn to the organized social movements of the period performed political ideals in social spaces far greener than were many others across the convulsing national landscape. Up and down California's coast—where there exists such dramatic proximity between dense urbanism and relative wilderness—the outdoors component of a general political meltdown necessarily weighed more heavily than elsewhere.

Although I am talking here about Northern California's cultural geographies, it bears mentioning that Southern California's countercultures, too, were organized around outdoor group activity and sociality. Frye recalls about her teenage years in San Diego hippie countercultures: "You would go to the beach, go surfing, be outside, play volleyball, active play. We weren't focused on 'things' or TV/videos for entertainment. We played in creeks, ocean rivers, parks, canyons, the mountains."[40] For her, countercultural life was about being in nature and locating an emerging social critique precisely in and through those outdoor places. Countercultural values, as she reports them, were "the clichés, but true: make love not war, do your own thing but don't harm others, question authority. Certain dreams and visions, hopes, turned out to be a sham, not trustworthy [like girls being tracked into home economics and away from math]. We saw so much hypocrisy ... students getting hosed down by police, getting shot.... My friends going to Vietnam, and I felt like, 'just tell me the truth, just tell me.'"[41] Frye's time spent in the water or mountains was one way to embody the impulse behind "question authority." In terms of the gendered experience of everyday countercultural life, Frye recalls it through "the clothing part of it—beautiful hippy clothing, colorful, fun, wild, playful, unusual, happy."[42] Hippie culture flew in the face of middle-class department store women's culture. Indeed, Frye's offices today on the twelfth floor of the City Administration Building in downtown San Diego show this playfulness dramatically. Plastic flowering plants and vines drape down from the ceiling and wind crazily around the seating area in which everyday city business is done. Along with the large surfing photos of her husband Skip, this wild tone helps Frye to "lighten things up."

Another younger Southern Californian whom I will call Marsha remembers the green and yellow psychedelic swirls on the deck of her first surfboard, a single-fin shortboard, and the drug culture that surrounded surfing in the early 1970s, in which she eagerly participated.[43] As a very young teen, her motto was: try everything, and try it *first*. In those years, she was a "tomboy . . . a flat-chested [girl] when there were only big-bosomed women on the beach," and she recalls the difference she felt from other girls who only cared about "getting a rich guy" and who "didn't do sport." She strategized about how to appear like a "good girl" and still have a lot of sex, and managed to cover her reputation by always having one or another boyfriend. For contraception, she collected urine samples and stored them in her school locker, submitting them later to Planned Parenthood for testing. *Roe v. Wade* had just made abortion legal, and if she was pregnant, she planned to have one. The antimaterialism and everyday outdoors life of the counterculture in Southern California fueled a growing critique of her family's wealth. "All I saw was emptiness, shallowness. . . . Being so content with surfing . . . [I thought] why would you choose anything else?" She made what was among her friends an unusual decision: not to "marry a wealthy man," and she stuck by it. Driven by her fury at the guys who gave her a hard time in the water, she pursued professional surfing. For her, payback time arrived when big-name companies began sponsoring her. At middle age, her core values still hold close to hippie antimaterialism; everyday life is tied to the rhythms of the ocean. She does a lot of community outreach, through surfing, to girls.

But it would be Northern California, ultimately, that became identified in the popular imagination with countercultural rebellions. From the pot growers in Humboldt County, to human potential people in Sonoma and Mendocino Counties (and in Big Sur at Esalen), the lesbian ecowitches like Starhawk or Z. Budapest of the East Bay, the People's Park advocates in Berkeley, the organic farmers of Santa Cruz, and to all of them alighting day after day in San Francisco's Golden Gate Park, the very notion of what it meant to be politically alive included, by default practice, some piece of an engaged human-nature epistemology.[44] Among counterculturalists, one went about the everyday (including out-of-door activities) *as a way* to effect new social and political values. But the mere doing of countercultural life alone was rarely the whole of its politics — since that to which it ran counter had to be effectively articulated and then transformed for countercultural constituencies to last and turn critique into new socialities.

The generational transfer of knowledge happening today between women surfers in Santa Cruz transmits this historical memory of California's countercultures, but with the hindsight of several decades seasoning it. Some of what has been learned has to do with sexuality—the conditions under which sexual relations occur, their risks, pleasures, and consequences. Older women's mature appreciations of how hard it was (and continues to be) to figure out "liberated sexualities" motivate some of their outreach to younger women—and that outreach is systematic and extensive.[45] The complicated memory of their own sexual coming-of-age creates awareness and sometimes a sense of worry about the potential traps into which their own symbolic or actual daughters might fall. Further confusion derives from today's youth culture and media being more "undressed" and sexually revealed in their body politics than ever before, as if enacting any form of sexual activity (no matter its gender politics) qualifies as female freedom. Many younger women embrace these forms of freedom and indeed take some example for doing so from baby boomer surfers who posed in *Playboy* and the like.[46] So the ongoing issue of how to do liberated femininity amid a subculture saturated by bikini ideals and the babe factor persists, and the problem of talking and listening to one another across generations is one to which I will return.

Other lessons seasoned by time are in the process of generational transfer too. One of the most significant has to do with being clear about the confusing fact that so much of the coastal region, in spite of its natural wonders, is urban space. Much like the Hawaiian islands, Santa Cruz confronts that curious form of urbanism—the resort-town "paradise." That it is a comparatively extra-urban location with a population of under sixty

thousand, and one free of high-rise development, mystifies its deep enmeshment in the urban sprawl of most of the Northern California littoral
zone. To live in Santa Cruz is to be living both removed from and right in
the heart of one of the most densely populated and highway-networked
regional centers in the contemporary United States. To be sure, the place is
idyllic, blessed with towering redwoods, the hoarse sound of barking sea
lions offshore, and no skyscrapers screening the ocean vista. It is a green
city, and like San Francisco it has accomplished everyday revolutions such
as the banishment of landfill-clogging supermarket plastic bags (one indicator of countercultural outrages converted into practical political intervention). At the same time, the homeless population in Santa Cruz is continually growing, as are cases of mental dysfunction and other signs of
urban crisis. Sky-high real estate prices, depressed local wages, and limited
work opportunities force many to make the daily drive "over the hill" on
Highway 17 for jobs. If one lives in Santa Cruz, one often works elsewhere
and commutes. Snarling traffic, road rage, intensely overtaxed highway
systems holding together Northern California's economies—it seems little
wonder that surfers offer "stress reduction" as one of the most often mentioned rationales for surfing.

The knowledges produced in this location, then, have to do with living as
female-gendered subjects inside a particular form of urbanism—city life in
very beautiful settings that everybody is scrambling to get a piece of. This
"scramble for the same piece of the pie" mentality is, in fact, a form of public trauma, chronically rehearsed in conversations about real estate prices
and the high cost of California living. One cannot visit California for long
without engaging that trauma. In this respect, the name Paradise for the
surf shop rings ironically, and the need for its mission of fostering female-
positive and healthy living is made all the more urgent: Surfing as *real* anti-
depressant, for example, in lieu of symptom-controlling drugs. Healthy
foods, and the right relations to food and its production, as a counter to
a female body politics enslaved to ideals of heterosexy thinness and to
humans' distance from nonhuman worlds. Group connections and human
relationships as *real* forms of security, in lieu of what Rosemary Reimers-
Rice in chapter 1 called "monster houses" and lives oriented to supporting
them (most surfers in fact rent their homes). Sisterly solidarity and friendship as the foundation of individual women's strength so that the chronic
pull can be resisted to put others first and relinquish leadership of one's

own life or of local/global community life. There is an enormous need for implementing just such girl localist philosophies and programs of human well-being that can address the challenges of gendered and urban life at this moment in history. Given this need, Smith's "right human relations" provide ethical direction, a template for establishing values that can compete with other, more mass-produced templates, especially that of neoliberalism's "the winner takes all."

The invocation of a "winner takes all" philosophy returns us to the fact that, notwithstanding my claims about Paradise as a feminist institution structured along community-center lines, the shop also operates as a for-profit business in an extremely competitive and rapidly consolidating global industry context. In the eleven years since Paradise opened its doors, industry giants like Billabong, Quiksilver, and Rip Curl have been busy throughout the surf world buying out established local shops, starting new ones, or forming partnerships between individual proprietors and themselves. The process of surfboard manufacture and garment making, too, has changed, as production grows and, to remain profitable, gets outsourced to the free-trade zones of China and to Indonesia. Local developments in Santa Cruz index these larger global trends. Stores with deep local roots have found it necessary or timely to sell off their businesses or to go corporate: the Santa Cruz Surf Shop now is a Rip Curl store; Freeline is associated with Quiksilver (though it retains its name); Schroebel turned over and is now an O'Neill shop. Industry clothing lines have expanded, too, along with their manufacturing and distribution networks. Top brands (O'Neill, Roxy, Hurley, Billabong) pay top dollar to advertise their wares in magazines like *Seventeen* or *Elle*; the products featured move through venues like Macy's or Nordstrom's. What does not sell in the uptown stores early in the season gets discounted and recycled through Ross, Costco, and Mervyn's.

Some of the industry's most aggressive expansion or consolidation can be witnessed in the bid for the female market, especially the lucrative fashion market. Billabong and Quiksilver emerged as early trendsetters by producing well-developed women's and girls' product lines, marketing them through innovative advertising campaigns such as the young adult Roxy novels featured in chapter 2. Their continuing sponsorship of global competitive tour events ranks them among the most powerful of forces influencing women's surfing today. These early efforts toward girl-friendly practices have since become the industry norm. Major brands like

Reef, Rip Curl, and O'Neill, many with freestanding stores in surf towns up and down the California coastline, have rolled out girl's fashion and accessories alongside guys' clothing and hard goods like boards and wet suits. The "girl store" section in brand shops these days often occupies as much space as the men's sections. Some longtime local businesses in prime real estate locations, like Jack's at the Huntington Beach Pier fronting the Pacific Coast Highway, have stand-alone separate stores like Jack's Girls. Surf shops have moved away from men-only environments that sell guys' trunks as a second thought to the main attraction: quivers of "sticks" (collections of surfboards).

These widespread changes pose challenges, at every level, to a place like Paradise Surf Shop. The economies of scale on which industry giants operate put small, independent retailers at an obvious competitive disadvantage. Smith, the owner of Paradise, reports: "My own employees would go up to Ross and come back with stuff I have in the store. They bought it at a fraction of *my cost!*"[47] Compounding this challenge, brand gear on display in retail venues is often available from online sources, again for a fraction of the price—a move welcomed by consumers, but one that shrinks independent retailer revenue sources further as it empowers megabusinesses. To meet this changed climate, Paradise has altered the way it does business and generates cash flow. Several years ago Smith bought out her friends to become the single proprietor of Paradise. She shifted the store's orientation more toward surf lessons and equipment rental—her biggest new income source, and one less subject to competitive disadvantage. The lesson and rental part of the business, Smith notes, has kept Paradise Surf Shop in the black. Paradise also started super-specializing its fashion offerings: cloth ing featuring the Paradise logo (a female surfer flying down the line), as well as brands created by local artists and/or companies (sustainable Santa Cruz businesses like Ocean Minded, No Enemy, or BluEmersion, using recycled rubber, organic cotton or hemp, and natural vegetable dyes). None of these products is made by Chinese or Indonesian women or girls in global garment sweatshops.

Beyond economic questions of scale, Paradise has faced other insidious forms of aggression from industry giants: the raging battle over who will control images of women's bodies in surf and mainstream media. This battle takes many forms, and some of them are indirect but structure the whole culture, like the new "look" of the subculture in brand outlet stores and global sports media. In the past five years, for example, the commercial corner on which Paradise sits at Pleasure Point has gone glossy. There is a kind of before and after version of this site that, on my last visit in March 2008, called to mind a transformation resembling the one in Sayulita. Surf globalization has arrived in Santa Cruz too. Brand storefronts (a gleaming Billabong was built across the street from Paradise), as well as the businesses that surround them (Internet cafés, trendy eateries), replicate, in their facades and interior layouts, the production values of glossy magazine advertising. The unscrubbed look of the guys' surf shop is gone, dated: floors are now not sandy, and the smell of resin no longer filters into front rooms from backdoor "ding repair" workshops. As they do into other boutiques or sidewalk mini-malls, shoppers now walk into surf stores with freshly ground coffees in cups made of recycled materials. These stores are heavily capitalized with (and surfers use this language) "product": jammed full with a diversified selection of hard and soft goods, clothing organized along brand lines. Whole walls, floor to ceiling, display flip-flops.

An unmistakable gender politics has come along with this new look, and notwithstanding the power of local feminism, Santa Cruz has not escaped it. Even here, now, it is possible to see posters of male professional surfers ripping in great surf—maybe "Damien" or "Raj" or "Kelly"—giving an endorsing nod to various brands of eyewear, sandals, trunks, hoodies. But in the female sections of stores, and in the all-important front windows of these retail locations, posters of women advertising products are as likely to feature teenage models in bikinis as actual women professional celebrities. Even when surfers, and not models, endorse products, it is a rare poster that pictures a woman actually surfing, or doing anything even associated with the sport. Most visuals are fashion and modeling shots or vaguely "lifestyle shots." While it is true that men professional surfers are also photographed in lifestyle visual genres, one very rarely sees male models in surf media who are not also surfers. And it is simply unthinkable that an ace male surfer would be told what the Australian professional surfer Pauline Menczer was told in 1999: that she did not have "the look sponsors wanted" and would therefore not receive sponsoring. At the time of this conversation, Menczer was the world champion.[48]

Such a changed context has forced Paradise to debate its future once again. Assuming it had the money to do so, should it "doll itself up" to appear "now" and therefore competitive, weathering the outlay of capital that such a face-lift requires? If yes, what disciplining effect would that *Seventeen*-ish visual economy and cultural logic exert on the alternative body politics that Paradise has striven to foster? A girl-identified shop like Surf Diva in San Diego has managed to bridge this gap between *Seventeen* and girl power, but would such a bridge be possible in Santa Cruz? If so, does an *Elle* visual economy do fatal violence to the women's center aesthetics of Paradise's conversational couches and inviting doorways of potted plants? Maybe it is just time for Paradise to fold—to look for a new buyer for the business, somebody with cash, energy, somebody "young." The fact is that business is slow, and has been for a while. Paradise is not making money. Smith believes the economy, especially for small business owners, has been in recession already for a year at least. A number of the local surf shops have noticed the downturn; they are ordering less new inventory or ordering it in-house to cut out sales representatives (Smith's husband, a former sales rep, has left the business). "I had high hopes of busting down some barriers, and I think I did to a certain degree," Smith notes.[49] "But industry giants with all of their financial resources are more than I can compete with. . . . If I were a non-profit center," she tells me wryly, "I think it would be a lot more 'profitable!'"[50] Currently Smith is pursuing a buyer for the business and hiring out the day-to-day running of the store. She has returned to full-time work as a court reporter to make ends meet.

Southern California and the Epicenter of Global Surfing

The seaside La Jolla street that houses Surf Diva—"the boutique" as the retail part of the business is called—has none of the hippie or alternative feel of Santa Cruz. No punk rock haircuts, no freshly painted outreach centers for the homeless. As I am driving down Avenida de la Playa on a sunny March day, out pulls a Rolls Royce from a local car wash. Once I see the store, I park. I take a table across the street from Surf Diva at Barbarella Café. Two very refined women in their late sixties lunch together, one under the broad brim of a sun hat. Nestled around their feet a patient standard poodle waits. Here women wear makeup, softly done to appear natural. Their hair looks finished. This cottage-styled commercial district surrounding Surf Diva exudes quietness, not the bustle or tension of Northern California. Bordering Barbarella's tables are rows of terra-cotta planters.

Geraniums, rununculus, and nasturtium grow up around the trunks of miniature orange trees. An edge is missing, and with it, a certain anger. The place has the sense of a giant, quietly pleasant suburb.

Kayak rentals do a brisk business on both sides of the street. Here is the put-in place for tours of the La Jolla Caves, or the Seven Caves series. Small flatbed and larger trucks driven by fit young men cruise up and down the street, hauling equipment. Kayakers, with paddles in hand and some still wearing life jackets, trudge the several blocks between the stores and the Pacific. Surf Diva is situated modestly, one of many shops, and has a somewhat less assuming street presence than I would have imagined given Surf Diva's splashy media personality and its clear status as the industry leader in the girl-business concept. Next to Surf Diva is Ocean Girls, offering fashion and tourist trinkets and displaying girl-related surf and water memorabilia like a 1950s swim cap collection. In its window a huge picture of a bikinied girl (no surfboard in sight) is posted. It too, like Surf Diva, offers surf lessons and equipment rental. Rusty Surfboards lies a few doors down, near San Diego Surf Systems, which is the oldest shop on the block (founded in 1979). Aqua Adventure, too, vies for business, next to kayak places. On the second floor above Surf Diva is Jet Set Models, specializing in models for athletic markets. That business shares second-level space with lawyers, architects, and caterers. Back on the first floor, patrons come and go, pull up, and then leave surf shops with rented boards sticking out of the trunks of BMWs or Lexuses.

Surf Diva's door has a "Save Trestles" campaign sticker, and a short stylish beach dress fitted on an entranceway mannequin. The boutique section offers clothes, its signature pink boards, a video and magazine display, and three dressing rooms. Visible through a door that opens onto the back of the shop are its soft top rental boards and wet suits. There is no women's center feeling about this social space, even though it clearly evidences girl-power products and causes. Its owners, the twins Isabel and Coco Tihanyi, are younger than Smith, very much Generation Xers to her baby boomer. Unlike women of Smith's generation, they surfed as part of the college team at the University of California, San Diego (UCSD), a result of Title IX. Their lifelong love of surfing, their experiences with the raunchy locker-room culture of the guys' surf team, and their business acumen, combined with a desire to do something to build girl power and feminist community in the surf world, led the twins to found this rather unique business.

34　Izzy Tihanyi teaching Surf Diva students. Photograph by Elizabeth Pepin.

Surf Diva began as a surf school (fig. 34), and its backbone identity and revenue source continue to be its schools. Currently Surf Diva officially runs two. The La Jolla Surf Camp tailors its program to younger children (five to ten years old), while the Australian Surf Academy reaches teenagers (ages eleven to seventeen). But the business also teaches classes to women of all ages from many life contexts. Every weekend brings the offering of two day clinics for women. Regular other classes include coed sessions, five-day clinics, private lessons, group lessons, and "boarding school" packages modeled on summer camp for both teens and adults that use the dorm facilities of ucsd as the camp base. Holiday family-centered events bring in new people too· Mother's Day clinics (moms surf for free), moms and kids as well as dads and kids clinics, Halloween events (with prizes), and Thanksgiving events (coupled with a food drive). Surf Diva uses surfing to do other kinds of team-building work as well, including coed corporate clinics that emphasize relationship building between coworkers and bachelorette parties that celebrate and honor female friendship. For women-only surfari-style lessons, one can book a trip to the Nicoyan peninsula of Costa Rica, where

Surf Diva instructors will provide a Costa Rican version of the Las Olas surf experience. Surf Diva actually had a formal relationship with Las Olas in its early years. Photographs of Mexican surf scenes in the late 1990s show both Izzy Tihanyi and Bev Sanders amid a group of instructors and staff—many of which came through Surf Diva employment channels. Today Surf Diva books twenty-two weeklong surf tours per year in Costa Rica.

If Surf Diva has embraced an unambiguous business model of girl empowerment from the start, the owners do tremendous civic outreach work at the same time. The list of nonprofit efforts to which Surf Diva lends its image, following, and volunteer labor power shows much the same tilt as that Paradise supports: female health organizations and environment advocacy groups (e.g., Boarding for Breast Cancer, Team Surf Diva: Avon Walk for the Cure, UCSD Cancer Association, UCSD Cancer Center, San Diego Baykeeper, Summer Solstice, Surfrider). But its outreach is broader or, one might even say, more "traditional," insofar as at least some of these organizations have long been underwritten by Chamber of Commerce and small business sources: the American Red Cross, Girl Scouts of America, various elementary schools (including the Archer School for Girls), hospitals, arts centers, public radio, historical societies, Kiwanis, and the equivalent of the surfers' chamber of commerce, SIMA, the Surf Industry Manufacturer's Association, and its specific black-tie fundraising events, like the San Diego Waterman's Ball.

Through these outreach efforts and the creativity of their surf school classes, Isabel and Coco Tihanyi have brilliantly promoted the business and, with it, women's and girls' surfing. Surf Diva has been written up in many big city and local newspapers and in major magazines and has received mention at numerous local, national, and international news stations. According to one Web site, these "include CNN, The Today Show, MTV, ESPN, MSNBC, KUSI and The Travel Channel . . . [as well as] *The New York Times*, *Vogue*, *Glamour*, *Cosmo*, GQ, *Newsweek*, *Oprah Magazine*, and *Condé Nast Travel Magazine*. In 2006, Surf Diva was recognized by the California State Assembly and awarded 'Small Business of the Year' for its district."[51] Spanish-speaking media have picked up the surf trend too, featuring the trilingual (French/English/Spanish) Coco Tihanyi on the Univision series "The Chicas Project," part of their daily show *Despierta América*, a pun of sorts on *Good Morning America*, retooled so that *America* designates the Americas to Univision's global Latino audience. The segment "Ellas tam-

bién quieren surfear" ("Girls Want to Surf Too") offers a quick survey from
Coco Tihanyi of Surf Diva history, what a "diva" is (a woman who does many
things "superwell"), and then a surf lesson from the Costa Rican instructor
Belén Alvarez for Univision's talk show hostess.[52]

Contributing to its own rise to prominence, Surf Diva produced a book,
Surf Diva: A Girl's Guide to Getting Good Waves (2005), which provided the
twins yet further occasions to appear on TV and in other media, and to distribute, in very friendly sound bites, what essentially is a thumbnail view
of the Surf Diva gender project.[53] As a guide to surfing as a feminist and
girl-powered way of life, the text shows remarkable breadth and ambition,
even while, as the author Izzy Tihanyi suggested to me in interviews, the
book was meant to be taken "lightly." Its tone and narrative style do not
contradict her claim. Still, it is as close as one is likely to come to a feminist
surf manifesto that also can do the job of a trade press book, which is to
sell. Formally, it crosses chummy how-to narrative with graphic-novel traditions: a kind of *Generation X* (Douglas Coupland) for surfers. Photographs,
illustrations, sound-bite bullet points, internal short essays, and humorous
lists together do the work of socializing readers into Surf Diva surf culture.

The text begins with the post-college work life of sister Izzy, who (in
typical Generation X fashion) works as an advertising executive and occasional show producer for *STV*, an independent TV show on extreme sports.
It is a "show shot by and for the kids that watched it . . . about dudes on
boards, punk rock music, and interviews of the top pro athletes. Classic
stuff" (10). The punk do-it-yourself ethos comes to the fore as does its preferred medium—popular culture. The problem is that the great interviews
Izzy lands with big-name women surfers—Rochelle Ballard, Megan Abubo,
Lisa Andersen—never see air time. The excuse given by her nearly all male
coworkers is that there is not enough action footage to show the female
athletes doing sport. In what becomes a recurrent move, the reader gets
the following response to the guys' claims: "Not that they couldn't get the
footage; it was just too much effort to film a girl, unless, of course, she was
running down the beach in a red swimsuit for the opening credits on *Bay
watch*" (11).

An opportunity for a more focused advocacy of female sport opens when
Izzy hears about Watergirl, the very first shop in Encinitas (not far north of
San Diego, and since closed) to risk a girls-only venture. "This is what I had
been looking for—a way cool yet subversive idea. Like the Lilith Fair Tour

or the all-women's America's Cup Team. Different and daring to the point of breaking some barriers" (11). As institutional contexts for locating feminist impulses, the Lilith Fair and America's Cup examples speak clearly to the new school dimensions of the sisters' feminist consciousness. In the founder of Watergirl, Ilona, Izzy encountered a woman "part hippie, part athlete, and part sexy mama, [who] resembled a brunette version of Barbie" (11). Combining 1990s punk-indie counterculturalism with girl power and athleticism, Izzy and Ilona started Water Women, an organization run out of the Encinitas shop which sponsored contests and promoted women's surfing. Inspired by the possibilities of this moment and a new gathering of energies, Izzy had the idea for a women's surf school.

To return to the notion of *Surf Diva* as a feminist manifesto, let me sketch quickly its gender politics and philosophy. Ultimately, they map the third-wave or new-school character that underlies the business in its local/global feminist work. As a rapid entry into all the big issues Surf Diva engages, I focus on the text's "Girls who Surf" blurbs appearing about twenty times in offset bold text. As one-liners, they range from the playful to the more serious. The first one stages the whole series in that familiar "light" register: "Girls who Surf: often hear about cool new bands from their friends in the lineup before anyone else" (11). Expanding on it quickly, the next one follows: "Girls who Surf: are more likely to respect the environment, listen to good music, have great fashion sense, and generally kick ass" (14). Between the two of these, we have the makings of a surfing girl-power philosophy: it is green, girls look good while doing it, it connects them to collective cares and the culture of other youth (music), it creates girls like Xena or Buffy who don't leave "kicking ass" to the boys. As the blurbs continue, they preach a more explicit antidote to the well-known effects of sexism on young women: surfing is a place for girls to develop "strength, flexibility, confiden[ce]" (28), one where they have "faced their fear and pushed their limits" (40). Surf girls do not go it alone (compete with other girls) but instead deepen their connections with both friends and the environment.

But if Surf Diva culture is friendly to fashion and consumer culture, this friendliness has its limits. In a world of increasing so-called super-performance alpha girls (the constant achievers in academics, sport, and social causes) we get a blurb about "slowing down, enjoying the day, being in the moment" (86) and "not sweating the small stuff" (surfing as "more important" than "washing the car or making the bed"). Surfing persists, then, in its 1950s and 60s countercultural intentions to rein in the work and conformist patterns of middlebrow Protestant capitalism. But everyday practice, in Surf Diva contexts, updates boomer era countercultural impulses so they speak to notorious Generation X "slacker" refusals of overwork and to a much broader generational sense of local/global community. Such multigenerational counterconsciousness is crucial to the final set of blurbs, which combine both "fun" (where to put surfing stickers) and a pedagogic pitch for transnational ecogirl community building. "Girls who surf remember: we all live downstream" (182), and "Girls who surf understand the importance of a global surf community—more female surfers equals more Surf Divas to take care of each other" (216). The book ends by bringing together its overall consumer-friendly ecoconsciousness and West Coast optimism ("positive thinking is one of the most powerful forces in the world") (223). But again, this western hopefulness comes with an edge; it is not a simple feel-good politics. The closing blurb, "Girls who surf take nothing for granted" (234), has safety implications—know what you are doing, be alert to the unexpected in a wilderness context. But as an overall gender politics, this text checks any postfeminist claim that all women's battles are already fought and won. Indeed, its purpose is to equip young women with tools and strategies to engage struggles of the present.

The Surf Diva project thus finds common cause between a politicized gender identity and consumer culture. Indeed, "inside" consumer culture—in its commercial networks of media, music, advertising, and products—Surf Diva performs a significant portion of its outreach to youth, creating constituencies in which green consciousness, brave femininity, and transnational female solidarity exist alongside a culture of loving sales on shoes and bags at Nordstrom's. Izzy Tihanyi hardly considers fashion "fluff." "Girls want to feel part of a community," she tells me.[54] "When you see colors—like our pink boards—it says someone thought enough to make things for you. It legitimizes interest in the sport, says you can do it. When I was growing up, I didn't have that." She adds, "I would have loved to have [surf] camp when I was growing up—at five years old or twenty. I'm jealous of my own camp instructors in Costa Rica—they're so ripped, glowing." The historic absence of girl-related surf products, she believes, "made you question your passion, which is why I'm so proud of our shop—some people walk in and say, wow, this is Girl Central!" Consumer demand has moreover created positions in the industry for women, yet big surf companies still staff their senior positions with men and hire women typically only for the women's fashion lines. Like most of the women running surf businesses, Izzy is a keen observer of gender politics in the surf industry's upper echelons.

In San Diego, it would be hard to escape that industry's radiating energy. When I ask Izzy about the numbers of local shops on her street alone (and there are other streets in San Diego with as much activity), she laughs a bit. "Yeah, we're at the boiling point here," she says, "the epicenter." Like parts of Hawaii and Australia, San Diego and the forty-five-mile stretch of coastline north to "Surf City" Huntington Beach centers the global surf trade. Quiksilver, Huntington Beach's second largest employer (with seven hundred employees) after Boeing, has its headquarters there; the U.S. surfing championships have been held at the Huntington Pier since the 1960s. The Huntington Beach Surfing Walk of Fame and the International Surf Museum at Huntington Beach do the work of institutionalizing surf history and archiving its memorabilia. Surfline wave forecasting service is located here, and five Webcams provide continuous live feed of the surfbreak, paying it more attention than any other place on the planet.[55] The Surfrider Foundation, with sixty U.S. regional chapters and eight international branches in surf-heavy nations, has its home base just south of here in San Clemente, near San Diego County's northern border.

In terms of fashion and the production of the surfer-girl look, this part of California is the absolute epicenter, and a girls' localism that did not address this fact in some meaningful way would have no relevance. But even if Izzy claims an investment in fashion and commercial culture—in the tradition of (as Izzy puts it) the Queen of Capitalism, Madonna—this investment is hardly uncritical. She expresses pained disdain for the five-foot poster in the window of another surf shop next door: it portrays a surfer who is too skinny, too much like a model. The visual gives no indication of the young woman doing sport—it is a straight bikini shot. Izzy's criticism goes beyond mere business competition. As does Paradise, Surf Diva prefers using instructors, not models, for photos, like one of the local girls from Kalaheo, Kauai, Savannah Sussman, who is a Surf Diva team rider.

I do not appreciate that this kind of model poster is hardly as bad as things get in the visual culture of girl's surf shops until the next day, when I drive up to Surf City to witness the Huntington Beach scene in all its current weekend glories. The day is sunny, and I park at the Pier. The parking lot scenario is per usual: people changing in and out of wet suits. It is mainly a longboard crowd since the waves are neither fast nor big. Still, there are plenty of takers. A huge car show of vintage Woodies—in fact the eighth annual Huntington Beachcruiser Meet—is taking place. More than three hundred antique cars are on display, some from as early as the 1930s, some for sale at shock prices ($350,000 and more), some complicating one's sense of who does surf collectibles, like the Low Rider Woodies. Huntington Beach in its identity as "Surf City USA" is churning out surf culture a mile a minute: sand volleyball tournaments (the girls playing in bikinis), collectible and used surfboards laid out on the sidewalk for sale, used surf posters and recent surf paintings, women's vintage wet suits, surf music, and on and on. All these items constitute the informal surf economy coming into public space on a festival-type day.

The formal surf economy is still to come—with its massive outlet stores, its overhead, and brands, all set on some of the most "location, location, location" real property on the planet, front and center on Pacific Coast Highway. There are too many posters with too many young women modeling bikinis (and no sport) to name names in Huntington Beach. One's hand gets tired scribbling down examples. The one that stood out to me, on a day of too many choices, hung in the front window of Jack's Girls. Jack's is a local institution; its doors opened in the 1950s, and during Huntington Beach's general overhaul in the 1980s, the current fifty-thousand–square-foot commercial structure was built.[56] The late Mike Abdemuti, who bought the business in the 1970s from Jack Hokanson, founded the Hollywood Walk of Fame. So Jack's carries a local clout that big-brand stores attach to and cultivate. In the picture window of Jack's one finds current male professionals getting tubed or doing aerials: they are pictured in some form of intense sport activity. By contrast, next door, at Jack's Girls, the window shows a teenage girl in a bikini, standing next to a barbecue grill. She is holding aloft a flaming hot dog, her mouth pouting open. She looks at the camera teasingly—should she or shouldn't she? Well. For me personally, this is an official moment of having come full circle back to the old days of those old images, yet now they are not just in *Surfer* magazine but occupy, poster-size, "girl-friendly" stores. If a difference exists between a Victoria's Secret ad and this one, I cannot see it. Thousands of people, on a festival weekend, are consuming this image of girls' beach culture that has no boards, no swimming, no female athletes, no girl power. Huntington Beach boasts some 16 million visitors a year and was ranked by the *New York Post* as one of the top five destinations for teens and their parents in the country.[57]

Certainly, the popularized soft-porn visual economy in surf media has offended surfing women for decades. As a Northern California feminist project, Paradise Surf Shop in Santa Cruz wanted to facilitate a store and visual environment that did not promote pubescent body types as sub-cultural ideals—which is why the bathroom sticker, "just because some designer cranked it out doesn't mean you have to wear it!," articulates a serious social critique. Smith, Paradise's owner, had seen enough thong-bikinied women and virgin-fetish early teenage girls "laid" across major surfing magazines. *Surfer* was but the most offensive of numerous options. Indeed, lots of women, in the years of interviewing them for this study, have reported canceling subscriptions to *Surfer*. They are fed up with the visual violence those images inflict on female body ideals. And they do not wish, in households with young people around, to expose them to a surf version of *Playboy*. Until very recently, these women had reason for hope: a new array of surf magazines by women, for women brought relief and optimism. Subscribers could leave these open on coffee tables, hoping their daughters and sons would pore over them in detail. Alongside those maga-zines the new girls' stores made a point of *not* fixating on size-6 or size-8 bodies—intentionally so, since neither Smith nor Izzy Tihanyi are size-8 women, nor are most women at *any* age past puberty.

By 2008, however, a new skepticism among women business owners has settled in. In recent years, images of girls have gotten younger, more sexualized, and less sporty. And the string of U.S. women's surf magazines that came to the fore to produce alternative surf stories and visual cultures have, one by one, been forced out of business.[58] Corporate giants and local stores with institutional status (Jack's, for example) have emerged as the players controlling the visual field. When it comes to girl markets and girls' fashion, and with them, the representation of women and girls, they are regressing to a former visual gender politics and spreading it further and wider than possible before globalization. *Surfer Girl* was the first magazine to be founded and then go down, the harbinger of how difficult it would be doing something *not* bikini-driven. *Surfer* contested *Surfer Girl*'s name, sued for copyright infringement, and won. Much talk circulated about why a cultural establishment with the clout of *Surfer* felt the need to go this route, and the answer that has stayed once the dust settled is: it could. Next came *Wahine*, which had management problems, its contributors will tell you in confidence. But *Wahine*'s fatal problem, shared later with *Surf Life for Women* and *sg: the girls' source for surf, snow, skate, lifestyle*, was simpler: industry giants enforced an impoverishing embargo by never spending advertising dollars. Sunshine Makarow, the former editor of *Surf Life for Women*, asserts, "I don't think there will be a successful magazine unless the priorities [of the surf giants] change drastically."[59] Looking through these magazines, one finds none of the supposedly girl-friendly Roxy, Billabong, Quiksilver, Hurley, or O'Neill brands.

This kind of industry pattern directly contradicts trade wisdom about the smarts of heavy marketing to core buyers in specialty surf and sports stores. Once brands hit secondary stores like Macy's, their coolness and authenticity quotients decline. Indeed, SIMA reports record-high profits in recent years deriving specifically from the specialty-market subsector.[60] So how to make sense of CFOs' decisions to routinely spend $15,000 a month in *Elle* or *Seventeen*, instead of advertising in a subcultural women's magazine, at the bargain price of, say, $2,500 a quarter for two pages? Obviously more is at stake than the bottom line here. Or rather, a different method of measuring the bottom line is needed. Images and their control centralize surfing's dominant political unconscious and its current internal struggles. Just try to go against the grain and see how much the "Cali girl" mascot operates as a kind of global transcorporate brand. Undermine the brand, feel the heat.

Expressing views shared by women up and down the coast, Elizabeth Pepin, a San Francisco surf photographer, documentary filmmaker, and writer, exclaims: "It's just completely and totally time to end it—this b.s. that comes out of Southern California. Look at the girls in the ads, they look like they are all fourteen-year-olds from Orange County—because they are. That's the surf ideal. It should be these six-foot-tall powerful Hawaiian women instead. Big. Incredible. Those women don't take any shit and look like they can kick some ass" (fig. 35).[61] Modeled loosely on notions of Hawaiian female power interspersed with Northern California realist style, Pepin herself has created several archives of alternative visualities, among them a portrait series in black and white drawn from the girl localism of Pacifica (figs. 36–40). The hard-core surfer ideal to which I alluded earlier in this chapter is personified through visuals like these, which seem to dignify the

35.1 Elizabeth Pepin at work.

35.2 Shooting.

36 Kim DaSilva, Pacifica, 1997.
Photograph by Elizabeth Pepin.

everyday practice of surfing and deemphasize the "babe" body politics; my hunch is that they and Pepin's statement above would get much cheering from rank-and-file girls.

At the same time, regional tensions between Southern and Northern California female surf cultures are right under the surface, pivoting on how different surfers or business owners respond to the beauty regimes of their respective regional cultures—how much they are perceived to collude with, profit from, or rebel against the sexist visual ideals coming out of Southern California. Again, a gold standard of feminist functioning exists in California surf culture, with Northern California women held up as the ideal. When I asked Izzy Tihanyi about differences in regional female surf culture, she responded: "I'm so entrenched in Southern California, but I love surfing up there. As a southerner looking north, I see in the women up there a different breed. More hard core, they surf all winter. They don't care that it's cold. We're fair weather surfers, but they are hard core. Like Zeuf. Or [the late] Cathy Oretsky—who surfed Stockton by herself. They are more dedicated because you have to be. The elements and the crowds are intense. There's an edge to that scene. Here there's a lighter tone, it's easier to be

37 Mollie Stilinovich
at Pacifica.
Photograph by
Elizabeth Pepin.

38 Judith Cohen, at Pacifica. Photograph by Elizabeth Pepin.

39   Sam, Chloe, and Carrie at Pacifica, 1997. Photograph by Elizabeth Pepin.

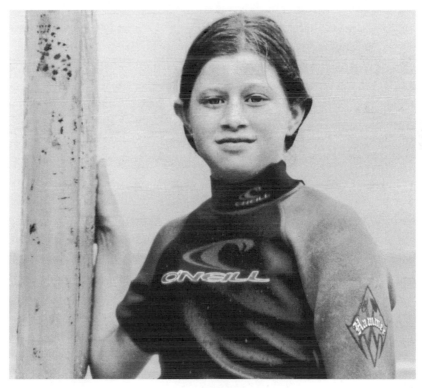

40   Rachel Klein at Pacifica, 1998. Photograph by Elizabeth Pepin.

a female surfer. The water temperature is less intimidating. Up there, it's sharkey, you get ice cream headaches. It's more intense. Here I will paddle out in the winter, if it's big, and won't see so many girls."[62]

Even if it is not tangibly on the table, Southern Californians are unquestionably on the defensive. Taken to task for wearing makeup, buying into the surfer girl mystique, and overemphasizing appearance and conventional sex appeal, Southern Californian surfers cannot compete with Northern Californians for feminist moral high ground. One prominent woman, who wished to remain unnamed because "I have to work in this industry," expressed disappointment about the presence of models, wearing makeup, in the visuals of female businesses and Web sites—why should women enforce "the look" in their own promotional archives?

But, as Pepin reports in a very telling exchange between herself and one of the female editors at Surfline.com, the environment Southern California presents to women is itself exceptionally hard-core in terms of sexist challenges. Pepin tells the story of reading an editorial penned by a new Surfline female editor, from down south, about aggravations in the lineup with men who cared more about the curves of her body than about how she carved the wave.[63] In a gesture of ultimate exasperation, the new editor concluded her column with the thought, what the hell, just get a boob job, and then you won't have to worry about looking good enough. Pepin reports being so outraged about this endorsement of "plastic tits" that she wrote the woman to say: how can you, as a new female editor, perpetuate this, encourage others to do it? And the woman responded: you don't understand, you don't have to live in Southern California.

Indeed, Pepin and others concede the truth of this. "I don't have to worry," she says. "We wear wetsuits, year-round."[64] She is skinny, she says, gesturing toward her own tall and lean frame, but still, she admits to body issues. What woman avoids them? "It would be really hard to live under the SoCal demands."[65] Smith of Paradise reports a similar appreciation for the constraints Southern Californians live with. "SoCal gals are way more body/fashion conscious than us NorCal gals are. They are bombarded with images of beautiful, thin women with silicon boobs every day. Here in Santa Cruz we don't have any billboards anywhere, and most of our weekly magazines don't have the ads like they do in SoCal—ads for breast implants, cellulite reduction, plastic surgery of all sorts to nip and tuck here and there—people here just aren't as interested in that as much as SoCal."[66] There's also a greater sense of collective female power to resist. If a poster resembling a Victoria's Secret ad went up at a Santa Cruz surf shop, Pepin suggests that "women would burn the place down!"[67] Not only that, she says, there are more guys in northern California who are "supportive." "They don't like all that Southern California makeup look"; they find the surfer girl ideal unattractive. "My husband," she says, "you know, likes the way I look."[68]

If a popular belief among subculturalists suggests that feminist history emanates from high-minded Northern California toward points in the unconscious south, I want to emphasize that such subregional stereotypes do not hold. The fact of the matter is that *Southern* Californians like Mary Setterholm, Jericho Poppler, and Mary Lou Drummy were responsible for officially founding the Women's International Surfing Association (WISA) in 1975, and holding its first event (a contest) at Malibu. While surf subculture during the golden age of the 1950s fostered collaborative male-female rebellions as features of its alternative gender formation, as I argue in chapter 1, the "alternative" aspects of subcultural masculinity had grown angrier and more territorial by the late 1960s and early 1970s. Feminism was "in the air," so to speak, making itself felt both onshore and in the water. For their part, some surfing women took the "question authority" impulse of countercultural life in the direction of challenging their gender status as either bikinis or subpar athletes. Like nonsurfing men, many male surfers very much disliked this unapologetic outspokenness.

Setterholm spoke to subcultural men directly in a 1974 article, "Equal Time," printed in *Surfer* magazine.[69] "Why is surfing considered a man's sport, and why are women the minority in surfing?" she asked.[70] "Well, there is a very dark side of surfing, and many people have been lost completely because of it. Surfing, which started out to be a cultural gathering of artists, has evolved into a state which reflects the paranoia, the prejudices and the hostilities of society as a whole."[71] The founding of WISA as a women's organization, Setterholm reasoned, would counter this hostility by celebrating female surfing, sponsoring purses for women's contests, expanding the female surf community by offering free lessons to women, linking surf culture to environmentalist advocacy, and promoting healthy living for women. Indeed, in the mission of WISA one sees the source from which both Paradise Surf Shop and Surf Diva would later take their leads. Very soon after this dramatic "coming out" of feminists in surf subculture, Setterholm was sexually assaulted by a group of surfers at a party—actions that further politicized many of the women associated with WISA's leadership. Setterholm exited surf culture for some years, and Drummy, who grew up surfing Malibu in the 1950s, took over WISA's leadership and presided until its last contest, in 1991.

By the late 1970s, it was also clear that professional women needed their own organization devoted to the specific issues of sexism and professional athleticism. Toward that end, the champion Poppler (from Long Beach) founded the Women's Professional Surfing Association (WPSA). As some measure of surf culture's backlash against mainland women's liberation efforts, Poppler names the period between the mid-1970s and the mid-1980s "the Dark Ages of Surfing."[72] Purse differences were notoriously large. For example, one Australian event awarded $35,000 to its male champion and $1,500 to the female champion. At that same event, "while women were competing in their final surfing heats, all eyes in the crowd—and of the media—were focused on the women competing in the bikini contest on the beach."[73] Though surfing hardly was the only place in the nation that liked its bikinied women, surf subculture of the 1970s and 1980s seemed to be in "open season" mode, a far cry from the gender harmony of the golden age era.

To return to my earlier discussion of countercultural sexuality, obviously a major historical shift was underway in the 1960s and 70s with regard to sexual mores. Hippie countercultures of both Northern and Southern California relaxed normative codes of female propriety, and sexual experimentation was understood to be at the cutting edge of social change. The frequent, sometimes excessive use of drugs and alcohol checked normative restraints further. Most surfers report increased sexual activity during these years. Most appreciated the practical and gender education those activities made possible and in no way would consent to returning to pre–sexual revolution constructions of propriety. Still, the majority of boomers seem to have experienced the time, at least in retrospect, as uneasy. Various threats always hovered. Social disciplining mechanisms could never quite be escaped (hence the show of having boyfriends to preserve a woman's reputation). Women report illegal abortions across the border with Mexico in Tijuana and anxiety about accessible and reliable birth control. And then there were the misgivings about coming forward honestly with me, so many years later, on the topic. One woman, in lowered tones, put it this way: "My husband [a well known California surfer] knows all of this, but he doesn't like for me to talk about it." She meant that he did not like to be reminded that she had a "past." And she herself was not sure, looking back, if that past was one in which to take rebel pride.

This "still working through it" perspective on the sexual revolution may be one reason why the cross-generational conversations happening today through female surf shops prove so important, even if they are fraught. At midlife, baby boomer women have clearly *not* figured out, in some final way, what "liberated sexuality" means. They have experiences and life lessons to share, to be sure, many of which they had before or while new vocabularies of *harassment* and *date rape* were invented or abortion became a female civil right. But there is more than a single generational speaker or listener in this conversation. Attitudes about sexuality held by Generation X surfers with punk countercultural histories do not square at all neatly with those of the boomers. Punk was never as much about "making love" as it was about "making war," even if the war waged was hard to identify in terms of who was at war with whom and why. And Madonna the material girl did not just signal a new third-wave embrace of power but also of the material female body. It is not that Generation Xers report no ambivalence or sexual angst. Even Madonna has disclaimed some of her own excesses. Rather, there is not the *expectation* of something clear-cut, something devoid of contradiction. And these disagreements over liberated sexuality represent key fault lines of generational conflict to which I return in the book's final chapter.

The broad point here is that the premium on "bikinis" and all that that visual regime suggests about women as objects of the male gaze constitutes a cultural context shared by Northern and Southern California women surfers across generations. Such contexts reflect a shared historical location (albeit unevenly shared, to be sure). That shared gendered location can and does create division and competition among women, but common strategies for resistance happen too. When one asks women what helped them withstand the sharp learning curve of surfing in the years that were *not* "golden," many recount other sharp learning curves undergone, like those required by incidences of violence, family trauma, or countercultural excess (including substance abuse). Sometimes these are public stories, as in the cases of Setterholm or Frye. Both women have used their personal experiences with violence to raise public awareness about women's issues and challenges.[74] Other female elders have come forward, in the interests of public education, to reveal long histories of sobriety.[75] More often, though, the resolve one develops as a consequence of sexist assault or substance abuse issues does not find expression on any public stage;[76] this is the stuff of private conversation, shared with trusted friends and lovers, recounted in snippets and half revelations as one sits bobbing in the lineup, waits for a contest heat to start, or drives to some new break with some new friends and talks across generational divides. This resolve and its transmission between generations makes for the backbone of everyday girl localism.

Again, it was Southern California surfing baby boomers—perhaps because of their proximity to Los Angeles beauty culture—who founded the first major organizations (WISA and WPS) that would take on women's liberation work in surfing. And the mission statement of WISA, as I noted earlier, maps the later institutional intentions of both Surf Diva and Paradise Surf Shop. On the collective activist shoulders of this earlier generation of second-wave women squarely stand the girl-power ideologies of the present. To those informed about surfing women's history, the leadership by Southern California women in feminist community building is clear. "My Southern California surf sisters have given me a lot," notes Pepin. "I will never forget my experience in 1997 (or was it '98?) at the first Roxy contest in San Onofre, back when Roxy was targeting real women surfers and not just preteens. It was a wonderful event full of camaraderie and cheer, and I met so many amazing women there. Roxy had invited many women surf legends, and I had the honor of photographing many of them [fig. 41]. Margo Oberg took me under her wing and introduced me. . . . I sat on the beach listening to them talk about the old days and the early women's pro circuit and all the hardships and discrimination they went through. I realized how their efforts really paved the way for me, even though I didn't know this at the time when I learned to surf [in the early 1980s]."[77]

Pepin's statement is important for its recognition of Southern Californians who paved the way for her as a San Francisco surfer. At the same time, this mechanism of assistance remains diffuse structurally, and Pepin knew nothing of these women when she started surfing that would help her understand herself as a member of a larger cluster of rebel-athlete California women. So then what *did* sustain her in the everyday interim of adolescent womanhood as she underwent the trial of learning to surf San Francisco's most challenging local break, Ocean Beach?

Pepin identified with the subculture of West Coast punk. As hippie cul-

41 Founding figures of women's professional surfing at San Onofre, 1998. Left to right: Joyce Hoffman, Debbie Hull, Linda Davoli, Mary Setterholm, Candi Woodward, Shannon Aikman, Margo Oberg. Photograph by Elizabeth Pepin.

ture did for Frye, punk culture gave Pepin the ability "to dress funny, drive funny cars, do a funny sport [surfing]."[78] She did as she pleased as a teen-age girl, and "no one batted an eye." "I was always into angry music—the X Ray Specs, Black Flag, Circle Jerk, the Dead Kennedys," Pepin reports. "I owned a record store on 7th and Folsom [in San Francisco] and had a lot of those Olympia bands down. And I would go up to the K Records Festival [the first label to sign the Olympia bands]." During those same early years of the 1980s, Pepin started surfing Ocean Beach. Like Steamer's Lane in Santa Cruz, Ocean Beach is cold and thick. Today it continues to be a nearly all-male lineup.[79] Pepin surfed by herself or with "other alternative punk rock types." But she clarifies, "I did it to *be* by myself—it was about escaping people" and coping with troubled life at home. The anger of punk, its public identity of unapologetic rage, expressed the pains of family disintegration and the particular pressures they put on her as a female. Punk gave Pepin, as the women's liberation movement of the 1970s gave Southern California's boomer women (including Frye), a cultural logic by which to organize rebellion and outrage.

Although quite differently inflected, this same Generation X punk culture underwrites the media-savvy and Madonna-proud feminism of Surf Diva in San Diego. Again, Pepin weighs in to admire the efforts of Southern California women in building a feminist surf community, this time referring to the significance of Surf Diva. It "paved the way for women's surf schools, and I think [Izzy Tihanyi] has created a nurturing and warm environment where women feel safe trying a new sport. . . . She has set up a good program which really does teach people how to surf—unlike some of the other surf schools. . . . She also has managed to shine a spotlight early onto women's surfing, letting the world know about the new sport women were/are flocking to."[80] Smith, Paradise Surf Shop's owner, agrees. She applauds the foresight of Izzy Tihanyi in focusing on surf lessons and a female surf school instead of relying on the sale of clothes.[81] Had Paradise done the same, Smith thinks now, she might even still be doing well enough in business to endure the current downturn.

Conclusions: Beyond Women as Consumer Demographics

Female surf shops are an outcome of two generations of countercultural life translated into present-day subcultural careers and then projected politically beyond the subculture proper to larger community programs and affairs. Paradise founded itself as much on the unconscious model of a Northern California women's resource center as on that of a for-profit organization, whereas the very language of a "surf diva" located itself comfortably in Southern California consumer culture from the beginning. But if Paradise and Surf Diva do business in some loose keeping with the generational and subregional inclinations of each shop's owners, I do not wish to overstate rivalries between Northern or Southern California, or to associate one subregion with a single generational or countercultural identity. In political outreach efforts, in their fights against sexism in surf media, and in the intergenerational transmission of girl localism, Paradise and Surf Dive ultimately share more purpose than not. Yet the fact that Surf Diva seems better suited to weathering the current political climate while keeping intact feminist intentions raises a host of concluding questions about strategic commercialism and the strengths or vulnerabilities of new political constituencies like those produced by such surf shops.

What is at stake in the continued good fortune of a business like Surf Diva? What does surf subculture stand to lose if an institution like Paradise cannot survive or if feminist surf media is systematically undermined? For girls and young women, Izzy Tihanyi sees the Surf Diva lesson as about "going for it, not being fearful of one's own strength [as a female]. Surfing teaches so many lessons: go with the flow, don't panic, respect locals, respect environment, practice/patience/confidence."[82] If a woman can "handle herself out there [in the water], it gives her confidence on land. . . . No one can take that away from you." Paradise Surf Shop— in the guise of living lives of "right relations"—counsels young women to be simultaneously community minded, independent, and connected to other women. In her films and photographs, Pepin emphasizes "strong, independent, brave women."[83] She hopes her work teaches that "you can do anything you set you mind to do. Resist what mass media . . . puts on you. . . . Don't let them co-opt what you love or make you feel bad about your body." Even on the smallest day, surfing requires bravery, Pepin believes. "A woman should take the fact that she's trying, even if she's just learning, and put it into other aspects of her life." Most of all, "surfing is a sport, not a beauty contest." If surf shops and feminist media are, overtly or covertly, undermined by industry giants, various sites of generational transfer of girl localist knowledges get lost, and the backbone of young women's feminist athleticism in California atrophies.

Why the need for industry giants to close things down so tightly on women's image production, women's media, and female-focused stores? Why the need to take the athlete out of the female poster, to efface the relation of women to sport and the outdoors and to the nonsexualized female body?

I doubt most producers of these images have occasion to pose answers to such questions, and if they did, they likely would respond: business is business. And it is precisely this answer that demoralizes and outrages not just women and girls, but also subcultural men. The most frequent complaint in surf culture, even more frequent than bad waves or crowded surf spots, concerns subcultural commercialism. Industry overcommitment to the bottom line—and the use of soft-porn visual economies to sell clothing is but one symptom—not only harms women but puts at risk men's abilities to support, sustain, and make clear *to themselves* their own historic push for alternative masculinities. One hardly needs to be a feminist to make a case against dominant surf industry commerciality.

And indeed, such a case would go against the grain of what the evidence of this chapter suggests by way of conclusion: that Surf Diva's strategic embrace of commercialism is partly responsible for its viability as a girl localist institution. What Surf Diva has managed to do is put generational savvy about media, marketing, and self-promotion toward a focus on feminist sport, surf camps, and surf lessons. As has been amply noted, "shopping" and fashion play supporting roles in this political project, and Surf Diva does not feel ethically torn about this fact (as do hippie boomers). Like so many members of Generation X, Surf Diva knows how to work the system; it knows such workings will corrupt somehow, but this given does not immobilize it.

To argue that Surf Diva acts with an awareness of compromise is not to excuse its operators from engaging all the ethical, political, and environmental implications of their social locations and everyday behaviors. But I want to be clear that the hardball game surf industry giants have played in recent years with independent retailers in general and with female-focused businesses specifically puts the ability of female-owned businesses to *do* business in jeopardy. So far Surf Diva is keeping pace with that battle, with nobody running a close second. Surf Diva is the only shop in Southern California to angle itself toward, or embody in its communities, Generation X feminisms. While Ocean Girls and Girl in the Curl indeed both market heavily to girls and also partner with people who do surf camps with an emphasis on girls, they are shops owned by boomers, and their institutional flavor has more to do with the vintage surf collectibles displayed in their stores and the golden age culture of the 1950s than with the present. They deal partly in nostalgia. By contrast, Surf Diva is maintaining itself and growing slowly, reaching out and politicizing young women in greater numbers with the possibility of continuing that trend precisely because the business can hold its own. Surf Diva speaks to young women where they live, about how they live, and about how new girl localist social worlds might be imagined, organized, and sustained in what looks to be a long battle. And if these women "shop," their whole female local/global subcultural life is *not* figured through shopping, but rather through female bodies doing sport and teaching one another how to teach one another to do sport.

Surfing the New World Order

What's Next?

Now that surfing is indisputably global big business, what fates await girl localisms? How might they push back against what seem very big odds? This final chapter offers some observations and thoughts toward the future. I have argued throughout this book that the local/global circuits of their subculture offer surfers a means by which to travel the new world order as global citizens. This kind of global citizenship has become tenable as earlier sub-cultural blind spots have been attended to—especially the notion that global surf breaks can serve the role of a kind of one-night stand to the itinerant dropout subculturalist. Even the rawest anti-social surfer today realizes that this kind of philosophy simply will not do. As history has proven repeatedly, the most beloved of surf spots become subjected to use and ugly overuse. Their future usability has required the invention of more responsible eco-practices than anyone originally suspected necessary or possible. Countless green projects have sprung from this basic dilemma and insight and have politicized the rank and file of surf culture.

Among sports communities, surf subculture is unique in its explicit local/global social movement intentions. The Surfrider Foundation's strategic plan for the following decade intends to "motivate a global movement of care for coasts."[1] It emphasizes that "significant protection of our waves and coasts . . . will [not] occur through the efforts of a few individuals. We must create an ethos of coastal care that is ingrained into our collective cultural psyche. It will take a movement to achieve our dream." This broad goal has put surfing in dialogue with other major globalist questions of the present concerning big capital, local communities, nation-based regulatory institutions, and the ability of these sectors to work with sustainable development projects. Gender issues have been fundamental to these discussions, and the most effective sites for articulating links between them have been feminist businesses and media. But between surf industry giants and women-centered surf activities a basic conflict has emerged about the logic that locates and legitimizes women's approaches to surf culture and to globalist thinking. The SIMA has repeatedly forecasted the existence of female purchasing power for lifestyle products as a crucial industry growth factor.[2] In official industry publications and trade shows, women are valued first and foremost as consumers.

The industry's inclusive gender philosophy—as though everything meaningful about surfing for women can be figured through shopping—falls short, however, of what most surfing women or girls have in mind. Spurred on by the missions of female-run businesses and media, rank-and-file female surfers have taken up the subculture's most fundamental offering: to bend the rules of normative gender while experiencing oneself, in everyday ways, as both connected to local/global ocean environments and to one's own physical intelligence and strength. The professionals among surfers, aware of opportunities for women's athletics more generally, see in surfing both a career path and a bully pulpit from which to make a difference on issues beyond surfing—issues concerning the environment, global health, poverty, and women's well-being, to name a few. Participating in surf microeconomies across the world, women gain opportunities for travel and new ways of making a living, in that way creating new launch pads for feminist advocacy. Relations with other female surfers across boundaries of class, nation, race, religion, and body type have required the development of new girl localisms and global citizenships conditioned by and responsive to those differences. As women's surfing expands, that requirement for flexibility and transnational educations grows more urgent. In every one of the categories indicated here—athletic embodiment, professional aspiration, labor power, transnational sociality, and local/global activism—gender issues figure significantly, global sexisms are highlighted, and the very meanings of surf life and/or globalist thinking are altered and reworked.

It is clear to many that women surfers must take on and effectively challenge surf industry giants. Surfing as big business must be called out, pressured wherever possible on the notion that women are nothing but either bikinis or consumer markets. At every age level this challenge must be waged—and the younger the girls who are doing it, the better. Such a task requires political savvy, since the livelihoods of many of surfing's most prominent spokeswomen are tied to industry sponsorship. That link has undoubtedly enabled female travel, influence within surfing, and the ability to make a living, but it also has regulated the terms of inclusion and critique. One must look a certain way and be an exceptional competitor. And whatever one produces that is real (like boardshorts), edgy, creative, or alternative will be quickly reproduced, folded back into the global brand. For girl localisms to flourish and for subcultural alternative gender formations to persist and deepen, the tendency of global capitalism to cannibalize the local and to then repackage it must be frustrated. This will require simultaneous efforts across multiple sites of the local, even if what works at one local site will not automatically work at another.

Women and girls are but one index of industry's controlling strong arm. Wherever the global surf industry is dense, social space tends to be extremely regulated. As a way to think through gender and surfing in the new world order, this final chapter reflects on the enmeshment of the surf industry (and girl localisms) in a few larger global issues of the twenty-first century. I here aim for synthesis rather than for thick description. I discuss Hawaiian, Mexican, and Indonesian surf worlds to pull into this final discussion the ongoing concerns of the book: the efforts of girl localisms to define their claims on public space, surfing's new female economies, and intergenerational communication.

To turn to perhaps the most intensively regulated of global surf spaces, let us begin at Pipeline, on Oahu's North Shore in the Hawaiian islands. Home to some of the world's best so-called barrel waves, as well as to the most concentrated population of resident surfers, Pipeline is the last leg of the men's professional tour. As the surf commentator Dibi Fletcher sees it, when the annual tour comes to town, the North Shore morphs into a corporate trade show.[3] Logos are plastered across every conceivable surface. Throngs of surfers, boogie boarders, photographers, tourists, film crews, and fans come and go via a route in perpetual disrepair, the two-lane Kam highway, named after Hawaii's first king, Kamehameha. It's a circus. Competition for space in the already-crowded lineup intensifies during this time and the volume of less experienced people increases the danger of an already dangerous wave. Onshore, industry palaces sit on the best pieces of local real estate, and from these privileged locations they cater to resident surf stars and executives while overseeing Pipeline's barrels 24/7.

But the real surveillance work is done by surf crews like the Pipeline Posse, local Hawaiian boys and young men hired by surf companies to "protect the experts in the Pipeline pecking order," as the Posse's Web site advertises.[4] Their job is to ensure that the Andy Ironses of the tour get plenty of wave time before contest day without being endangered by "kooks" (amateur surfers). When rules of surf etiquette break down and nonlocals give offense, the Posse steps in as an enforcer to make sure that it does not happen again. They represent themselves as guardians of the break, as peacekeepers. If the Posse is on the corporate payroll, it also extracts its own tributes and favors. Surfboards or "donations" are demanded to settle slights. When the Posse's terms are not met, it simply denies access to Pipeline. In the dance between these native Hawaiian locals and outsider *haole* (foreigner) industry people, we catch another glimpse of access issues and regulatory processes that emerge with surfing as big business. The Posse agrees to tolerate on its turf people and crowds it does not want in exchange for respect and material goods; the surf industry nods toward indigenous local rights or sovereignty issues without actually having to give up much.

What about women at Pipeline? Readers will recall the blockbuster *Blue Crush* I took up in chapter 2, which featured Anne Marie (Kate Bosworth) surfing Pipeline assisted by a fictionalized group of Posse boys, suggesting again to whom Pipeline belongs. A local Pipeline regular still paying his own dues, the (white) surfer Kahea Hart told ESPN,

> There can easily be a hundred people out there [at Pipeline] on any given perfect good day.... The pecking order starts off with, I'd say, the women bodyboarders at the bottom of the food chain. And then you've got a lot of international male bodyboarders who come over, and they're all sitting on the inside blow flapping their flippers, mushing the wave out, getting in the way. Then you've got some Brazilian surfers, stand-up surfers, who are trying to pick up the scraps. Then you've got a few mainland and U.S. surfers who come over, and they get their fair share of waves, they get a lot of good surf. Then you've got the local [Hawaiian native] boys, the guys who grew up here and who have been surfing here all their lives, and it's their spot.[5]

Although a few women have surfed Pipeline as regulars since the 1970s, this renowned break undoubtedly constitutes a hypermasculine social geography, and women therein occupy a place, as Hart describes it, "at the bottom of the food chain." Not even the Association of Surfing Professionals (ASP) tour has a stop there for professional women, arguing that the wave is too powerful and that women cannot handle it.[6] The controversy about Pipeline and its aggressive masculinity has raged for many years. Challenging other women to "go big or go back to the kitchen," the Pipeline regular Betty Depolito ("Banzai Betty" and a founding member of WISA in the 1970s) organized stand-alone contests for local women in 2005 and 2006. Speaking to a local audience who knew the liberties taken by Hollywood, she declared her contest would be "Better than Blue Crush!" Without a special event of some kind, Depolito argued, women would never see wave time due to crowds and the low status of females in the pecking order.[7] The women's Pipeline contest crowned winners and garnered press coverage. It showed women's talent and power. But it turned out to be a two-time affair only. In 2008, contest permits were declined—and women like Depolito expressed public concern that big money players were monopolizing the available permits.[8] For reasons of ocean health, Pipeline hosts only so many contests a year, and Depolito understands the need for regulation as she herself sat on the local board making those rules. But was it ocean health or questions of economy that forced the issue? She and other disappointed women will need to restrategize and probably find more monied sponsors.

If men keep the best breaks for themselves, if local turf wars between men activate in subcultural life the larger issues of Hawaii's colonization and the struggle of locals to survive in a high-cost paradise and to control what belongs to them, women (including native women) generally are forced to go elsewhere to surf, to places not so policed. The point is not that no girl localisms exist on the North Shore—they do, and Depolito's work illustrates one version of them, as does that of Rell Sunn's Makaha, to which I will turn shortly. The point is that girl localism here is intensely caught up with other turf wars that make for some of the most complicated obstacles to female entry on the surfing planet. In the late 1950s, *Gidget* indexed the first stage of surfing's mass popularization and *The Endless Summer* spoke to that trend by abandoning places like Malibu and creating new global male homosocial subcultural imaginations. In the twenty-first century, girl localisms—whether they are sites of pure consumerism forwarded by industry giants to make money or whether they articulate the real presence of groups of girls and women—put pressure for access on already pressured places such as Pipeline. The heat gets hotter. What recent women's businesses and surf camps and the network of staff supporting them have thus done, in effect, is to enter the opening provided by the new economy and enact a girl-driven dream of endless summer, a social space of *female* homosociality in places where neither the surf industry nor established male locals already regulate social space. Given that women's oppression works fundamentally by controlling women's bodies and mobility, girl localisms have appealed en masse by putting women's bodies into motion.

If the girl localisms featured in this book have been largely centered on a few California instances, it is not because other examples do not exist. California localisms figured in the present work because they are the ones I know best and to which I had access. But I would estimate that hundreds of girl localist communities now exist around the world, in fact, in most places where there are surf breaks. Surf schools or clubs representing themselves online suggest communities on both the east and west coast of the Americas, in Europe, Israel, Australia and New Zealand, Africa, Japan, Indonesia, and so on. Some places such as Hawaii and California, where women's surfing is established, have histories of girl localism much longer than the recent girl boom. Others, such as Indonesia or Mexico, where surfing for girls is now just arriving due to globalization, owe their girl localisms to that boom. Many of them could serve to discuss different forms of girl localisms doing battle with the global surf industry and its sense of women as merely a consumer demographic. The ability of localist communities like that of Sayulita and Las Olas to frustrate global capital's conversion of distinct places into an uncritical or homogenized whole is crucial. Moreover, the global surf industry is only one source of trouble, and often not even the worst one. In Hawaii or Mexico, one encounters problems for locals from unchecked tourism, and in California, as I noted in chapter 4, locals faced the TCA and toll roads. Localist communities often play one lesser evil off a bigger one. They team up with surf industry giants in southern California or Hawaii to oppose toll roads or touristic overdevelopment threatening surf spots even as they battle industry efforts to control representations of surfing girls or drive out of business the smaller shops or media projects that produce alternative femininities.

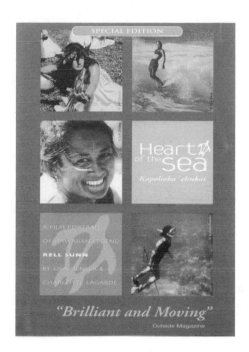

42 Queen of Makaha, Rell Sunn,
memorialized in *Heart of
the Sea* (2002).

To think through one example of effective girl localist strategy, let us
return to the island of Oahu, but this time not to the North Shore and Pipeline, but to the east side of the island, to Makaha, the birthplace of surfing
legend Rell Sunn.[9] Here another mythic surf break exists by a town known
to be poor, rough, marked by unemployment, and largely native. Locals
have gotten used to not expecting anything, but Sunn hoped to change that
during her lifetime. Sunn grew up diving, investigating the reefs around
her home, and watching the Makaha International Surf Championships
come to town in the mid-1950s. Women surfed at this championship, including Linda Benson from Encinitas, who won it in 1959. But Sunn learned
to surf in the Hawaiian way from greats like Duke Kahanamoku, Wally
Froiseth, and Rabbit Kekai. She heard their fabulous stories of world travel,
waves, and Aloha. As she puts it in the documentary about her life, *Heart
of the Sea*, she believed women could tell those stories too (fig. 42).[10] After
making a name for herself in the 1970s as a competitive surfer and one of
several founders of wisa, Sunn responded to local malaise by beginning a
one-person outreach program for teenagers in her neighborhood who got
into drugs, got into trouble with the law, got pregnant early, or dropped out

of school. She herself had had the best of surfing mentors, traveling in the 1960s as a young teen to California with the great Duke himself. Creating the Menehune Surf Contest in the late 1970s—a contest for the local kids of the islands—Sunn hoped to use surfing to inspire youth toward healthier ways of living and potential new work possibilities. She wanted to pass Aloha on to the next generations.

Throughout the years Sunn's reputation for having an open-door policy at her house grew. Something was always cooking on the stove, and young people could come over, hang out, and "talk story." She knew everyone. Sunn shared her wealth of knowledge about Hawaiian history, cosmology, and the old ways, she taught hula, and she used the traditional three-pronged spear to free-dive (no air tanks or spear gun) to bring fish home for dinner. Her own radio show spread her reputation further. When she was diagnosed with breast cancer in 1982, at age thirty-two, she was ranked number one on the professional tour, a woman at the peak of an athletic career and a subculture figure of enormous international stature. With the clock on her life now ticking, she seemed more committed to young people than ever. She continued to compete. But by now the Menehune Surf Contest had become an institution, and the locals were alive to its possibilities. As a conduit of hope, it was working. Sunn's longtime work with women's issues in surfing expanded to include breast-cancer–awareness seminars and work on environmental racism—as a child she had run behind a truck spraying DDT thinking it was selling ice cream or children's candies; no precautions had been taken to screen locals from the truck's spraying rounds. The surf industry's T&A obsession showed its ugliest face when, after a mastectomy, Sunn was dropped from sponsorship. Without breasts, she was no longer the surf industry's principal Polynesian goddess, the one featured for more than a decade in industry photographs.

Undeterred, but with recurrences of the cancer, Sunn carried on. In 1995, very sick and likely dying, she took some twenty local kids to the annual surf festival in Biarritz, France. As she had so many times before, she raised the money for her projects through surf events. The crew's presence in Biarritz generated press, giving the young people hope, direction, and a sense of thinking big about surfing as a way to see and be in the world. Looking back on it later, the young people did not realize "Aunty Rell" was so sick. She seemed to them invincible, coming through a bone marrow transplant, surfing emaciated and bald wearing a skullcap after chemo. Yes, she felt embarrassed by the baldness and the prosthetic breasts. But she was always laughing, telling stories. Once, after losing the breasts in a tumble of whitewash, she joked she needed a "boob leash" (like a surfboard leash). When she passed on, in 1998, she left behind a surf community galvanized by her life example. If Sunn symbolized to her many mourners the particular situation of colonized Hawaiians and especially of native women, her story became much larger than that of a single life because her fight did not stay local; she did not go down as its outraged victim. The Rell Sunn Education Fund and Menehune Surf Contest continue her vision.

In the community Sunn founded we see the center through which the many other girl localisms visible today in Hawaii travel. These include communities on Kaui (both on the north shore at Hanalei and on the south shore at Poipu Beach), on Maui (on the east shore at Hana and on the west shore near Lahaina), on Oahu (on the North Shore around Halewia and on the west side, as well as surrounding Makaha), and on the Big Island of Hawaii at Hilo.[11] Many current professionals—Megan Abubo, Rochelle Ballard, Keoni Watson, and Melani Bartels—consider themselves schooled at least in part by Aunty Rell and to have been nurtured by the Menehune Surf Contest. Some, like Ballard, have what might be considered second-generation girl localisms circulating specifically around them (Ballard's is located through her own surf school on the south shore of Kauai). Still others are led by Sunn's generational peers such as Margo Oberg (on Kauai) or Depolito (on the North Shore). Those communities of girls were developed alongside Sunn's own and in collaborative dialogue. In its thirty-second year of operation in 2007, the Menehune Surf Contest has institutionalized in the islands a place for young people, and for young women and girls, to center their hopes and sense of possibility.

The politics operating through these combined communities share practices and ideals that map for the future some of the problems and possibilities of girl localism. First of all, each of these constitutes an independent community reflective of the social and coastal profile of the local place. Kauai is home both to a heavily Christian surf scene associated with Oberg and to a very in-your-face brand of girl power associated with professional big-wave surfer Keala Kennelly. What is important in this definition of the local is the fact of its internal diversity. But if independent and internally diverse, these local communities remain aware of one another; they are linked. Links come through mentors (Ballard claims both Oberg and Sunn), contests (the Menehune draws all islanders, not just those from Oahu), and a shared vision for the fate of the islands in the context of heavy touristic development, military presence, and the global surf industry. Concerning development, everybody will say that less is better, but how that "less" shakes down differs from case to case.

Take for instance a current problem faced by the surf camp, Maui Surfer Girls, on the island's west side, near Lahaina. This is one of the world's best-known camps, doing instruction locally but also coordinating surf trips off the island. Its blogs, newsletters, surf-for-peace decals, and local and off-island activities make it a business that other girls' surf camps emulate. In a recent letter to the editor of the *Maui News*, Dustin Tester, the owner of the business and a Maui local, urged officials to create what she calls "win-win" scenarios between the need for the local regulation of beach parks and the need for local people like herself to make a living as small businesspeople. Her school faces possible closure because of new rules under review by local authorities. Tester writes: "As a lifetime resident and small-business owner on Maui, I feel for both sides. . . . I understand the need for regulation to protect our beach parks and kamaaina [Hawaiian residents]—but to close down businesses all together would be unconstitutional. . . . From the start, I've run my surf camps with respect to the community—we shuttle our students to the park, eliminating using more parking stalls; we do beach cleanups and teach ocean ecology and respect; and we offer scholarships to underprivileged girls through programs like Kuina and Boys and Girls Clubs of Maui. . . . We can abide by rules and respect hours of use and numbers of students per class. But to take our permits away all together doesn't seem fair. And if this is the case, how will the county pick what schools retain their permits? Will it be a bidding war that forces the smaller schools to fold?"[12]

Tester asks the question on the mind of everybody who is making a living in the microeconomies of surfing: will big business win out and swallow up everybody else, only to then hire them back as cogs in the wheel? Clearly Tester has already made some kind of deal with Billabong, since she advertises a two-week camp, the Billabong Boarding School, as part of her own offerings. On Kauai, Ballard's camp is called the Rochelle Ballard O'Neill Camp, so some deal with major industry has been cut there too. It is very hard to stay in business without making a deal in Hawaii, given the crowds and competition for limited beach space.

So Tester is going public, advocating for herself and the larger political project of her business in the language most at issue in Hawaii—the language of locals' rights and community respect. The use of this language is complicated by the fact she is white, not a native—but still, it likely will track to some degree with her audience since she was born and raised in Maui. In Hawaii whiteness does not denote a single identity or politics. Whites born in Hawaii who grow up paying tribute to the language and customs of its native inhabitants are understood differently than *haoles* (meaning foreigners more generally).[13] Whiteness is not an unmarked or normative experience as it was for an earlier generation of surfing men from southern California, and girl localisms therefore struggle openly about whiteness as racial identity and history with ties to the histories of colonialism that *haole* denotes. In effect Tester articulates her whiteness as critical whiteness and in so doing, she links herself to native *and* resident locals.

But her brand of localism is not just local. She is making her case in the official world of "letters to the editor," where I found it, but also on blogs, in newsletters, and on other Internet sites where younger people, from any place, travel for information. Sympathetic responses to her letter are coming in from other small businesses doing ecotours such as whale watching, which face similar fates if regulatory decisions go the way of big business. No doubt Banzai Betty on the North Shore is feeling Tester's pain too—both of them facing the industry's resistance to sharing. This version of local advocacy is crossing boundaries to other industries and locations, meaning that it is allying itself with people and causes elsewhere. In the grand scheme of things, the skirmish outlined here is a minor one in the larger battle over who makes decisions about the use of space, its ownership, and the profits derived from it. But the strategy used to wage this fight is not minor—it constitutes a basic one that seems likely to keep girl localism alive.

Independent local places must thus be linked to one another, through a language of shared values. In the case of Maui, Tester insists on the rights to make sustainable livings for local Hawaiians. But this battle between locals and global industries must be articulated to groups beyond the home group, that is, one must develop political allies. Ideally, allies will have one foot outside the surf industry, as, for example, the whale-watching companies mentioned above. When one's livelihood is directly tied to industry sponsorship (as is Ballard's), it is harder to be a whistle-blower. Still, whistle-blowers exist (Sunn, Depolito, or, Kennelly). Yet much of the work of girl localism at this moment simply concerns surviving, existing, laying claim to social space, and strategizing about deepening it.

One conclusion I hope readers draw from my discussions of global play is that what is at issue for women, as much as it was for men at in the mid-twentieth century, is work, an economic life. Economies of play are about fun and desire, to be sure, but they also concern work, a wish for agency in relation to work, and for respite from the unpaid labor of social caring. Economies of play that revolve around women's travel index the ongoing problem of First World gender and its exploitation. At a historical moment at which Western societies claim that their gender formations are the world's best and should be exported, feminist efforts to expose Western sexisms of the present do battle against Western cultural imperialism. Economics of play also bring to light the needs and character of many non–First World women, in particular those living in less regulated places where surfing is gaining a new foothold as a result of globalization. How should we measure the new female economies generated by surf subculture but existing apart from it? While sima reports the annual profits of member organizations, these numbers cannot begin to account for many other economic transactions and exchanges crisscrossing global subcultural microeconomies. These, too, are features of girl localisms ripe for future investigation.

Take for example the women at the corner of Niños Heroes and Primavera in Sayulita. These women do not know any surfers, and yet surfing as a microeconomy has altered their lives permanently. It has brought to town small-scale efforts to globalize from below like those of Las Olas. On their heels more intensive forms of the tourist and development industries have arrived, a land boom has taken hold, and social space in Sayulita has been reorganized, often displacing locals to the fringes of town. As do Hawaiian natives, Sayulitans find everyday life ever more expensive. People travel outside town to buy food. Ritual local festivals are fading in communal importance. At the same time, local women have gained in terms of their earning power, public presence, possibilities for education, options for medical treatment, and connections with other women beyond extended family.

Sayulitan women's preferred places of employment are those that are least regulated: cleaning the private homes of American women, not employment at a Villa Amor or working in a shop for specified hours. The freedom of such workplaces can cut both ways, one could imagine, permitting abuses no one sees or can stop. But for now, these new economies provide one way for local women to remain on ejido lands to which they have claim and enjoy relative security without having to take economic refuge across the border. As Sofia told me, her three siblings all went north to California, without papers. The grassroots forms of surf globalization we see in Sayulita may offer Sofia enough economic reason *not* to get pulled into other kinds of mobilities (and to be mobile in this way she would be traveling without her children). She may be able to stay put on the corner, not become a woman who cleans U.S. women's houses in the United States.

Or we might think about the economies running through the sweatshop wage of Laura Beatriz, a Huichol Indian from a rancho in Jalisco who came to Sayulita to work as a maid at Villa Amor.[14] Very tall, with blue-black hair done up in braids, one on each side of her head, Laura Beatriz is a dancer and her family does the beadwork of her people in the old way, as they do it in the mountains. But she has a baby to support, the father having fled, so she had to give up dancing. Her mother is sick, and her parents have two small children they have taken in with medical problems, one of them the bug-infested child of a prostitute. There is no money on the ranch. So Laura Beatriz came to booming Sayulita at the invitation of a family friend with whom she stayed, but then they parted company. She rather enjoys living alone, she has discovered, but for missing her young daughter. It feels good to send home money. One of her friends, a Mexican woman, knows how to surf, and though Laura Beatriz has not had a chance yet, she wishes to learn. Her daughter would like it, she thinks. But how that might happen, after long workdays and trips to the rancho, is not clear.

The invocation of beadwork and indigeneity here recalls a less familiar story about new economies related to women and surfing than the one above may suggest. In a case of reversals, Lulu Alberto, a colleague of mine doing research in Oaxaca on the transnational character of Mexican indigenous communities, learned of a young California surfer in Mexico selling beadwork in the local marketplace.[15] Characteristically, the surfer had found herself out of money and in need of something quick. Being handy with needle and thread and seeing the tourist trade in trinkets in Oaxaca in which women figure prominently, she decided to embroider local handbags with kitschy items and beads. Her products proved an instant hit among tourists. The Oaxacan women, hardly strangers to producing trinkets for tourists, knew a good idea when they saw one. Seizing on her example, they began to reproduce her bags themselves, knowing that coming from *them*, tourists would value the bags even more. The last we heard, this new product was moving out the door nicely and bringing handsome new revenues into Oaxacan women's hands.

The above case of reversal finds a curious echo in yet a different kind of reversal. This one involves a Mexican woman who leaves coastal Guerrero to go north, in search of work, in the 1950s. She crosses the border into the United States without papers, then finds work and stays. But in the summers she returns to the Mexican Pacific, bringing her young sons home to visit. Driving the rough road to Guerrero she spies from high above a little coastal town that one cannot access from the highways of the 1960s. She gets out of her car, hikes down to the beaches, and says: I like this place. The place is Sayulita. As a Mexican national she is able to buy two properties, one on the ocean front. In 1984, one of her sons, Mario—a three-time Olympian in martial arts frustrated to the extreme by the U.S. boycott of the Olympics in 1980 since it has dashed his career prospects—comes down to Sayulita to imagine what else he might do with his life besides hope to win a gold medal. He stays in the oceanside property and puts out some kayaks on the beach for rental. That is where it started. Today, Mario and his brother run the Duende Hotel and surf concessions and lessons on the beach. The brother runs the hotel, while Mario oversees the surf staff, equipment, and schedules. Mario also has the other property up on the hill, where he lives with a dozen Chihuahuas. It has five rooms to let.

What is also remarkable about this story is that I learn it from "the gringa," Mario's wife of the past ten years.[16] This woman, a blonde-gray baby boomer whose name is Linda, sits under the awning of Duende's Hotel and Surf Stand. Linda is the person tourists first see when they look at the business. She seems familiar, English-speaking, and her presence draws in the newer kind of tourist to Sayulita, the one coming down from Vallarta resorts in a bus for an afternoon of shopping and maybe a surf lesson. Linda surfs some and has been a counterculturalist for most of her life. Most recently, with her children grown, she lived alone, for a dozen years before marrying Mario, on Oregon's Mount Hood, tree farming, in a trailer without electricity. During the rainy season, she would travel to Mexico and stay for a few months. About ten years ago, she chanced on Sayulita. She met an old woman, Silvia, a local legend run out of the United States by McCarthyism and who spent her time walking Sayulita's beaches. They would walk, talk, and swim together at the Playa de los Muertos. Silvia died in Sayulita at age ninety-five, after introducing Linda to Mario. Now "la gringa" makes her home here, because of her husband. She has learned about Mexico from him, but the person who really knows "everything," says Linda, is her mother-in-law. She used to live with the pair on the hill, but the ninety stairs up proved too much for her, at eighty-five. So she returned to the United States, now living in San Luis Obispo, on California's central coast. Life these days for Linda in Sayulita is hard work. She orders all the equipment, has a lot to keep track of in running this business. Her U.S. siblings tease her that she works uncharacteristically long hours. In any event, she says, it feels strange to live in so urban a place. Sayulita is the most hustling town she has ever lived in.

I want to say a few things about graying blonde women in Sayulita as a way to reflect on the phenomenon of "Californication" and the problems it poses for effective girl localist politics. Tracking economic trends in postwar U.S. western states, geographers for some years have noticed the migration of Californians to other choice western spots: mountain towns in Colorado, art towns in New Mexico, green towns in Washington State, theater towns in Oregon. These towns have attracted professional baby boomers whose financial profiles have been supplemented handsomely by California real estate markets. If the fluctuation of California housing markets has sometimes led to financial ruin, it has also led to the massive increase in individual families' net worth as home equity doubles or triples in very short time spans. Finding themselves with windfall profits, Californians have bought second homes or relocated permanently to nearby western regional areas, altering these local economies by the fistfuls of dollars they have at their disposal. Bumper stickers like "don't Californicate Oregon" register the frustration of locals who find themselves priced and crowded out by monied Californians on the move. The blonde-gray baby boomer women one sees in Sayulita also make the local scenes of Ashland, Boulder, Santa Fe, Steamboat, and Seattle.

In the wake of NAFTA, the opening of Mexico to this kind of California travel has barely begun. An obvious question we must raise concerns the upper limits the Mexican government might be willing to impose on

Americans as they buy land in Mexico—how far will neoliberal definitions of global freedom, the right of people and companies to do business across borders without government hindrance, be allowed to go? But alongside this inquiry, another emerges: what is going on in California that so many people flee it? Surely the presence of U.S. families on Gringo Hill in Sayulita stands as much as a critique of everyday life in California as it indicates an embrace of Mexico and all the U.S. dollar can buy there. As someone in part raised on California beaches, I find a disturbing poignancy in recognizing that "la gringa" in Sayulita looks so much like me. There is a sense of embarrassing cliché about "us" in Sayulita, we California baby boomers. We are very far from home, on Mexican cobblestone streets, but so similar in our middle-aged hip and fitness, women wearing jeans and, if they still can, belly shirts; men not yet retired and powerful still in the chest; all of us walking up and down village streets, so exposed to one another in our graying search for something real. We are getting old, we boomers, and it is a new century with new ways, but who knows how to be old? We are still dressing the part, hawking ourselves, trying so hard. As much as are the young women, we second-wavers are in the grip of the neoliberal too. We may be fighting it, but the hand is strong and its grip tight. Who are "we" here in Sayulita? Tourists, transnationals, New World *doñas* with places on Gringo Hill? Like Carlos Fuentes's "Old Gringo," have we given up on the United States, on California, and journeyed to Mexico to die?

If in universities we might judge such travels skeptically, as politically regressive, what is less clear is why these spaces prove so seductive, and for whom. I, too, when I first went to Sayulita, had such a sense of "homecoming" to some regional feeling now gone from California that I wanted to buy property, wished to have my children spend time there. I bumped around over dirt roads with a real estate agent doing the numbers for the better part of a day. There are no strip malls, no prepackaging, no fast anything, no driving across town. People walk. Young people are at liberty to do whatever—the town and the beach are open to them. One of my closest girlfriends since teen years has actually bought a place. There, she and her family all surf. But as I have discovered with favorite records, the old songs seem old now, dated, not "classics." We were taught to believe in early childhood that we were the deserving center of the world (all the primal training that went down before the civil rights movement reorganized it all), but now it is impossible, for me anyway, to feel deeply for such generational innocence. Too much has happened, and there is so much yet to answer for. So there will be no colorful Mexican concrete work in my future. The complications of it all, and what I finally see as the better politics of girls localism, counseled me away.

Effective girl localisms dig in and fight whatever fight is there to face. They do not abandon local places, as Malibu was abandoned. The California coast has many girl localist communities to sustain surfers—up north, through central California, and down into Santa Barbara, Ventura, even Oxnard, that raw men-only scene of my own coming-of-age. When surfers move their money and energies from, say, towns in California to Sayulita, there is a greater challenge for them to stay available for the battles that remain in California. And to be sure, that one is the harder political battle to fight. The kinds of political machines that grassroots groups face in California (most often related to development) put the global surf industry into focus as certainly not the worst enemy to have, and in some cases, the force best able to power critical localist programs.

Indeed, to name the surf industry a friend or foe in some blanket way is too easy—and my final example of developing girl localisms in Indonesia raises new as well as predictable questions along these lines. Indonesia, or "Indo" as surfers say, has what is considered today the best surf in the world, displacing Hawaii as the gold standard of waves. Clean, long, thinner, more plentiful and reliable, and less crowded than those in Hawaii, the wave resources of this archipelago nation of 17,500 islands have attracted a mountain of recent industry investment—surf camps, shops, inns, eco-resorts, and so on. Much of that most recent investment has been in new girl-targeted markets. Indonesia's 222 million people (it is the world's fourth most populous country) represent enormous potential purchasing power. And then there is the market of tourists from Australia and Japan. The Asian financial crises of 1997–99 hit Indonesia particularly hard. When the infamous General Suharto was forced to resign his despotic reign amidst the crisis, it seemed the perfect opportunity for surf giants to flood a demo craticized post-Suharto Indonesia with girl-powered surf intentions.

Up went the largest girl-focused shop in the world in 1998 in Kuta on Bali—twelve thousand square feet of hot pink retail space operating under the brand Surfer Girl (fig. 43).[17] This megastore has eighty-two labels (all major global brands are represented), and a live emcee and deejay to keep the place jumping. The business offers surf camps for girls, lessons (surf

43   Surfer Girl Retail Extravaganza, Bali.

s'cool), equipment, and surf treks aboard a heavily logoed surf bus to other spots around Bali. Surfer Girl sponsors team riders, posting their photos from a recent surfari to Scar Reef at Sumbawa and Desert Point at Lombok. One of these riders is Bonnie, from Nias, Indonesia; of the other two, one is Australian, the other hails from Uruguay. Like so many other shops I have examined, this one links the megastore to outreach programs—for example, MUM (Manusia untuk Masyarakat, or People for the Community), a development initiative that fundraises for the village children of nearby Karangasam, sending them school materials and healthy foods. The brand also heavily promotes GUS, Gelombang Udara Segar (meaning "breath of life" in Indonesian), an environmental organization that cleans local beaches, provides organic trash cans at surf breaks, does educational work with children in local schools, and builds special projects like the "cool waste water garden toilet" at the surf spot Ulu's. In fact, the Kuta store provides headquarters and office space for GUS. This megastore is the flagship for retail businesses in other areas: two additional stores on Bali, two in Jakarta, one in Surabaya.

As noted earlier, Bali is a haven for Australian and Japanese tourists. From the start, Bali's growth as a surf economy centered on the international traveler. In the 1960s, male flight attendants from the United States and Australia arrived and tested the breaks at Kuta.[18] By the 1970s and 1980s, local Balinese were surfing in larger numbers, opening shops, competing internationally, and organizing Indonesian contests and surfing groups like the Bali Surf Club.[19] This was an all-male local crew. Meanwhile, non-Indonesian surfers had fanned out to explore the outer islands and set up businesses, changing local economies along the way. The responsible tourism movement came out of changes of which surfers were not proud. As the Suharto regime collapsed and Indonesia democratized, the girl fashion market was targeted for growth—every other global market was reaping benefits from targeting girls, after all. To keep the global surf industry booming, a national consumer base needed to be created to supplement the international one. But for there to be viable national sales in fashion, some real-life girls actually needed to surf. Without that, there would be no brand authenticity. So the industry set about the task of creating real-time girl localisms to do the work.

But there have been complications, the full force of which is still settling in. Advocates of the new post-Suharto era wanted to show that democratization was real and thus opened other borders, including those that permitted the return of formerly exiled radical Islamists.[20] Spending time on Bali, a historically Hindu island, non-Indonesian surfers could in fact forget that the country is overwhelmingly Muslim; indeed, it is the world's most populous Muslim nation. Known for religious tolerance and the fact that it was not an Islamist state, Indonesia was now touted as an experiment in Muslim democracy.[21] But shortly after the return of the exiled radicals, the terrorist attack in Kuta, Bali, occurred, killing more than two hundred Western tourists. The attack was blamed on Jemaah Islamiyah, a terrorist network with links to al-Qaeda. Further attacks followed in both Bali and Jakarta in 2005, this time less lethal, but still leaving twenty-five dead. In total, some five hundred people were wounded. A jihadist Islam is currently trying to establish a foothold in Indonesia. Islamic observances have turned more conservative in recent years. For example, in Banda Aceh women are publicly caned under local law for "morality crimes" like gambling. More women are wearing the veil. On the whole, the Indonesian government continues to hold fast to tolerance as its official state policy, even as it contends with a larger process of neoliberal economic reform so un-even it likely creates the very climate of displacement and need from which Islamist converts are recruited.

However unexpectedly, the surf industry has come to play a serious role in the fight against jihadist terror. The MUM foundation, initially promoted through Surfer Girl, now is a fully accredited NGO seeing to the "further-ance of social development" in Indonesia.[22] The foundation pursues an ex-tremely broad mission of "providing aid and assistance to the people with the greatest need." It aims for the direct delivery of aid to communities hard hit by natural disaster (like the tsunami of 2004 around Sumatra or the massive earthquake in Aceh), by extremist activity, and by poverty. Its board members include members of the medical professions, surf industry executives, village council leaders, and professionals working in finance. Some are Indonesian nationals, but others are Australians, such as Stephen Palmer, the vice chairman, who also owns Surfer Girl and cofounded GUS.[23] First-response activities following the terrorist attacks on Bali were coordi-nated by MUM, which organized volunteers and air evacuations, gathered accurate information as the events unfolded, and implemented follow-up plans after the crisis passed. Palmer has advocated a memorial to the dead to be built in the form of a pedestrian mall at Kuta so that foreigners will return, and as he said in an Australian radio interview, "think about where we are headed as a human race."[24]

In this turbulent context, one wonders about the project of developing girl localisms from above. If Muslim men do not face a conflict between surfing and religious observance, observant Muslim women might very well do so. To the degree that practices of covering the female body at puberty are on the increase, there would seem to be a very provocative conflict between an industry committed to bikinis, babes, and immodest femininity and an emergent conservative Muslim gender regime. The surf industry, in its own way, has made concessions to bridging this gap. In its efforts to create girl localisms, one sees a visual economy designed to be appropriate to Indonesia, meaning relatively modest. Though the subcul-tural press never mentions the words "Muslim female" anywhere, the idea nonetheless seems to structure the look and feel of the Surfer Girl enter-prise. Surfer Girl is not the only company at Kuta vying for girl markets. Rip Curl School of Surf (and its Sister Surfers) is doing similar work.[25] Although these businesses occasionally show women in bikinis, most often they do not. The mascot of the Surfer Girl brand is "Summer," a yellow-haired cartoon character in the visual style of Japanese anime. She wears shorts and a T-shirt (belly not showing) and is not sexualized. Other anime-styled girls and boys populate this Web space as well, ambiguously raced as sometimes white, sometimes Asian, and most often mixed.

Yet in spite of all the glitz and hip sparkle attached to surfing here at Kuta, so far it seems a very difficult sell. In the press briefs issued about local girls and surfing, we have the sense of patient fathers working against their daughters' litanies of fears and reservations. One article in the *Jakarta Post* from 2005, "Indonesian Gals Hit the Surf," quotes the Rip Curl head coach, Jonni Morrison-Decker: "Contrary to what people might think, being a girl is generally not a physical disadvantage in surfing but rather a benefit."[26] He goes on, "Girls naturally keep their balance better and are easier to teach." Girls are fascinated by surfing and know about its fashion, but they "might need some extra encouragement and support in order to actually get out in the water." What is keeping girls back, he says, are "mental barriers." Girls "can surf just as big waves as guys can, if only they set their minds to it." To "empower these girls by showing them *how* to step into [the water]," as the Rip Curl Indonesia public relations man Clemens Berger puts it, the company has for three consecutive years sponsored the annual Girls-Go-Surfing Day, which brings together lots of girls in a festival environment at Double Six Beach in Seminyak.[27] In 2005, the third year, two sponsored young surfers were invited as role models, Herlani Theresia (Niki) of Indonesia, and Madeleine Taylor from Australia. Papers quoted Indonesian teenagers, who took lessons during the event and vowed to return to surf more in the future. They said it was hard but fun.

In general, local media reports female surfing to be on the rise, and there is reason to believe that this is the case. No doubt the new girl localisms I found in Sayulita among a group of transnational friends are happening to some degree in Bali too. But the fact that Indonesia is home to an active jihadist movement that has twice bombed local spots well known as surfing hangouts requires some digestion for the world of girl-powered surfing. Travel advisories counsel people to avoid nonessential travel. Indonesian authorities report arrests and a lessening of the power of the Jemaah Islamiyah. But as long as the unevenness of globalization remains, so will the environments from which recruits hail. In this insecure context, new girl localisms go forward. The few sponsored young women of whom I have seen photographs on Web sites or in subcultural magazines are light-skinned, wear bikinis, and have non-Indonesian names, even if they are Indonesian nationals. I assume they are not Muslim or that, anyway, they are not observant. A few girls' photos actually surfing in bikinis appear in local magazines, and they look more classically Indonesian—they claim Bali as home and are likely Hindu (fig. 44). But these do not make for details anybody talks about.

Many younger, prepubescent girls also show up in photo galleries. They might hail from the outer islands or from Bali. They are pictured in shorts, active, seemingly inclined toward "exercise," if by that we mean hugely energetic movement. Whether or not they are Muslim is not indexed here by covering, since they are too young to have to cover themselves. In its bid to develop youth global markets, Rip Curl has for the past few years been eyeballing the world in its "Rip Curl Grom Search" (fig. 45). *Grommet* is slang for a very young surfer. In a surfing version of *American Idol*, the Grom Search surveys the global landscape for promising surf competitors. Touring surf Meccas of the world, crowning young champs along the way and then sending them to larger surf-off contests with the promise of sponsorship and celebrity, the Grom Search in Indonesia recently identified Pacitan as a "hotbed" of girls surfing, with "four brave young girls really getting into the surf."[28] Young "Selina" won the day's event. Pacitan is located in East Java, a generally Muslim area, though the blended religious traditions of earlier eras—Hinduism mixed with animism mixed with Islam—remain strong.

It seems possible that some of the girls at Pacitan might claim the local/global coordinates of a new Muslim surf girl localism. Recently, in where else but Surf City USA, Huntington Beach, an observant Muslim woman, Shereen Sabet, a microbiologist at California State University, Long Beach, began a small business (Splashwear) out of her home to address what she saw as a conflict.[29] She and her Muslim American friends wished to remain observant, but they did not want to avoid water activities because of modesty concerns. Many of them were second- and third-generation children of immigrants who have grown up in U.S. coed contexts, where there is no separation of the sexes in pools or beaches, as there might be in many Muslim countries. At puberty, when they began to cover, they found themselves unable to do things they once loved as girls: swim, snorkel, or in

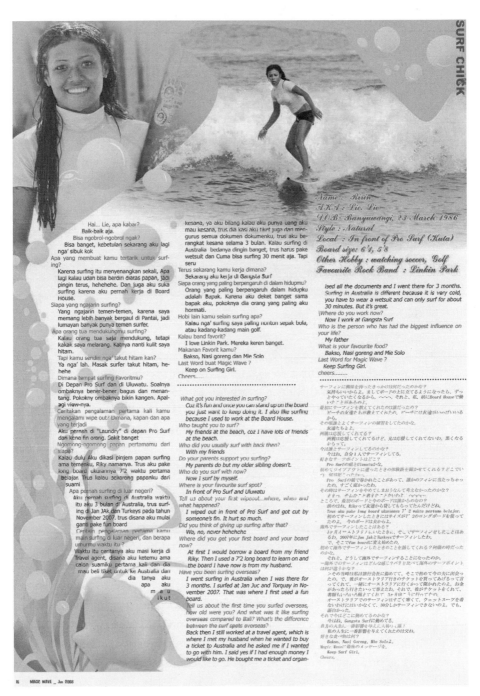

SURF CHICK

Name : Ririn
A.K.A : Lie, Lie
D.O.B : Banyuwangi, 23 March 1986
Style : Natural
Local : In front of Pro Surf (Kuta)
Board size : 6'4, 5'8
Other Hobby : watching soccer, Golf
Favourite Rock Band : Linkin Park

Hai... Lie, apa kabar?
Baik-baik aja.
Bisa ngobrol-ngobrol ngak?
Bisa banget, kebetulan sekarang aku lagi nga' sibuk kok
Apa yang membuat kamu tertarik untuk surfing?
Karena surfing itu menyenangkan sekali, Apa lagi kalau udah bisa berdiri diatas papan, jadi pingin terus, hehehehe. Dan juga aku suka surfing karena aku pernah kerja di Board House.
Siapa yang ngajarin surfing?
Yang ngajarin temen-temen, karena saya memang lebih banyak bergaul di Pantai, jadi lumayan banyak punya temen surfer.
Apa orang tua mendukungmu surfing?
Kalau orang tua saja mendukung, tetapi kakak saya melarang. Katnya nanti kulit saya hitam.
Tapi kamu sendiri nga' takut hitam?
Ya nga' lah. Masak surfer takut hitam, hehehe
Dimana tempat surfing Favoritmu?
Di Depan Pro Surf dan di Uluwatu. Soalnya ombaknya bener-bener bagus dan menantang. Pokoknya ombaknya bikin kangen. Apalagi viewnya.
Ceritakan pengalaman pertama kali kamu mengalami wipe out? Dimana, kapan dan apa yang terjadi
Aku pernah di "Laundry" di depan Pro Surf dan kena fin orang. Sakit banget
Ngomong-ngomong papan pertamamu dari siapa?
Kalau dulu Aku dikasi pinjem papan surfing ama temenku, Riky namanya. Trus aku pake long board ukurannya 7'2 waktu pertama belajar. Trus kalau sekarang papanku dari suami
Apa pernah surfing di luar negeri?
Aku pernah surfing di Australia waktu itu aku 3 bulan di Australia, trus surfing di Jan JAk dan Turkeys pada tahun November 2007. trus disana aku mulai ganti pake fun board
Ceritain pengalaman pertama kamu main surfing di luar negeri, dan berapa umurmu waktu itu ?
Waktu itu ceritanya aku masi kerja di Travel agent, disana aku ketemu ama calon suamiku pertama kali dan dia mau beli tiket untuk ke Australia dan dia tanya aku apa aku mau ikut

kesana, yo aku bilang kalau aku punya uang aku mau kesana, trus dia kasi aku tiket juga dan mengurus semua dokumen dokumenku, trus aku berangkat kesana selama 3 bulan. Kalau surfing di Australia bedanya dingin banget, trus harus pake wetsuit dan Cuma bisa surfing 30 menit aja. Tapi seru
Terus sekarang kamu kerja dimana?
Sekarang aku kerja di Gangsta Surf
Siapa orang yang paling berpengaruh di dalam hidupmu?
Orang yang paling berpengaruh dalam hidupku adalah Bapak. Karena aku deket banget sama bapak aku, pokoknya dia orang yang paling aku hormati.
Hobi lain kamu selain surfing apa?
Kalau nga' surfing saya paling nonton sepak bola, atau kadang-kadang main golf.
Kalau band favorit?
I love Linkin Park. Mereka keren banget.
Makanan Favorit kamu?
Bakso, Nasi goreng dan Mie Solo
Last Word buat Magic Wave ?
Keep on Surfing Girl
Cheers.......

....

What got you interested in surfing?
Cuz it's fun and once you can stand up on the board you just want to keep doing it. I also like surfing because I used to work at the Board House.
Who taught you to surf?
My friends at the beach, coz I have lots of friends at the beach.
Who did you usually surf with back then?
With my friends
Do your parents support you surfing?
My parents do but my older sibling doesn't.
Who do you surf with now?
Now I surf by myself.
Where is your favourite surf spot?
In front of Pro Surf and Uluwatu
Tell us about your first wipeout...where, when and what happened?
I wiped out in front of Pro Surf and got cut by someone's fin. It hurt so much.
Did you think of giving up surfing after that?
Wa, no, never hehehehe
Where did you get your first board and your board now?
At first I would borrow a board from my friend Riky. Then I used a 7'2 long board to learn on and the board I have now is from my husband.
Have you been surfing overseas?
I went surfing in Australia when I was there for 3 months. I surfed at Jan Juc and Torquay in November 2007. That was where I first used a fun board.
Tell us about the first time you surfed overseas, how old were you? And what was it like surfing overseas compared to Bali? What's the difference between the surf spots overseas?
Back then I still worked at a travel agent, which is where I met my husband when he wanted to buy a ticket to Australia and he asked me if I wanted to go with him. I said yes if I had enough money I would like to go. He bought me a ticket and organ-

ised all the documents and I went there for 3 months. Surfing in Australia is different because it is very cold, you have to wear a wetsuit and can only surf for about 30 minutes. But it's great.
Where do you work now?
Now I work at Gangsta Surf
Who is the person who has had the biggest influence on your life?
My father
What is your favourite food?
Bakso, Nasi goreng and Mie Solo
Last Word for Magic Wave ?
Keep Surfing Girl.
cheers........

....

サーフィンに興味を持ったきっかけは何だったのかな?
気持ちいいからよ。そしてボードの上に立てるようになったら、ずっとやっていたくなるから。へへへ。それと、私、前にBoard Houseで働いたことがあるの。
最初にサーフィンを教えてくれたのは誰だったの?
ビーチの友達かしら教えてくれたの、ビーチでは友達がいっぱいいるから。
その頃友達とよくサーフィンの練習をしたのかな?
友達たちよ。
両親は応援してくれてる?
両親は応援してくれてるけど、兄は応援してくれてないわ、黒くなるからって。
今は誰とサーフィンしてるのかな?
今は、自分1人でサーフィンしてる。
好きなサーフィンポイントはどこ?
Pro Surfの前とUluwatuかな。
初めてのワイプアウトに遭ったときの体験談を聞かせてもらえる?どこでいつ何が起きたの?
Pro Surfの前で遭ったことがあって、誰かのフィンに当たっちゃったの。すごく痛かったわ。
その時はサーフィンをやめてしまおうなんて考えなかったのかな?
わ。そんなの。私がサーフィンやめるわけないじゃない。へへ。
ところで、最初のボードと今のボードは誰からなの?
前のは、Rikyって友達から貸してもらってたんだけど。そして、True aku pake long board ukurannya 7' waktu pertama belajar。初めてサーフィンしたときにはサイズが7'2のロングボードを使ってたの。今のボードは夫からよ。
海外でサーフィンしたことはある?
3ヶ月オーストラリアにいたときに、そこでサーフィンをしたことがあるわ。2007年にJan JukとTurkeysでサーフィンしたわ。そこでFun boardに変え始めたの。
初めて海外でサーフィンしたときのことを話してくれる?何歳の時だったのかな。
それと、どうして海外でサーフィンすることになったのかな。
—海外でのサーフィンはどんな感じ?バリと比べて海外のサーフポイントはどう違うかしら。
つその当時はまだ旅行会社に勤めてて、そこで初めて今の夫に出会ったの。で、彼がオーストラリア行きのチケットを買ってあげるって言ってくれて、一緒にオーストラリアに行くかって聞かれたのよ。お金があったら行きたいって答えたら、それで、彼がチケットをくれて、書類もいろいろ揃えてくれて、3ヶ月間"いてきたわけ。オーストラリアでのサーフィンはすごく寒くて、ウェットスーツを着ないといけないかなくて、30分しかサーフィンできないのよ。でも面白かった。
それで今はどこに勤めてるのかな?
今は、Gangsta Surfに勤めてる。
自分の人生に一番影響を与えた人って、誰?
私の人生に一番影響を与えてくれたのは父よ。
好きな食べ物は何?
Bakso, Nasi Goreng, Mie Soloよ。
Magic Waveに最後のメッセージを。
Keep Surf Girl,
cheers。

16   MAGIC WAVE _ Jun 2008

44   Local surfer Ririn at Kuta featured in *Magic Wave*, June 2008.

45 Global scouting for surf talent.

Sabet's case, scuba dive. Sabet's solution to this problem was to design and manufacture a swimsuit covering the whole body and head while allowing full mobility. Today about a dozen stores sell this all-body suit in the United States and abroad. Interviewed on local television stations, Sabet says non-Muslim women also buy the all-body suit.[30] Some women have skin problems or scars that make them self-conscious. That the suits are stylish and colorful makes them appealing. Some women object to how sexualizing skimpy bikinis are. Taking the discussion of the babe factor in surfing around the world and back again, Sabet asks the television audience: "Are we really free if we don't fit into that bikini, tankini mold?"[31]

In February 2007, an Associated Press photo of twenty-three-year-old Sama Wareh, at Newport Beach, brought Sabet's modest "burkini" to the world of surfing.[32] Wearing a Splashgear suit, Wareh headed into the water with her board. Before buying the suit she had gone into the water in jogging pants, a skirt, and long-sleeved shirt—not functional clothing to wear while surfing. Recently, a life guard, noticing her stylish new all-body suit and head scarf, came up to her and asked, "Dude, are you like a Muslim surfer girl or something?"[33] His question, she imagined, was on the minds of many people on the beach. Now, she says, they ask instead where they might buy such a suit.

Does this figure of the Muslim surfer girl suggest appropriation, empowerment, consumerism, or new forms of social imagination? Is she a hybridized neoliberal girl par excellence? Perhaps Splashwear suits turn Muslim women into girls? Are there risks run whose consequences may come home one day, in a fateful encounter? Might this girl localism collaborate with other girl localisms in Surf City to get rid of the Victoria's Secret models posing as surfers at Jack's Girls? Whatever answers might be given to these questions, one certain thing is that if Muslim girl localisms grow, their gear will be picked up and mass-produced by Surfer Girl Bali or any other manufacturer who can develop markets in places like Australia, Great Britain, France, or Canada, where surfing and large Muslim immigrant populations overlap.

I would like to close on a quieter note, and on a different coast—the so-called third coast, the Gulf Coast, near my own home in Houston. The term *third* suggests its "other" status as coastline between the U.S. West and East Coasts. Over time I have come to love this otherness, the muddy waters, the wind waves, the marshy wetland birds, the not-glamour of Galveston. The water is very alive with jumping fish, swooping birds, and the occasional shark. There is no heavy surf industry pressure for space here, no contests, not so many beautiful people, and, at middle age, I find it all a relief. Girl localisms from Galveston, Port Aransas, Corpus Christi, and Padre Island are powerful enough that young women's pictures in community and major local papers are not so novel anymore (fig. 46).[34] The Texas Surfing Museum at the beginning of June 2008 began an exhibit on women in surfing.[35] While progressive political victories in Texas are hard to come by, one that Surfrider Texas has earned is the ongoing battle to keep the Texas beach public.

I tell my sons about these victories, but maybe most important, I tell my young niece Samantha, or Sammie. She is eleven, a shy girl not yet come into herself. But she is proud of a few things. One of them is that she has learned how to swim. About five years ago, we started—Samantha did not want to get water in her nose. She did not want to put her head underwater. She is a working-class, Mexican American girl, and she and her friends do not go to swim camps during the summer. But over time, we got in the local pool, then into its deep end, then out at Galveston, even as the summer storms came on and whipped up the water, and it all seemed like too much. It was not too much. Along the way, Sammie has claimed something

46 North Shore Surf Club, Houston, Texas, 2007. Photograph by Jimmy Johnson.

for herself. On her most recent birthday, she invited her friends to a beach party at Galveston, and without me present, they went swimming, took a room in the bungalow motel where my own family usually stays, and had themselves a great girly time. I am proud of her for everything she is figuring out, and she knows it. I am proud of all these moments of intergenerational exchange and learning—they provide real resources in whatever fights feminists wage in the present.

Notes

Introduction

1 Joni Martin, "Women on the Waves: Surf Vacations for Women Fulfill Gidget Fantasies," *San Francisco Chronicle*, 22 September 2002; Charis Atlas Heelan, "Surf Girls Rule: Riding the Big Kahuna in Bikinis," *Frommer's*, 4 September 2004, www.frommers.com. Reviews of Las Olas have appeared in *Oprah*; *Travel Woman*; *Elle*; *Self, Body, and Soul*; *Surf Life for Women*; *Harper's Bazaar*; *Sports Illustrated for Women*; *Women Sports and Fitness*; *Spa*; *Shape*; *Time*; *Newsweek*; *Condé Nast Traveler*; and *Travel and Leisure*. See the media section of the Las Olas Web site, www.surflasolas.com.

2 For one of many Web sites designed to attract U.S. investment, see Avalos Sayulita Realty, www.move2sayulita.com.

3 For visuals of Villa Amor, see the Villa Amor Web site (www.villaamor .com).

4 Carroll, "Boom!!!," 98.

5 More recently, the business has expanded and goes under the name "Manifesta Retreats," encompassing "golf safaris" and "artistic safaris." But in 2002 the "Manifesta" appeared as an explicit manifesto published online detailing the Las Olas mission. My interviews with Bev Sanders reinforced the mission statement (Sanders, conversation with the author, 22–24 October 2002, 24–30 November 2002). Chapter 3 takes up these matters in full.

6 Sanders, promotional brochure, 2002.

7 Ibid.

8 Peralta, *Dogtown and Z-Boys*.

9 On "responsible tourism," see the International Center for Responsible Tourism at Leeds Metropolitan University (www.icrtourism.org).

10 With the language of the "new" new social movement, I suggest post-identity political formations that formulate strategic goals for explicitly globalist or transnational contexts. For a survey of theories of social movements that distinguish between what might be called "theories of mobilization" focusing on the "how" of gaining specific

ends (associated with some global identity-based social movements) and per- spectives developed recently in Western Europe that use the term *new social movements* to denote protest working through "why" questions, aiming at an emancipatory transformation of society, not specific problems of the nation- state, see Mayer and Roth, "New Social Movements and the Transformation to Post-Fordist Society."

11 James, *Beyond a Boundary*. A fundamental difference between surfing and cricket is that Western imaginations initially positioned surfing as antithetical to colonial and capitalist Protestant work ethics as well as to related gender rela- tions. James's famous question, "What do they of cricket know who only cricket know?," pertains (preface). But surfers today often do not only surfing know. Moreover, if surfing as globalist rhetoric at times does the cultural work of con- temporary coloniality, its infusion with precolonial and anticolonial lifeways and cultural memory makes for unexpected political and ethical interventions.

12 I am grateful to the communications scholar P. David Marshall for brief but influ- ential early conversations about surfing as metaphor. See Marshall's "The Surf, Cultural Production, and the Value of Cultural Studies."

13 Nick Fielding, Matthew Campbell, and Nicholas Rufford, "Bin Laden Paid for Bali Bombing," *Sunday Times* (London), 20 October 2002.

14 Also see Catherine Munro, "Surfboards Used as Stretchers," *Australian Financial Review*, 14 October 2002.

15 The first and most influential print media representation of the subculture is *Surfer Magazine: The Bible of the Sport*, founded in Southern California in 1960. But some four hundred magazines—in eight languages and located in twenty- seven countries—have seen print since that time. For a record of their runs, see Matt Warshaw, "Appendix 4: Surfing Magazines," *Encyclopedia of Surfing*, 754– 57. Film production preceded magazines, and its history is available widely. For an interesting look at the U.S. scene via poster art, see Warshaw, *Surf Movie To- nite!* On Australian cinema, see Thomas, *Surf Movies*. Of the dozens of surf mu- seums in existence, the best known include the Bishop Museum (Honolulu), the Surfworld Museum (Victoria, Australia), the Huntington Beach International Surfing Museum (California), and the Santa Cruz Surfing Museum. Excellent popular histories include Warshaw, *Surfriders*; Kampion, *Stoked*; and Young and McGregor, *The History of Surfing*.

16 The feminist subcultural work in process at that time resulted most notably in Gabbard, *Girl in the Curl*. Several magazines had runs in these years, includ- ing, in the United States, *Wahine* (1995–2001) and *Surfer Girl* (1998–2000); in South Africa, *Saltwater Girl* (1999–present); in Australia, *Shred Betty* (1998); in Brazil, *Fluir Girls* (2001–present). A range of action and documentary videos and films were made, the most revered being a tribute to Rell Sunn, the "Queen of Makaha," whose untimely death from breast cancer created new awareness about environmental racism in Hawaii. Sunn's example also powerfully testified to novel strategies of political intervention possible for women surfers in areas

of women's health, youth advocacy, and native cultural integrity. See Denker and Lagarde, *Heart of the Sea*. The original novel *Gidget* was reissued in 2001 with both a foreword by the historical Gidget, Kathy Kohner Zuckerman, and an introduction by Deanne Stillman that briefly historicizes the Gidget phenomenon. See Frederick Kohner, *Gidget*. Surf museums, too, made the representation of women in surf history a priority, and to do so women surfers' private archives often suddenly became official public history.

17 Stockwell, *Blue Crush*; Giddens, *Runaway World*.

18 A search on the World Cat database reveals that between 2000 and 2006, more than 250 mass-market books were published on various aspects of surfing (my thanks to one of the reviewers at Duke for researching this and doing the math). While the majority does not deal with overt gender issues, an opening for girl-aware books has nonetheless occurred. Representative texts in this vein include Afcari and Osborne, *Sister Surfer*; Tihanyi and Tihanyi, *Surf Diva*; and Hamilton, *Soul Surfer*.

19 Important exceptions include Willard (on the racializations of the legendary Duke Kahanamoku), "Duke Kahanamoku's Body." Also see Moser, *Pacific Passages*. I am also aware of several dissertations in progress from students of anthropology, sociology, and literature. Two other critically informed works, neither of them produced in university contexts, are the two parts of Finnegan, "Playing Doc's Games." Finnegan's is the best auto-ethnographic piece to date written on surfing. Also see Duane, *Caught Inside*. Duane pursued a PhD at the University of California, Santa Cruz, in American studies but ultimately has taken up a writing career in literary and sports journalism.

20 Warshaw, *Encyclopedia of Surfing*; Warshaw, *Surfriders*; Kampion, *Stoked*; Young and McGregor, *The History of Surfing*.

21 The Captain Cook journals are addressed often in such sources as Duane, Finney and Houston, and Moser. Frequent topics also include the experiences of Twain and London learning to surf, and Tom Wolfe's representations of surfing subculture in *The Pump House Gang*. The point about two hundred years of writing in English is taken up in Warshaw's "Paperweight."

22 A collaborative project between the anthropologist Ben Finney and the late writer, literary scholar, and surfer James D. Houston, *Surfing* was originally published 1966 and revised and reissued in 1996. This text remains the principal anthropological and folkloric source used by popular histories produced in the United States. Also see Pearson, *Surfing Subcultures of Australia and New Zealand*. For an early classic about the Australian scene, see Irwin, "Surfing."

23 Booth, "Ambiguities in Pleasure and Discipline." Also see Booth, *Australian Beach Cultures*; Henderson, "The Big Business of Surfing's Oceanic Feeling"; Stedman, "From Gidget to Gonad Man."

24 Shields, "Surfing"; Preston-Whyte, "Constructions of Surfing Space at Durban, South Africa."

25 The cofounding editors include Alex Leonard (a surfer and anthropologist cur-

rently living in Vietnam), Stuart Nettle (a surfer and writer in southern Australia), and Clifton Evers (a research fellow at the Centre for Social Research in Journalism and Communication, University of New South Wales, Sydney, Australia).

26 Ford and Brown, *Surfing and Social Theory*.

27 The phrase "real existing identities," in an ethnographic sense, comes from Angela McRobbie, in her call for a more ethnographically informed practice of social theory and cultural studies ("Postmarxism and Cultural Studies," 730).

28 Future scholarship on Hawaiian surfing would be usefully informed by texts and interventions (none so far about surfing) such as Trask, *From a Native Daughter*; Hereniko and Wilson, *Inside Out*; Silva, *Aloha Betrayed*; Holt, *On Being Hawaiian*; and Diaz and Kauanui, "Native Pacific Cultural Studies on the Edge."

29 Many texts on at-risk white young femininity exist. See Pipher, *Reviving Ophelia*; Wiseman, *Queen Bees and Wannabes*; and Brumberg, *The Body Project*. The at-risk texts aimed at working-class or poor young women of color are memoirs aimed directly at young adult audiences, not popularized psychology texts for parents. See, for example, Murray, *Locas*; Asugha, *Little Sisters, Listen Up!*; Miranda, *Homegirls in the Public Sphere*; Jones, *Between Good and Ghetto*. Also see Kindlon, *Alpha Girls*; Meadows, "The Rise of the Gamma Girl"; and Gottesman, *Game Face*.

30 The NWSA hosted an embedded Girls Studies and Activism Institute at its conference in 2007, with featured speakers (including a keynote by Rebecca Walker), local tours of activist outreach organizations, and instructions about developing girls' studies research agendas. The AAUW sponsors the ongoing National Girls Collaborative Project, emphasizing girls' education in math, science, and technology. In 2008 it hosted the National Conference for College Women Student Leaders. The Ms. Foundation for Women oversees an initiative called Girls, Young Women, and Leadership, which extends funding to projects and supports youth-led social change. The Feminist Majority Foundation works with college and high school youth through Web sites, e-zines, blogs, and so forth.

31 Harris, *Future Girl*, 136–38. For Canadian activity, see Jiwani, Steenbergen, and Mitchell, *Girlhood*, ix–xvii.

32 A cursory search of online engines reveals activity across global cities and across social sectors like religion, criminal justice, education, and so on.

33 Mignolo, *Local Histories/Global Designs*.

34 Jameson and Miyoshi, *The Cultures of Globalization*.

35 Ibid., xvi.

36 Ibid., xi.

37 Ibid., xii.

38 Ibid., xvi.

39 Ibid.

40 Although I work from Jameson, many would see links to new theories, cultures,

and politics. Those from whom I have most taken a lead include Lipsitz, *American Studies in a Moment of Danger*; Appadurai, "Grassroots Globalization and the Research Imagination"; and Appadurai, "The Right to Research." Also see Gordon, *Keeping Good Time*; and Harvey, *Spaces of Hope*.

41 Jameson, xvi.

42 Basu et al., "Editorial."

43 Freeman, "Is Local:Global as Feminine:Masculine?"

44 Basu et al., "Editorial," 943.

45 Ibid., 944.

46 See Harris, *Future Girl*; Aapola, Gonick, and Harris, *Young Femininity*; Harris, *All about the Girl*; Harris, *Next Wave Cultures*.

47 Harris, *Future Girl*.

48 Ibid., 13–36.

49 Qtd. ibid., 14.

50 On neoliberalism, see Harvey, *A Brief History of Neoliberalism*; also Ong, *Neoliberalism as Exception*.

51 A clear rendering of postfeminism as opposed to third-wave feminism can be found in Heywood and Drake, *Third Wave Agenda*, 1–20.

52 Walker, *To Be Real*; Findlen, *Listen Up*; Edut, *Body Outlaws*; Hernández and Rehman, *Colonize This!*; Nam, *YELL-Oh Girls!*.

53 Heywood and Drake, *Third Wave Agenda*; Garrison, "U.S. Feminism—Grrrl Style!"

54 Harris, *Next Wave Cultures*, 1–2.

55 Appadurai, "Grassroots Globalization and the Research Imagination," 6.

56 Wilson and Dissanayake, *Global/Local*, 1.

57 *Global Girl* is a term associated with McRobbie's Global Girl Project, a research initiative at Goldsmiths, University of London, related to girlhood and its interface with human rights discourse, the Internet, labor markets, new psychoanalytic perspectives on body morphology, and neoliberalism and globalization. The Global Girl is an image circulated in world edition fashion magazines of female mobility, beauty, and capability. She "bears no grudges," meaning that she is postfeminist. See McRobbie, "Four Technologies of Young Womanhood." On young women, sexuality, and what McRobbie sees as a new social contract between women and the state, see *The Aftermath of Feminism*, esp. 54–93.

58 Mayer and Roth, "New Social Movements and the Transformation to Post-Fordist Society."

59 Appadurai, "Grassroots Globalization and the Research Imagination," 3.

60 Mignolo, *Local Histories/Global Designs*. On the synergy between the American West and Western civilization, see Comer, "West." On narratives of settlement and space at odds with the conflation of the regional West, national salvation, and global Western civilizing missions, see LeMenager, *Manifest and Other Destinies*.

61 The phrase "colonized Hawaii" intends to foreground Hawaii's presence in west-

ern American geographical contexts as a feature of westward trends of Manifest Destiny. Of course Hawaii is only "west" from a mainland perspective. From the vantage point of the Pacific Rim, the California mainland is "East Coast." For a brilliant if quirky rendering of Hawaii at the center of a world geography conceived through islands rather than land masses, see Okihiro, *Island World*. Such a reconception echoes recent though already-classic works theorizing the geographical imaginations of Oceania such as Hau'ofa, "Our Sea of Islands."

62 Herman, "Literature, Growth, and Criticism in the New West."

63 Comer, *Landscapes of the New West*.

64 Keywords like *borderlands, glocal, deterritorializations,* and so forth speak to celebrated critical rhetorics of the 1990s. For this project, my thinking was most shaped by texts like *Postmodern Geographies,* in which Edward Soja sees the regional as able to synthesize the social spaces of the global with the urban. Or by Appadurai, in *Modernity at Large,* for whom the regional or local is less a spatial than a relational concept produced by disjunctive flows of capital through various "scapes" of the new world-system (178–79). Anna Tsing in *Friction* works not from the site of the village, or the nation, or flows between them, but from frictions or interconnections that draw together worldly differences and utopian global encounters. Feminist explications shifted the focus of the regional not only to the fate of subaltern women in contexts of new forms of labor, global movement, and various crises (like sexual slavery or AIDS) affecting them but also to the power differences obscured by related critical rhetorics of the 1990s — nomadology, hybridity, migration, diaspora, exile, border crossing. See, for example, Ehrenreich and Hochschild, *Global Woman*; Sassen, *The Global City*; and Kaplan, *Questions of Travel*.

65 Connery, "The Oceanic Feeling and the Regional Imaginary," 286.

66 Campbell, *The Rhizomatic West*. See also Campbell, *The Cultures of the American New West*.

67 Tatum, "Spectrality and the Postregional Interface"; Tatum, "Topographies of Transition in Western American Writing"; and Tatum, "Postfrontier Horizons."

68 Allen, *Blood Narrative*.

69 See also Kollin, *Postwestern Cultures*; Handley and Lewis, *True West*; Comer, "Everyday Regionalisms in Contemporary Critical Practice"; Comer, "Taking Regionalism and Feminism toward the Third Wave."

70 Pennybacker, "Surfin' Surfari."

71 Deloria, *Playing Indian*.

72 The phrase "not condemn people for the contradictions they face" is George Lipsitz's (e-mail correspondence with author, 17 July 2005). Avery Gordon's work in *Keeping Good Time* also aided my thinking here, especially her discussion of Toni Cade Bambara, to which Lipsitz directed me. I am indebted to Lipsitz for suggesting Peter la Chapelle's dissertation on country music and whiteness in Los Angeles and Lisa Cacho's dissertation on "defensive whiteness" in California. For cautions as to how far such claims might be applied, see Lipsitz's own *The Pos-*

sessive Investment in Whiteness. For an overview of the field of critical whiteness studies, see an early collection, Delgado and Stefancic, *Critical White Studies.*

73   Kolodny, *The Land before Her*; Comer, *Landscapes of the New West*; Norwood and Monk, *The Desert Is No Lady.*

74   Clifford, *Routes.*

75   The biography of Duke Kahanamoku has been widely canonized in surf print media and museums. See Warshaw, *Encyclopedia of Surfing*; Kampion, *Stoked*; Finney and Houston, *Surfing*; and Ford and Brown, *Surfing and Social Theory.* Also see the Bishop Museum in Honolulu.

76   Brown, *The Endless Summer.*

77   Numbers reflect my computation of national scenes as reported in Warshaw, *Encyclopedia of Surfing.*

78   Ibid.

79   Ibid., xix. Numbers on women surfers are exaggerated in mainstream and surf media. One report claimed 37 percent of surfers in the United States were women in 2003, which may be the case in a few surf spots in the world (two of them in Northern California: Pacifica and Santa Cruz), but on the whole this is inaccurate. See Jordana Lewis, "New Wave of Surf Girls," *Newsweek*, 2004, 10. Inflated figures are encouraged by surf industry efforts to expand and capture female markets. The Surf Industry Manufacturing Association reports female buying power as one of its key growth factors in the recent economic boom. See Surf Industry Manufacturers Association (SIMA), "No Slowing Down for Surf Industry," www.sima.com.

80   See SIMA, "No Slowing Down for Surf Industry," www.sima.com.

81   See SIMA, "Surf Industry Riding Out the Economic Storm," www.sima.com.

82   McRobbie, *Postmodernism and Popular Culture.*

83   Mascheroni, "Global Nomads' Network and Mobile Sociality."

84   Harris, *Next Wave Cultures*, 1–13. Maira and Soep, *Youthscapes*; Bennett and Kahn-Harris, introduction.

85   Harris, *Next Wave Cultures*, 4. Guidikova and Siurala, "Introduction."

86   Some surf spots post rules of the water on beach or cliffside signs. "Surf etiquette" is the core curriculum of surf camps and schools. A variety of definitions of surf etiquette are available online, such as the "Bill of Rights and Lefts," Surfline.com, www.surfline.com. Traveling surfers will find online sources a must to consult regarding the "vibe" in breaks where one is not a local, especially where historic turf issues (Hawaii, for example) make for an unwelcoming scene to outsiders. The subculture's surf travel books, now numbering in the hundreds, recurrently speak to this topic as well, as do Ford and Brown, *Surfing and Social Theory.*

87   Generosity between surfers reportedly was the norm of the 1940s and 1950s, making for what Greg Heller calls a "distinctly Polynesian sense of hospitality and selflessness," the founding historical ethos of the subculture. "Aloha," December 2000, surfline.com (accessed 15 July 2006).

88   The official homepage of the Surfrider Foundation is www.surfrider.org.

89 Patagonia's business plan is no growth, and sustainability in its global stores includes on-site child care for its 85-percent-female workforce as well as on-site healthy foods and surf and mountaineering flextime for workers. See Chouinard, *Let My People Go Surfing*. Chouinard is a cofounding member of the One Percent for the Planet Organization, whose signatories donate 1 percent of all annual sales to environmental programs and protests.

90 Nihiwatu has been profiled in surf media and visited by surfing's luminary figures, who are asked (in addition to paying resort prices) to contribute to the Sumba Fund (see www.nihiwatu.com).

91 Point 4 of SIMA's mission statement reads: "[The surf industry will grow by] supporting oceanic environmental efforts through SIMA's Environmental Fund to ensure future growth of the sport and understanding of environmental activism." On guidelines defining "responsible tourism," see www.icrtourism.org.

92 On translocal social movements, see Buell, *The Future of Environmental Criticism*. On diasporic identities reconfigured as special political interests, see Appadurai, *Modernity at Large*.

93 Dirlik, "The Global in the Local."

94 Mayer and Roth, "New Social Movements and the Transformation to Post-Fordist Society"; see also La Feber, *Michael Jordan and the New Global Capitalism*. For a useful review of La Feber, see Mayer and Roth.

95 Touraine, *Can We Live Together?*

96 Jameson, *Postmodernism*.

97 Clark, "Where the Wanderers Stopped," 111.

98 The language of out there/in here comes from Giddens, *Runaway World*.

Californians in Diaspora

1 Kohner, *Gidget*.

2 Finney and Houston, *Surfing*. Given the importance of the relation of Hawaiian lore to surfing, it remains an understudied topic. Future research will benefit from critical perspectives alert to the exoticizing impulses governing representations of the Pacific. For hopeful directions (though not related to surfing) see Bacchilega, *Legendary Hawai'i and the Politics of Place*. Also see Okihiro, *Island World*.

3 Ehrenreich, *The Hearts of Men*.

4 In total, Frederick Kohner wrote eight Gidget novels, which were reprinted in ten languages, some selling a million copies. See the bibliography for details. Films include *Gidget* (1958), *Gidget Goes Hawaiian* (1961), and *Gidget Goes to Rome* (1963).

5 A list of the most influential books in establishing this picture for women's history include Hartmann, *From Margin to Mainstream*; Echols, *Daring to Be Bad*; Evans, *Personal Politics*; Hull, Scott, and Smith, *But Some of Us Are Brave*; and

textbooks rehearsing a similar narrative. For the latter, see Schneir, *Feminism in Our Time*. The phrase "bright and committed" is drawn from Davidson, *Loose Change* (preface, n.p.).

6 The most visible being the Civil Rights Act of 1963, Title ix (especially relevant to women's sports in educational contexts) and *Roe v. Wade*. The two were ignored by Davidson when she noted in 1973, "the center has held." *Loose Change* (preface, n.p.).

7 For example, see Radner and Luckett, *Swinging Single*.

8 Marsh, "Surfer Girls."

9 Kristin Finan, "Texas Surfer Girls Are Shooting the Curls," *Houston Chronicle*, 26 June 2006.

10 Joni Martin, "Hey There, Surfer Girls: The Best Women-Only Surf Camps," *San Francisco Chronicle*, 22 September 2002.

11 Rachel Barron, "Wave of Women Surfers, Filmmakers Hits Town," *Santa Cruz Sentinel*, 25 June 2003.

12 Mark Sauer, "Tubular Belles: Surfing Moms Find a Swell Way to Relax," *San Diego Union-Tribune*, 6 January 2000.

13 Lester Chang, "Teen-Age Surfing Star Attacked by Shark at Makua," *Garden Island News*, 1 November 2003. Also see Patricia Leigh Brown, "Surfer on Her Way Up, Brought Down by a Shark," *New York Times*, 4 November 2003. The book version of this incident is Hamilton, *Soul Surfer*.

14 "Women of Malibu," *Longboard Magazine*, May/June 1999, 52. But discrepancies between these figures and other reports exist. Kathy Kohner claims a half a million copies of *Gidget* were sold. See Beverly Beyette, "Riding That Wave Again," *Los Angeles Times*, 14 October 2001. Warshaw uses the latter number too in *Encyclopedia of Surfing*, 224–26.

15 Janet Cobb, "Female Surf Bum," *New York Times*, 10 November 1957. Also see Janet Cobb, "The Going Is Rough for Father Too," *New York Times*, 2 January 1960.

16 Reiss, *Gidget Must Die*. This is an offensive novel, and perhaps its most telling offense is that it resolves the white surf protagonist's murderous rage at Gidget by way of a fantasy sexual encounter with a Polynesian woman predictably exoticized.

17 Douglas and Glazner, "Gidget is 40!"

18 Reported in Warshaw, *Encyclopedia of Surfing*, 226.

19 For a time John Travolta was reported to be starring in the Kahoona role; see Douglas and Glazner, 33. For other information about the musical as it was actually staged, see Paul Clinton, "An Offer He Didn't Refuse: Francis Ford Coppola Stages High-School Musical Based on Teen Novel 'Gidget,'" cnn.com, 7 August 2000, http://archives.cnn.com.

20 McParland, *Cowabunga!*

21 Hugo Martin, "Surfer Girl, Forever," *Los Angeles Times*, 17 June 2006.

22 Ibid.

23 Warshaw, *Surfriders*, 123.

24 McParland, *Cowabunga!*, 1. Available online at http://www.sandradeefans.com/newgidgetbook.html (accessed 24 June 2008).

25 Martin, "Surfer Girl, Forever."

26 May, *Golden State, Golden Youth*. Whitney, "Gidget Goes Hysterical." The definitive work on the film series at present is Nash, *American Sweethearts*. In particular, Nash addresses the convention of father figures in teen pictures and those figures' interest in and control of daughters' emergent sexuality.

27 Kohner, *Gidget*. Further references to this work will be made parenthetically in the text and refer to the 2001 edition.

28 Kohner, *Cher Papa*, 1.

29 Jeff Duclos, "In Trim: Women of Malibu," *Longboard Magazine*, May–June 1999, 50–58; Gabbard, *Girl in the Curl*; Sam George, "Five Hundred Years of Women's Surfing," *Surfer*, 19 January 1999, 112–23; Douglas and Glazner, "Gidget is 40!"; Spurrier, "A Generation of Gidgets."

30 Morrissey is the only woman featured in Doc Ball's classic *California Surfriders*.

31 Duclos, "In Trim," 55–56.

32 Ibid., 54.

33 Denise Carson, "Surfer Girls," *Westside Weekly*, 9 July 2000. My thanks to Alice Echols for sending me this article.

34 Kohner Zuckerman did not get rich from the Gidget phenomenon. Her father sold the movie rights to Columbia for $50,000 and gave his daughter 5 percent, essentially buying the rights to her story. See Stillman's "The Real Gidget" and her "Introduction" to *Gidget* (2001). Stillman's interview offers rare insight into mid-century anti-semitism in surf culture. Gidget and many of the young Malibu girls were Jewish, which goes unremarked in popular films and novels, and Kohner and his wife were Czechoslovakian-born Jews who had fled the Holocaust to make new lives in Los Angeles.

35 A close consideration of these films is fruitful future research ground, especially in tandem with related films like the Elvis Presley trio *Blue Hawaii* (1961), *Girls, Girls, Girls!* (1962), and *Paradise, Hawaiian Style* (1965).

36 Materials about the legendary Malibu men of this era are widely available in magazine, film, and online sources. See Surfline.com or Warshaw's *Encyclopedia* for quick biographies.

37 For the phrase *set the tone* see Warshaw, *Encylopedia*, 224. The introduction to the version of *Gidget* republished in 2001 also briefly lays out this local history. See Stillman, "Introduction."

38 For excerpted materials from Twain and London, see Finney and Houston, *Surfing*, 97–110. Also see Duane, *Caught Inside* and, especially, Moser, *Pacific Passages*.

39 On Kahanamoku, see Warshaw; *Encyclopedia*, 308–10; Kampion, *Stoked*, 39–43; Finney and Houston, *Surfing*; and Ford and Brown, *Surfing and Social Theory*, 83–95.

40 On controversies surrounding statehood and annexation, see "How State-

hood Violated Kanaka Maoli Self-Determination," *Hawaii School Reports*, http:// www.hawaiischoolreports.com (accessed 15 December 2006). Also see Kelly, "A Kingdom Inside"; Sai, "American Occupation of the Hawaiian State"; Kauanui, "Hawai'i in *and* out of America."

41 Peter Bart, "Fellini of the Foam," *New York Times*, 12 June 1966; the phrase "Bergman of the Boards" appears in Bob Thomas, "Bruce Brown Rides a Perfect Wave after 'Endless Summer' Success," *The Washington Post, Times Herald*, 27 January 1967.

42 Vincent Canby, "On Any Sunday," *New York Times*, 29 July 1971.

43 Vincent Canby, review of *The Endless Summer*, *New York Times*, 16 June 1966.

44 Vincent Canby, "It Surfs Them Right," *New York Times*, 21 August 1966.

45 Vincent Canby, "Surfing Film Earns Its First Million," *New York Times*, 13 June 1967.

46 Ibid. Also, in his review of *The Endless Summer*, Canby comments on the "golly-gee-whiz" school of remarks of Bruce Brown and on his inadequacy at formulating a narrative line for surfers when they aren't surfing.

47 May, *Golden State, Golden Youth*, 4–5, 15. Also see Starr, *Embattled Dreams*.

48 May, *Golden State, Golden Youth*, 12.

49 Warshaw, *Surfriders*, 43.

50 Maki is best known for his 1950s black and white water shots of the last of the great Hawaiian beach boy surfers, "Blue" Makua and "Scooter-Boy" Kaopuiki. He took the final photograph of Duke Kahanamoku surfing (on his sixty-fourth birthday) at Waikiki. See Warshaw, *Encyclopedia of Surfing*, 358.

51 "Surfin' USA" and "Surfin' Safari" (1962), hit singles of the Beach Boys, predate Brown's *The Endless Summer*; by the mid-1960s the Beach Blanket film genre had reached the end of its run.

52 Drew Kampion, "Bob Simmons: King of Balsa," Surfline.com, 2000, http://www .surfline.com. Kampion finds that Simmons, a crack engineer and mathematician working at Douglass Aircraft during the war, applied his sense of objective hydrodynamic theory to surfboard construction (the balsa board) and, using fiberglass technologies developed by the navy, began the practice of glassing boards, making them fast, durable, and light.

53 Jason Borte, "Bud Brown: The Man Who Put the Surfing Picture into Motion," Surfline.com, 2000, http://www.surfline.com.

54 "Bruce Brown—The Story," http://www.brucebrownfilms.com (accessed 12 January 2010).

55 Drew Kampion, "John Severson: Surfer Magazine's Founder," Surfline.com, 2000, http://www.surfline.com.

56 Bailey and Farber, *The First Strange Place*.

57 Ibid, n.p.

58 Both Brown and Tom Blake are featured in many online and print biographies, but also see Lynch and Gault-Williams, *Tom Blake*.

59 A substantial literature treats the politics of the rush to statehood. See Sai,

"American Occupation of the Hawaiian State"; also Kauanui, "Hawai'i in *and out of America.*"

60 Kelly arrived in Honolulu from San Francisco with his artist parents at age four in 1923 and died at Diamond Head in 2007. He started surfing at nine on a discarded ironing board of his mother's until receiving a nine-foot redwood plank board shaped by one of Duke Kahanamoku's five brothers, David. He was a graduate of Juilliard. He lectured in economics at the University of Hawaii and wrote for the Honolulu papers for over fifty years about a range of issues, often including reparation. Warshaw reports in *Encyclopedia of Surfing* that Kelly was a Communist Party member during the early Cold War years (320). He founded SaveOurSurf, the first environmental surfing group, in 1961 in Oahu. In a representative *Honolulu Advertiser* op-ed piece from 1994, "Landowners, Tourism Have Wrecked Hawaii," Kelly wrote, "I got fired from four jobs for telling the truth—so I figured if I couldn't support my family telling the truth, I was gonna kick ass." Available online at www.legendarysurfers.com (accessed 15 January 2010). Surfrider honored him in 2003 with its inaugural Environmental Award for lifetime activism. Surfrider then renamed the annual honor the John Kelly Environmental Achievement Award. Kelly is also featured in a film about surfing and aging (he surfed daily into his 80s), *Surf for Life*, directed by David Brown (1999). For additional reminiscences about and regard for Makaha and Waimea of the 1950s and 1960s, see Noll and Gabbard, *Da Bull.*

61 Again, the pushback of surfer locals at the arrival of large numbers of tourists should be a topic for further research.

62 In none of the Vincent Canby reviews previously cited does he make any mention of decolonization.

63 Bart, "Fellini of the Foam."

64 The story of Aikau among South African surfers is well known. My account relies upon Coleman, *Eddie Would Go* (108–11). Jeffrey's Bay surfers whom I interviewed also recounted the story to me. Most memorably, see Chadwick, oral history. As one of the few local white African National Congress (ANC) party members in Jeffrey's Bay, a conservative Afrikaner town, Chadwick recalls that the Hawaiian team disgraced itself by failing to protest the racism directed at Aikau's. Evidence of the event's importance in popular memory can also be seen in an exhibit at the J-Bay surf museum on the second floor of Quiksilver's flagship store (Chadwick is the museum curator). On display behind glass is a page from the hotel register where Aikau finally was lodged. It bears his signature.

65 Jeffrey's Bay surfers report that unofficial segregation continues in the era after apartheid. When surfers do cross the color line, as Kim Meyer reported about surfing Kitchen Windows, formerly a colored break, she feels the spot doesn't belong to her, it is "their" spot. See Meyer, oral history. Rupert Chadwick remembers that during the years of apartheid local white surfers including himself urged nonwhites to surf white-designated Supertubes because the waves were so much bigger, longer, and faster. Chadwick eventually convinced the reluctant

Jaggles brothers to give Supertubes a try, but as the white and colored surfers together were about to enter the water, the "fish police," meaning Jackie Vosloo, the official from the Nature Conservancy who had legal jurisdiction on the coastline, stopped them and turned the Jaggles brothers away. To this day, the Jaggles don't often surf Supertubes even though they are serious enough surfers that they run a surf school and make their livings in surf microeconomies. The legal prohibition has been lifted but the memories continue to racialize the spaces. See Chadwick, oral history.

66 Canby, "On Any Sunday."

67 Reimers-Rice, oral history; Benson, oral history. All subsequent quotes from Reimers-Rice refer to these collected histories. Materials about Benson are drawn principally from the oral history unless otherwise noted.

68 Benson, oral history.

69 Gabbard, *Girl in the Curl*, 29.

70 Reimers-Rice, oral history.

71 Encinitas became a city only in 1986 when the previous communities of Leucadia, Cardiff-by-the-Sea, and Olivenhain all were incorporated into Encinitas.

72 Lipton, *The Holy Barbarians*.

73 Benson, oral history.

74 Ibid.

75 Reimers-Rice, oral history.

76 Ibid.

77 Gabbard, *Girl in the Curl*, 43.

78 Benson, oral history; see also Gabbard, *Girl in the Curl*, 45.

79 Gabbard, *Girl in the Curl*, 44.

80 Duclos, "In Trim," 55.

Wanting to Be Lisa

1 Qtd. in Joni Martin, "The Woman Who Rides Mountains," *Wahine* (1999), 40. See also Gerhardt, oral history. She talked with me a few months following her Mavericks event. In its wake, Gerhardt has been the subject of much media coverage. See, for example, the documentary *One Winter Story* (2006), directed by Sally Lundburg and Elizabeth Pepin. The film's title is in dialogue with the surf film classic, *Five Summer Stories* (1972), directed by Greg MacGillivray and Jim Freeman. *One Winter Story* made its European debut at the International Surf Festival in Saint Jean De Luz, France, winning the festival's best film award. It was also selected as best film of the Fourth Annual Ocean Film Festival in San Francisco. Currently, Gerhardt and the film are making rounds in San Francisco's schools and at-risk youth programs such as GirlVentures as part of ongoing outreach programs.

2 Smith, *Nike is a Goddess*, xix.

3 See, for example, Zimmerman and Reavill, *Raising Our Athletic Daughters*; Gottesman, *Game Face*. For a popular magazine example of such claims related

to surfers, see Susannah Meadows's *Newsweek* cover story profile of a "gamma girl" athlete who is also a surfer girl and is shown wearing a T-shirt sporting the Roxy logo (Meadows, "The Rise of the Gamma Girl"). For a well-known academic survey of gender and self-esteem (in which sport figures to some degree), see AAUW, "Shortchanging Girls, Shortchanging America."

4 Key popular texts contributing to the moral panic include, on the discourse about "Ophelia," Pipher, *Reviving Ophelia*; on girls and body issues, Brumberg, *Body Project*; on "mean" girls and female competition, Wiseman, *Queen Bees and Wannabes*.

5 I am working closely with as well as expanding the argument made in the prologue to Heywood and Dworkin, *Built to Win*.

6 Nicholson, *The Tribes of Palos Verdes*; *Blue Crush* (2002), directed by John Stockwell.

7 The Roxy Girl series includes Lantz, *Luna Bay #1*; Lantz, *Luna Bay #2*; Lantz, *Luna Bay #3*; Lantz, *Luna Bay #4*; Lantz, *Luna Bay #5*; Lantz, *Luna Bay #6*; Dubowski, *Luna Bay #7*.

8 Marsh, "Surfer Girls."

9 Ibid., 1.

10 Ibid.

11 Sam George, "Five Hundred Years of Women's Surfing," *Surfer*, March 1999, 115.

12 Gottlieb and Wald, "Smells Like Teen Spirit"; Leblanc, *Pretty in Punk*; Juno, "Interview with Kathleen Hanna." Wikipedia's entry on "Riot Grrls" also provides an excellent overview (accessed 12 December 2007).

13 Schilt and Zobl, "Connecting the Dots."

14 The businesses listed all had Web sites as of approximately 2000, but as chapter 4 shows, increased competition has forced many to close. Also see "Women's World," *Surfer*, March 1999, 102; and Gabbard, *Girl in the Curl*.

15 Smith, oral history; Marquez, oral history; Schiebel, oral history 1999 and 2002.

16 For surf club information I have relied on Gabbard, *Girl in the Curl*, 143–44.

17 Smith, oral history. As Heywood and Dworkin note, no official enforcement mechanism exists to score compliance, leaving bodies like the Women's Sports Foundation in the role of institutional police (*Built to Win*, 177n3). In an effort to publicize the inadequacy of most schools' attempts to meet Title IX guidelines, the foundation published the "Gender Equity Report Card: A Survey of Athletic Opportunity in American Higher Education" in 2000. For a look at the contentious and uneven implementation of Title IX, see Bouttilier and San Giovanni, "Politics, Public Policy, and Title IX."

18 At the same time the WCT voted in 1995 not to require a women's division, a move many think will lessen interest in women's contest events. The men's tour involves a two-tier system, in place only since 1992. See, for more information, Alisa Schwarzstein, "Qualifying Times: the 1995 Women's Pro Surf Tour," *Wahine*, 1995, 5.

19 Most numbers are derived from the Surf Industry Manufacturing Association
   or its commercial research businesses, for example, Board-Trac. Coralie Carlson
   quotes numbers from Paul West, the president of the United States Surfing Fed-
   eration in 2002, who reports a 120 percent increase in actual numbers over the
   years 1999–2002 (meaning about 150,000 females between the ages of twelve
   and nineteen surfing). See Carlson, "Surf's Up, Girls, with a Lot More Females
   Hanging Ten," *Houston Chronicle*, 1 September 2002. Jordana Lewis, relying on
   Board-Trac, reported in *Newsweek* that women made up 37 percent of the board-
   riders in the United States in 2002, which seems inaccurate in the extreme. See
   Jordana Lewis, "New Wave of Surf Girls," *Newsweek*, 19 July 2004, 10.

20 See Gabbard, *Girl in the Curl*, 105; see also Ben Marcus, "Lisa Andersen: Still Looking for a Home," *Surfer*, February 1996.

21 Gabbard, *Girl in the Curl*, 106.

22 Ibid., 108.

23 Elizabeth Glazner, "Lisa Andersen," *Wahine* (1995), 8.

24 Gabbard, *Girl in the Curl*, 105.

25 Ibid., 110.

26 Ibid., 107.

27 Ibid.

28 Chris Mauro, "The Man Behind *Blue Crush* Touches on the Women's Surfing
   Pulse," *Surfer*, March 1999, 100.

29 The notion of being "just a girl" informs a provocative memoir written by a run-
   ner, weightlifter, and scholar of third-wave feminism, Leslie Heywood (*Pretty
   Good for a Girl*). The protagonist's struggle to name and resist internalized sexism has helped me formulate my own understanding of Generation X versus
   Generation Y feminist challenges and attitudes.

30 Other subcultural figures of rebel femininity (e.g., Queen Latifah, Shakira,
   Jennifer Lopez) have also been recuperated as "good" and thereby assured con-
   tinuing commercial appeal. See, for example, Cepeda, "Shakira as the Idealized,
   Transnational Citizen"; Baez, "'En Mi Imperio'"; Guzman and Valdivia, "Brain,
   Brow, and Booty."

31 Warshaw, *Encyclopedia of Surfing*, 16.

32 In addition to these sources, see also the biographies of teenaged surfer girls profiled in Carlip, *Girl Power*, 219–45.

33 The Australian Pam Burridge is the first female surfer to write a memoir of her
   rise to surfing fame. See Stell, *Pam Burridge*. The work is out of print and largely
   unread among U.S. surfers. I did not interview a single woman who had read the
   memoir or even knew about it. Yet it is quite possible that this memoir will be
   reissued to take advantage of the new market for surf stories.

34 In response to public desire for more information about her extraordinary life,
   Andersen consented to a biography published in 2007. See Carroll, *Fearlessness*.

35 Much has been written about Oberg. Oberg herself writes about women's surf-

ing in "Strategy for Females." Also see Jim Kempton, "Margo Oberg," 36–44; Gabbard, *Girl in the Curl*; Warshaw, *Encyclopedia of Surfing*; and online sources like Surfline.

36 I have written about this text elsewhere in ways both relevant to and not overlapping with this discussion. See Comer, "Taking Regionalism and Feminism toward the Third Wave," esp. 120–27. Also on Generation X literature, see Comer, "Western American Literature at Century's End."

37 Nicholson, *The Tribes of Palos Verdes*, 24. All subsequent references to this source will be made parenthetically in the running text.

38 Reed, "Roseanne."

39 The phrase "a young girl's power to save herself" appears on http://books.google .com (accessed 18 January 2010).

40 Kearney, "Girlfriends and Girl Power," 125.

41 For a survey of some of the films in which Pipeline figures significantly, see Warshaw, *Encyclopedia of Surfing*, 463–66.

42 For the girl power sensibility—its mix of bold humor, friendship, and sexuality—see the outtakes that follow the conclusion of the documentary.

43 Bettijane Levine, "Riding Wave of Fiction-Fashion Marketing," *Houston Chronicle*, 22 April 2003.

44 Lantz, *Luna Bay #1*.

45 Lantz, *Luna Bay #5*.

46 Moretti, *The Way of the World*.

47 Concerning the gender dimensions of the Bildungsroman, I rely specifically on Fraiman, *Unbecoming Women and the Model of Development*. On the politics of maturation, see George, "But That Was in Another Country." Also see George, *The Politics of Home*.

48 I am indebted to Fraiman's work on Nancy Armstrong here. See *Unbecoming Women and the Model of Development*, 14–15.

The Politics of Play

1 Directed by Peter Wier, 1982.

2 See the Wikipedia entry for Hurricane Kenna, http://en.wikipedia.org (accessed 24 June 2008).

3 My first visit to Sayulita occurred 24–30 October 2002. A second visit followed 24–30 November 2002. On the combined visits I formally interviewed Beverly Sanders (Benicia, California), Lara Beutel (Australia), and Alayna Schiebel (Santa Cruz, California). My field notes from both visits include conversations with about twenty camp participants, among them the Hot Flashes, as well as conversations with the instructors Sandra (from New Jersey), Meagan (from Australia), and Kara (from Hawaii).

4 Field notes from 2002 include conversations with Patricia and Paul Southworth of Captain Pablo's, with Mary Ingram of Villa Amor, and with many real-

estate agents, including those at Avalos Realty. I also traveled to Puerta Vallarta in November 2004 and March 2005 to measure growth in tourism in Nayarit State. In January 2008 I returned to Sayulita. Field notes include conversations with hotel workers at Villa Amor, including Laura Beatriz; clerks in local stores; service providers in the massage and manicure industries, including Graciela Navarro of Nirvana; and with Miguel Guerrero Arce, a taxi driver for Transportación de Servicios Turísticas. I returned again to Las Olas, speaking to surf staff Bianca Valenti (from Santa Barbara, California) and Naomi (from British Columbia, Canada).

5   Janelle Brown, "Journeys: Their Little Secret, But for How Long?," *New York Times*, 7 March 2003. Steve McLinden, "Mexican Haciendas Becoming Hot Targets for Americans," *Seattle Times*, 27 March 2005. Alfredo Corchado and Laurence Iliff, "More U.S. Citizens Putting Down Roots South of the Border," *Dallas Morning News*, 14 March 2005.

6   Christopher Petkanas, "Nueva Rivera," *Travel and Leisure*, October 2007, http://www.travelandleisure.com.

7   Golson, *Gringos in Paradise*. The article version of the book, "La Vida Cheapo," won the prestigious 2004 Lowell Thomas award for travel writing.

8   Surfers and surf camps seem to suggest a pattern of development akin to urban revitalization inspired by artists. They create bohemian cultural capital that then becomes an investment commodity for urban professionals and/or developers. See, for example, Zukin, *Loft Living*, Podmore, "(Re)Reading the 'Loft Living' *Habitus* in Montréal's Inner City"; Smith, "Of Yuppies and Housing"; Smith, "New York City, New Frontier."

9   Harvey, *A Brief History of Neoliberalism*, 99.

10 Bev Sanders, "Our Manifesta," Las Olas company Web site, http://www.surflasolas.com (accessed 24 June 2008).

11 Ibid.

12 Ibid.

13 Promotional materials of Las Olas, 2002.

14 Coke is illegal to burn in the United States, and the company planned to ship the product to various Third World countries. But even in a dry form its particles contaminate air. Sanders's group discovered, just days before the vote, that their new "neighbor" had been sued by the federal government five hundred times within the past three years for pollution violations. This information, when presented to the Benicia City Hall members, changed their minds, and the building of the plant was blocked (Sanders, oral history, 29 October 2002).

15 Qtd. in Bernard R. Thompson, "Fonatur Is Planning Two New Resort Destinations," Mexidata.info, 21 July 2003, http://www.mexidata.info.

16 "Responsible tourism" is also discussed in my introduction. For further information, see the International Center for Responsible Tourism at Leeds Metropolitan University, http://www.icrtourism.org.

17 Although the Punta Mita development did not proceed by way of exploiting

Hurricane Kenna victims, the frequency of hurricanes in this hospitality corridor of Mexico makes it seem prudent to be alert to development strategies allying government and tourist tycoons that exploit disaster victims by appropriating land and displacing locals. See Klein, "Blanking the Beach"; and Sánchez, oral history.

18 Qtd. on Four Seasons Punta Mita Golf Web site, http://www.fourseasons.com.

19 Polly [last name unknown], conversation with author, 29 November 2002.

20 The following is drawn from my interview with three sisters, their aunt, a neighbor (Sofia), and various passersby on the street corner, January 14 2008.

21 I am grateful to Linda of Duende Surf Shop for introducing me to the political history of Sayulita's "big families." Linda learned it from her husband Mario Duende's mother, a Mexican woman who crossed the border for work in the 1950s, but who ultimately returned and bought property in Sayulita in the 1960s. Both women figure in chapter 5.

22 Harvey, *A Brief History of Neoliberalism*, 99.

23 Josue Pelayo Martinez, "An American Is No Longer Tolerated in Sayulita," *Meridians*, 8 October 2004. See also Brown, "Journeys."

24 Often the best sources of practical information about ejido transfers and current law are real-estate companies. I consulted with Avalos Realty. Other sources on ejidos and legal issues include Creekmore, "Ejido Land vs. Private Property." The politics or ethics of such changed laws, however, are another matter. I address those concerns in chapter 5.

25 Sánchez, oral history.

26 The fluid nature of the beach scene made such matters as first and last names difficult to verify unless competitors were written up in media. One is Adrian (last name unavailable). Dylan Southworth was featured on the cover of *Planeta Surf*, www.planetasurflarevista.com.

27 I have used the complex language of "mestizo indigeneity" because it seemed closest to Sofia's meanings, though she herself did not use it. Discussions of identity politics in human rights or antiracist groups in Mexico run strong, as does awareness of a certain neocolonial attitude or mestizo paternalism toward "our Indians." I have little doubt that Sofia would have spoken somehow to these issues given more time, but we did not engage them.

28 I learned this from Las Olas surf staff, most of whom are blondes from the North American West Coast, from California to Vancouver (conversations with author, January 2008).

29 I have changed the name of "María" to ensure her privacy.

30 See Martinez, "An American is No Longer Tolerated in Sayulita."

Countercultural Places

1 On cultures of political secrecy, see Valeria Alvord, "Surfer-Activist May Win San Diego Mayor's Post," *USA Today*, 7 November 2004. In 2004 Frye boycotted closed-session meetings of the City Council, sponsoring an open-government City Charter ballot measure that passed with overwhelming popular support (82 percent). New rules now require more public access to the meetings, a transcription of meeting proceedings, and the right for the public to testify in any closed-session agenda matter. For her efforts at government transparency Frye received the Beacon Award from the California First Amendment Coalition. See "About Donna Frye: Open Government and Quality of Life," City of San Diego, http://www.sandiego.gov/citycouncil (accessed 24 June 2008).

2 John M. Broder, "Sunny San Diego Finds Itself Being Viewed as a Kind of Enron-by-the-Sea," *New York Times*, 7 September 2004. For financial crises and Frye's mayoral candidacy, see the *San Diego Union Tribune*'s interview with Frye ("Write-in Candidate for Mayor of San Diego," *San Diego Union Tribune*, 17 October 2004).

3 Philip J. LaVelle and Daniel J. Chacon, "First Review of Ballots Turns Up 4,854 with Frye's Name," *San Diego Union Tribune*, 14 December 2004.

4 Miriam Raftery, "Exclusive: Citizens Request Recount in San Diego Mayoral Race," *Raw Story*, 18 August 2005, http://rawstory.com.

5 The "Save Trestles" homepage of surf culture's grassroots campaign can be found at the Surfrider Foundation Web site, http://www.surfrider.org/savetrestles (accessed 24 June 2008).

6 Qtd. in David Reyes and Dan Weikel, "Panel Rejects Toll Road through San Onofre State Beach," *Los Angeles Times*, 7 February 2008.

7 "Council Wrestles with Trestles Toll Road: Votes 4-3 Not to Oppose Proposed Freeway Extension," NBCSanDiego.com, 26 September 2006, http://www.nbcsandiego.com.

8 Popular press coverage on the victory in publications like the *San Diego Union Tribune* has remained very limited. Official transcripts of the resolution are available online at http://docs.sandiego.gov/councildockets_attach/2007/September/09-25-2007%2520Item%2520330.pdf (accessed 25 June 2008).

9 For an informative list of supporters of the campaign, including cities and counties, statewide organizations, and elected officials, see the supporters link under "*Save the Park . . . Stop the Toll Road*," a project of Save San Onofre, a coalition of political advocacy groups. http://www.savesanonofre.com (accessed 25 June 2008).

10 For Surfrider's protest of the appeal, see "Trestles Update: Tell the Folks in DC to Protect Trestles," Surfrider Foundation, San Diego chapter, http://www.surfridersd.org (accessed 25 June 2008). Such a move was widely expected; see "Toll Road Decision Might Face Appeal," 7 February 2008, http://www.10news.com.

11 The Surfrider Foundation San Diego chapter is not only available to give talks at schools but it also facilitates connections between young people and a host of local environmental organizations with specific youth outreach visions. Surfrider San Diego also sponsors local/global projects designed and implemented by young surfers. For instance, twelve-year-old Cobi Emery of San Diego and his friends do local beach cleanup and link their work to ocean health and surf subculture in Bali. They have established an initiative *Pick Up 3 and a Difference You Will See* that encourages beachgoers to make a contribution to environmental health by picking up three pieces of trash each time they go to the beach. They report on these activities on their Web site pickup3.org (accessed 25 June 2008). They also provide a video of their efforts at Hui300.com (accessed 25 June 2008).

12 Qtd. in Scott Bass, forum comment, *Surfer* magazine, http://forum.surfermag .com (accessed 25 June 2008).

13 Pete Thomas, "Trestles, San Onofre State Beach Saved," *Los Angeles Times*, 18 December 2008.

14 Frye, oral history, conducted in her offices in downtown San Diego's City Administration Building. For a quick overview of the overlap in women's rights agitation and ecosurf commitments, also see Matthew T. Hall, "Frye Caught Political Fever at Surf Shop," *San Diego Union Tribune*, 7 July 2005.

15 Frye, oral history.

16 Many texts on the 1960s see the New Left and various countercultures as mutually contradictory if not mutually exclusive. For example, the sds activist and commentator Todd Gitlin questioned, after Woodstock, "whether the youth culture will leave anything behind but a market." Qtd. in Echols, *Shaky Ground*, 47. For cautions about countercultural politics see Lipsitz, *American Studies in a Moment of Danger*, 57–114. An uneven and sparse literature exists on the hippies themselves; on matters of gender and women, that literature remains largely silent (e.g., MacFarlane, *The Hippie Narrative*). Histories and analyses addressing counterculture and gender more directly include the innovative study of Janis Joplin by Echols, *Scars of Sweet Paradise*; and Echols, *Shaky Ground*. For a fine article on the leanings of counterculturalism into New Left radicalism, see McBride, "Death City Radicals." See also Connery, "The World Sixties" (106–7) who urges scholars not to downplay the contribution of countercultures in the Western world to global trends of opposition and refusal.

17 Most U.S. chambers of commerce will link local businesses to local schools and nonpartisan organizations (e.g., Girl Scouts, Kiwanis, ymca). In developing economies, microcredit loans and small business enterprises can provide economic guards against female and child poverty and undereducation and can be associated with politically liberal or leftist change. But in the United States the presence of businesses at the center, or as sources, of new progressive political constituencies is far less common. Bookstores, especially left-wing and women's bookstores, have often served these community-building and informing roles.

18 My work on the surf community in Santa Cruz is informed by oral histories, film documentaries, and long-term observation. I did formal interviews with a few dozen surfers of all ages and skill levels in July 1999, followed up select surfers in Sayulita in 2002, and then followed up again in Santa Cruz and San Francisco in 2008. Over the years, we also traded e-mails and occasional phone calls. Several documentary films have been made that focus on Santa Cruz, the Santa Cruz–Pacifica women's scenes, or on Santa Cruz–Hawaii links, including San Francisco filmmaker Charlotte Lagarde's *Zeuf* (1994), *Swell* (1996), and Lisa Denker's and Charlotte Lagarde's *Heart of the Sea* (2002), all produced by Swell Cinema. There is also Georgina Corzine's mystical and sassy ecolesbian film *The Source* (1996). Finally, archival work of local women recording their life histories is available at the Santa Cruz Surfing Museum (http://www.santacruzsurfingmuseum.org).

19 Though I have not emphasized either of these stores in this chapter because I highlight Surf Diva instead, I am grateful both to Terry Kraszewski at Ocean Girl in La Jolla and to Mary Hartmann at Girl in the Curl in Dana Point, for conversations. Like Paradise Surf Shop and Surf Diva, these stores transmit to girls the skills of sport alongside those of living as young females able to challenge authority and to organize feminist and green activist projects.

20 I have not done the same kind of extended ethnography of women circulating around the Surf Diva shop as I did for Paradise because their daily rituals of social belonging do not track through the store as much. Geographies of cultural identification and group affiliation generate more through cultural productions and media representation, as the chapter attempts to show. Santa Cruz is understood as more contained or defined as a local identity, whereas La Jolla local cultures are more diffuse, mobile, and not as centered on legend.

21 Bumper stickers are also remarked on in Heather Knight, "Girls on Board: Paradise Surf Shop in Santa Cruz is the Only Surf Shop Owned by Women," *San Francisco Chronicle*, 17 January 2003.

22 Not a lot has been written about social life in Santa Cruz. Published materials typically focus on the coast, the mountains, mountain biking, the history of the Santa Cruz Beach Boardwalk, and so forth. A notable exception is Duane, *Caught Inside*.

23 Steve Hawk, "Introduction," *Surfer* magazine, March 1999, 10.

24 I was fortunate to do oral histories with all but Robin "Zeuf" Janiszeufski in July 1999.

25 The younger women are identified as role models in Hill, *The Women of Paradise*. Concerning the Pitts sisters, see Lagarde's documentary *Swell*. During the period of its filming, Beth Pitts drowned, and the surfers of Santa Cruz mourned her in public rituals.

26 The founding members included Sally Smith, Kristina Marquez of the legendary Van Dyke family, and Alayna Schiebel, a competitive longboard surfer. See the oral histories of Smith, Marquez, and Schiebel, July 1999. Sara Brae, another

founding member, had begun to discontinue her work with Paradise at the time of the above interviews, instead teaching surfing lessons at the school Surf Like a Girl. Brae and I did a surf lesson together in July 1999 and our conversations added to my sense of local women's surf culture. The story of Paradise's founding is also recounted in Hill, *The Women of Paradise*.

27 Qtd. in Hill, *The Women of Paradise*.

28 Ibid.

29 Ibid.

30 Ibid.

31 This story is featured in ibid.

32 Paradise initially received support from male investors, and in an initial large vote of confidence, Yvon Chouinard, the founder of Patagonia, praised the Paradise concept and storefront.

33 See "The Shop: Our Mission," Paradise Surf Shop Web site, http://www.para disesurf.com (accessed 8 March 2008).

34 MacKenzie, oral history; also subsequent conversations with the author. Mackenzie features as well in the film *Swell*.

35 Rodgers, oral history, July 1999. I visited the Santa Cruz Hotline factory warehouse and showroom in 1999, a subcultural workplace employing mainly surfers.

36 Zeuf is featured in the documentary *Zeuf*, directed by Lagarde. Also see Gabbard, *Girl in the Curl*; and Chase and Pepin, *Surfing*, 168–70.

37 Bayley, oral history.

38 Research is needed to investigate relations between surfing and sovereignty. On cultural revitalization as a strategy for healing the effects of colonization on the body, see Marshall, "Remembering Hawaiian, Transforming Shame."

39 Bederman, *Manliness and Civilization*; Cronon, "The Trouble with Wilderness."

40 Frye, oral history.

41 Ibid.

42 Ibid.

43 "Marsha," oral history. Quotes here are from the same woman whose name has been changed for reasons of privacy.

44 For a landmark book on Esalen, see Kripal, *Esalen*. Less familiar to scholars might be the pagan influence on emerging 1970s feminisms. Underground classics in Bay Area women's communities that gave history and feminist direction to paganism include: Budapest, *The Holy Book of Women's Mysteries*; and Starhawk, *The Spiral Dance*.

For memoirs that detail the period from the vantage point of Generation X children born to boomer hippie parents, see Michaels, *Split*; Gore, *The Hip Mama Survival Guide*; and Zappa and Cain, *Wild Child*.

45 Most of the women in this book are involved in organized outreach activities (not one-on-one outreach) through surf schools, contests, clubs, and the like.

Some women (like Elizabeth Pepin) participate in nonsurf organizations doing girl advocacy work (like Girl Ventures in San Francisco [www.girlventures.org]).

46 These include Laura Blears, in 1973, and Wendy Botha, in 1987 (Australian *Playboy*). See *Surfer* magazine, March 1999, 114–15.

47 Smith, personal correspondence with author.

48 For this story, see Warshaw, *Encyclopedia of Surfing*, 705.

49 Smith, personal correspondence with author.

50 Ibid.

51 See the Surf Diva Costa Rica Web site, http://www.surfdivacostarica.com (accessed 17 April 2008).

52 Clip available at Univision.com, www.univision.com (accessed 25 June 2008).

53 Tihanyi and Tihanyi, *Surf Diva*. Subsequent references to this source will appear parenthetically in the text.

54 Tihanyi, oral history. Subsequent quotes of Tihanyi refer to this oral history.

55 These two facts come from Warshaw, *Enclyclopedia of Surfing*, 280–81.

56 "Pier Pressure Junior Pro," *Surfing*, http://www.surfingthemag.com (accessed 25 June 2008).

57 "Awards and Accolades," City of Huntington Beach, http://www.ci.huntington-beach.ca.us (accessed 25 June 2008).

58 The demise of women's surf magazines has not been charted much in surf media (see the next note for an exception). My account here draws mainly from anecdotal conversation. If one searches online for information (enter *wahine*, for example), one is automatically redirected to new Web sites that offer no information about the closure of the magazines and attempt to recapture, toward some new consumer ends, that former market.

59 Qtd. in Michael Kew, "Higher Ground," Transworld Surf, http://www.transworldsurf.com (accessed 25 June 2008).

60 Surf Industry Manufacturers Association (SIMA), "No Slowing Down for Surf Industry," http://www.sima.com (accessed 25 June 2008).

61 Pepin, oral history. Although I did not interview Pepin in 1999 as part of the initial cohort of Northern California surfers, I have maintained contact with her since about 2000. We have traded ideas, visited the female-friendly breaks at Pacifica, and kept one another abreast of developing issues in women's surfing.

62 Tihanyi, oral history.

63 Pepin, oral history.

64 Ibid.

65 Ibid.

66 Smith, personal correspondence with author.

67 Pepin, oral history.

68 Ibid.

69 I am working closely here from the way this story is reported in Gabbard, *Girl in the Curl*, 54–55.

70 Ibid., 54.

71 Ibid.

72 As reported in Gabbard, *Girl in the Curl*, 84.

73 Ibid.

74 After some years in New York City, Setterholm returned to California and to surf subculture. Today she surfs and does activist work through her school, Surf Academy, in Manhattan Beach. She runs one of the most ambitious current youth outreach surf programs in the world—the LA Surf Bus—taking inner-city kids to the beach for surf lessons. For the inspiring mission statement of the LA Surf Bus, see its Web site, http://www.lasurfbus.org. Frye will tell you that she does not like talking about her own years in a first marriage marred by domestic abuse, but she lets it stand as part of the record anyway, alongside her public acknowledgment of a history of alcoholism. See Frye, oral history.

75 Frye, oral history; Benson, oral history. Both women have made public statements to this effect. For Frye, also see Alvord, "Surfer-Activist May Win San Diego Mayor's Post." Benson, see Gabbard, *Girl in the Curl*, 41–46.

76 Interview materials reveal many kinds of resolve as a consequence of sexist assaults: sexual violence against a twelve- or thirteen-year-old girl, which makes her hyperaware ever after and more effective as a surf journalist; the male bullies on the school playground who prompted a girl to fight back against boys' aggression and hone advocacy skills that eventually translated into voter registration drives, equal rights work, and surf environmental advocacy; girls whose mothers could not survive the collapse of 1950s marriages, giving them models of dependent femininity that encouraged surfing daughters not to "rely on some guy," as one put it; or those whose fathers' disappearances left mothers and their multiple children in poverty and for whom surfing offered a way out of the shrinking sense that the world was not theirs, putting in its place a spirit of going after big goals.

77 Pepin, e-mail correspondence with author, 5 March 2008.

78 Pepin, oral history. Subsequent quotes refer to this oral history.

79 The all-male lineup of Ocean Beach has changed a bit in recent years and a few exceptional women can be seen surfing such as Anastasia Shilling, Beth Price, and Diana Mattison. Diana Mattison specifically identifies as a fan of the local city punk scene and additional research would be fruitful concerning links between punk culture and the kind of tough athleticism required at a spot break like Ocean Beach. See Jane Ganahl, "Women on Waves: Ocean Beach's Female Surfers Aren't the Bikinied Barbie Dolls You See in the Movies," *San Francisco Chronicle*, 19 August 2002.

80 Pepin, e-mail correspondence with author, 5 March 2008.

81 Smith, personal correspondence with author.

82 Tihanyi, oral history.

83 Pepin, oral history.

Surfing the New World Order

1 See Surfrider Foundation, "Strategic Plan," http://www.surfrider.org (accessed 25 June 2008).

2 Surf Industry Manufacturers Association (SIMA), "No Slowing Down for Surf Industry," http://www.sima.com (accessed 25 June 2008).

3 On the North Shore during the tour, and for the link between industry and the Pipeline Posse, see Dibi Fletcher, "The Pipeline Posse: She's Surfing's Boswell, a Woman Who Can Tell You Everything You Ever Wanted to Know about the Sport, Its Heroes, and Its Villains," Interview, October 2004. Fletcher is a member of one of surf history's most illustrious and quirkiest families. She is mother to the competitors Nathan and Christian Fletcher and the wife of Herbie. The briefly-run television drama *John from Cincinnati* (2007), produced by David Milch, loosely based its series' family on the Fletchers, and both grandfather Herbie Fletcher and grandson Greyson Fletcher made surfing appearances.

4 Pipeline Posse, "History," http://www.pipelineposse.com (accessed 25 June 2008).

5 Qtd. in Jeff Merron, "Reel Life: *Blue Crush*," ESPN.com, http://espn.go.com (accessed 25 June 2008).

6 Lane Davey, "Better Than *Blue Crush*," *Surfer*, http://www.surfermag.com (accessed 25 June 2008.

7 "Banzai Women's Pipeline Championship," Banzai Surfing, http://www.banzai betty.com (accessed 25 June 2008).

8 "Shattered Dreams, No Pipeline Contest for Women Surfers," Banzai Surfing, 19 August 2007, http://www.banzaibetty.com.

9 Sunn has been profiled widely in books, subcultural magazines, online articles, biographies, and documentary film. See Gabbard, *Girl in the Curl*; Chase and Pepin, *Surfing*; Denker and Lagarde, *Heart of the Sea*.

10 Qtd. on the Rell Sunn Web site that serves as a tribute to Sunn but also as a center for announcements related to the Rell Sunn Educational Fund and Menehune Surf Contest, http://www.rellsunn.com/asianlifestyle.htm (accessed 25 June 2008).

11 On Kaui, the Hanalei surf team and its many strong young woman surfers, including Bethany Hamilton and Alana Blanchard, constitute one girl localism, as do the clusters of young women on the south shore at Poipu Beach associated with Margo Oberg and her surf school, as well as the Rochelle Ballard O'Neill Surf School. On Oahu, on the North Shore one finds among others the North Shore Surf Girls Camp and surf lessons with Sunset Suzy, in addition to the communities working through Rell Sunn in Makaha. On Maui, the east shore at Hana is home to the girls featured in Susan Orlean, "Maui Surfer Girls." On Maui's west shore, at Lahaina, are surfers affiliated with Maui Surfer Girls Surf Camp. On Hawaii, one finds the Big Island Surf Girls at Hilo.

12 Dustin Tester, "Nix Ocean Recreation Permit Law and Find Some Middle Ground," *Maui News*, 13 March 2008.

13 For insight into the complex racial order in Hawaii, see Judy Rohrer, '"Got Race?"' Also see Okamura, "Aloha Kanaka Me Ke Aloha 'Aina."

14 Laura Beatriz, oral history.

15 Lourdes Alberto, personal communication with author, 12 June 2007.

16 Duende, oral history.

17 "Support G.U.S.," Surfer Girl, http://www.surfer-girl.com (accessed 25 June 2008).

18 Warshaw, 288–89.

19 Warshaw; *Encyclopedia*, 288; also see Jenny Backstrom, "Surf Fashion Industry Making Waves," *Bali Rebound*, 1–15 May 2004, available online on Backstrom's Web site, http://bahinibianco.com/surffashion.html (accessed 25 June 2008).

20 Calvin Sims, "Indonesia: Gambling That Tolerance Will Trump Fear," *New York Times*, 15 April 2007.

21 Ibid.

22 MUM Bali Foundation (http://www.mumbali.org).

23 On Palmer and GUS, see Backstrom, "Surf Fashion Industry Making Waves." Richard Flax, another MUM board director, also founded GUS. See Tim Hain, "Helping Hands: Keeping Bali Clean," Hello Bali, http://www.hellobalimagazine .com (accessed 25 June 2008).

24 Anne Barker, "Bali Bomb Site Re-opened," *AM on ABC Local Radio News*, 28 October 2002, transcript available at http://www.abc.net.au/am/stories/s712326 .htm (accessed 25 June 2008).

25 Of several businesses, Rip Curl is the best known (see http://www.schoolofsurf .com).

26 Jenny Backstrom, "Indonesian Gals Hit the Surf," *Jakarta Post*, 4 August 2005.

27 Ibid. "Girls Go Surfing Day," *Beat*, 5 November 2008.

28 "Rip Curl Grom Search 2008 Lights Up Pacitan in East Java!," Rip Curl Asia, 10 February 2008, http://www.asia.ripcurl.com.

29 Peter Prengaman, "Muslim Women Keep Faith and Enjoy Water Sports in Style," *Lincoln Journal Star*, 24 February 2007.

30 Shereen Sabet, interview by Maria Hall-Brown, *Real Orange News Program*, KOCE, 14 March 2007.

31 Ibid.

32 Prengaman, "Muslim Women Keep Faith and Enjoy Water Sports in Style."

33 Ibid.

34 Select members of the North Shore Surf Club at North Shore High School in north Houston were recently invited to feature in an upcoming museum exhibit. They were chosen for their surfing ability and dedication to environmental and humanitarian efforts, including their involvement in the Surfrider Foundation, Texas chapter, in the Galveston Bay Foundation, in Texas Adopt-a-Beach, and in Surf-Aid International.

35 Texas Women, Texas Waves, exhibit at Texas Surf Museum, Corpus Christi, 6 June–28 October 2008.

Bibliography

Oral Histories and Interviews

Baraway, Anna. Oral history, Santa Cruz, California, 20 July 1999.

Bayley, Anne. Oral history, Santa Cruz, California, 21 July 1999.

Benson, Linda. Oral history, Valley Center, California, 16 November 1999.

Beutel, Lara. Oral history, Sayulita, Mexico, 29 October 2002.

Brae, Sara. Interview, Santa Cruz, California, 22 July 1999.

Chadwick, Rupert. Oral history, Jeffrey's Bay, South Africa, 15 January 2006.

Coccoli, Cindy. Oral history, Santa Cruz, California, 21 July 1999.

Comer, Jeannie. Oral history, Santa Cruz, California, 23 July 1999.

Duende, Linda. Oral history, Sayulita, Mexico, 14 January 2008.

Frye, Donna. Oral history, San Diego, California, 7 March 2008.

Gerhardt, Sarah. Oral history, Santa Cruz, California, 24 July 1999.

Gerkey, Denise. Oral history, Santa Cruz, California, 21 July 1999.

Kraak, Cheron. Oral history, Jeffrey's Bay, South Africa, 11 January 2006.

Laura Beatriz [no last name given]. Oral history, Sayulita, Mexico, 11–14 January 2008.

Mabetshe, Samuel. Oral history, Jeffrey's Bay, South Africa, 16 January 2006.

MacKenzie, Jane. Oral history, Santa Cruz, California, July 22, 1999.

Marquez, Kristina. Oral history, Santa Cruz, California, 20–21 July 1999.

"Marsha" [pseudonym]. Oral history, Santa Cruz, California, 21 July 1999.

Mayer, Kim. Oral history, Santa Cruz, California, 20 July 1999.

Meyer, Kim. Oral history, Jeffrey's Bay, South Africa, 17 January 2006.

Pepin, Elizabeth. Oral history, San Francisco, California, 3 March 2008.

Polly [no last name given]. Interview, Sayulita, Mexico, 28 October 2002.

Reimers-Rice, Rosemary. Oral history, Santa Cruz, California, 20–21 July 1999.

Rodgers, Brenda Scott. Oral history, Santa Cruz, California, 21 July 1999.

Sánchez, Sofia Silva. Oral history, Sayulita, Mexico, 15 January 2008.

Sanders, Beverly. Oral history, Sayulita, Mexico, 28–29 October 2002, 24–30 November 2002.

Schiebel, Alayna. Oral history, Santa Cruz, California, 20–21 July 1999.

———. Oral history, Sayulita, Mexico, 24–30 November 2002.

Scromme, Julie. Oral history, Corralitos, California, 22 July 1999.

Smith, Sally. Oral history, Santa Cruz, California, 20–21 July 1999.

Southworth, Patricia. Oral history, Sayulita, Mexico, 27–28 October 2002, 25–28 November 2002.

Thuysman, Andy. Oral history, Jeffrey's Bay, South Africa, 15 January 2006.

Tihanyi, Izzy. Oral history, San Diego, California, 6 March 2008.

Useldinger, Jenny. Oral History, Santa Cruz, California, 22 July 1999.

Versfeld, Paul. Oral history, Jeffrey's Bay, South Africa, 10–13 January 2006.

Williams, Brenton. Oral history, Jeffrey's Bay, South Africa, 16 January 2006.

References

Aapola, Sinikka, Marnina Gonick, and Anita Harris. *Young Femininity: Girlhood, Power, and Social Change*. New York: Palgrave Macmillan, 2005.

Afcari, Kia, and Mary Osborne. *Sister Surfer: A Woman's Guide to Surfing with Bliss and Courage*. Guilford, Conn.: Lyons Press, 2005.

Allen, Chadwick. *Blood Narrative: Indigenous Identity in American Indian and Maori Literary and Activist Texts*. Durham: Duke University Press, 2002.

American Association of University Women. "Shortchanging Girls, Shortchanging America." Washington, D.C., 1991.

Appadurai, Arjun. "Grassroots Globalization and the Research Imagination." *Globalization*, ed. Appadurai, 1–20. Durham: Duke University Press, 2001.

———. *Modernity at Large: Cultural Dimensions of Globalization*. Minneapolis: University of Minnesota Press, 1996.

———. "The Right to Research." *Globalisation, Societies, and Education* 4.2 (2006), 167–77.

Asugha, Ruby. *Little Sisters, Listen Up!: A Message of Hope for Girls Growing Up in Poverty, Racism, and Despair*. Boys Town, Nebr.: Boys Town Press, 2004.

Bacchilega, Cristina. *Legendary Hawai'i and the Politics of Place: Tradition, Translation, Tourism*. Philadelphia: University of Pennsylvania Press, 2007.

Baez, Jillian M. "'En Mi Imperio': Competing Discourses of Agency in Ivy Queen's Reggaeton." *Centro Journal* 18.11 (2006), 63–81.

Bailey, Beth, and David Farber. *The First Strange Place: The Alchemy of Race and Sex in World War II Hawaii*. New York: Macmillan, 1992.

Ball, Doc. *California Surfriders*. Los Angeles: Whale, 1946.

Ballard, Bill, dir. *Blue Crush*. Billygoat Productions, VHS, 1998.

Basu, Amrita, et al. "Editorial." *Signs* 26.4 (2001), 943–48.

Bederman, Gail. *Manliness and Civilization: A Cultural History of Gender and Race in the United States, 1880–1917*. Chicago: University of Chicago Press, 1996.

Bennett, Andy, and Keith Kahn-Harris. Introduction to *After Subcultures: Critical Studies in Contemporary Youth Culture*, ed. Bennett and Kahn-Harris, 1–20. London: Palgrave Macmillan, 2004.

Booth, Douglas. "Ambiguities in Pleasure and Discipline: The Development of Competitive Surfing." *Journal of Sport History* 22.3 (1995), 313–27.

———. *Australian Beach Cultures: The History of Sun, Sand, and Surf.* London: Frank Cass, 2001.

———. "From Bikinis to Boardshorts: Wahines and the Paradoxes of Surfing Culture." *Journal of Sport History* 28.1 (2001), 3–22.

Bouttilier, Mary A., and Lucinda F. San Giovanni. "Politics, Public Policy, and Title IX: Some Limitations of Liberal Feminism." *Women, Sport, and Culture*, ed. Susan Birrell and Cheryl Cole. Champaign, Ill: Human Kinetics, 1994.

Brown, Bruce, dir. *The Endless Summer*. DVD. Bruce Brown Films, 1966.

Brumberg, Joan Jacobs. *The Body Project: An Intimate History of American Girls.* New York: Vintage, 1998.

Budapest, Zsuzsanna Emese. *The Holy Book of Women's Mysteries*. San Francisco: Red Wheel Weiser, 2007.

Buell, Lawrence. *The Future of Environmental Criticism: Environmental Crisis and Literary Imagination*. Malden, Mass.: Blackwell, 2005.

Cacho, Lisa. "Disciplinary Fictions: The Sociality of Private Problems in Contemporary California." PhD diss., University of California, Los Angeles, 2002.

Campbell, Neil. *The Cultures of the American New West*. Chicago: Fitzroy Dearborn, 2000.

———. *The Rhizomatic West: Representing the American West in a Transnational, Global, Media Age*. Lincoln: University of Nebraska Press, 2008.

Carlip, Hillary. *Girl Power: Young Women Speak Out!* New York: Warner Books, 1995.

Carroll, Nick. "Boom!!! How Surfing's Newbie Explosion Will Change Your World." *Surfing*, November 2002, 98.

———. *Fearlessness: The Story of Lisa Andersen*. San Francisco: Chronicle Books, 2007.

Cepeda, María Elena. "Shakira as the Idealized, Transnational Citizen: A Case Study of Colombianidad in Transition." *Latino Studies* 1 (2003), 211–32.

Chase, Linda, and Elizabeth Pepin. *Surfing: Women of the Waves*. Layton, Utah: Gibbs Smith, 2007.

Chen, Martha, et al. *Progress of the World's Women 2005: Women, Work, and Poverty*. New York: United Nations Development Fund for Women, 2005.

Cheslock, John. *Who's Playing College Sports: Trends in Participation*. New York: Women's Sports Foundation, 2007.

Chouinard, Yvon. *Let My People Go Surfing: The Education of a Reluctant Businessman*. New York: Penguin, 2005.

Clark, Katy. "Where the Wanderers Stopped." *Surflife for Women*, winter 2006.

Clifford, James. *Routes: Travel and Translation in the Late Twentieth Century*. Cambridge: Harvard University Press, 1997.

Coleman, Stuart Holmes. *Eddie Would Go: The Story of Eddie Aikau, Hawaiian Hero and Pioneer of Big Wave Surfing*. New York: St. Martin's Press, 2004.

Comer, Krista. "Everyday Regionalisms in Contemporary Critical Practice." *Post-

western Cultures: Literature, Theory, Space, ed. Susan Kollin, 30–58. Lincoln: University of Nebraska Press, 2007.

———. *Landscapes of the New West: Gender and Geography in Contemporary Women's Writing*. Chapel Hill: University of North Carolina Press, 1999.

———. "Taking Regionalism and Feminism toward the Third Wave." *A Companion to the Regional Literatures of America*, ed. Charles Crow, 111–28. Oxford: Blackwell, 2003.

———. "Wanting to Be Lisa: Generational Rifts, Girl Power, and the Globalization of Surf Culture." *American Youth Cultures*, ed. Neil Campbell, 237–65. Edinburgh: Edinburgh University Press, 2004.

———. "West." *Keywords for American Cultural Studies*, ed. Bruce Burgett and Glenn Hendler, 238–41. New York: New York University Press, 2007.

———. "Western American Literature at Century's End: Sketches in Generation X, Los Angeles, and the Post–Civil Rights Novel." *Pacific Historical Review* 72.3 (2003), 405–13.

Connery, Christopher Leigh. "The Oceanic Feeling and the Regional Imaginary." *Global/Local: Cultural Production and the Transnational Imaginary*, ed. Rob Wilson and Wimal Dissanayake, 284–311. Durham: Duke University Press, 1996.

———. "The World Sixties." *The Worlding Project: Doing Cultural Studies in the Era of Globalization*, ed. Rob Wilson and Christopher Leigh Connery, 77–108. Santa Cruz: New Pacific Press, 2007.

Corzine, Georgina, dir. *The Source*. 1996.

Creekmore, Mitch. "Ejido Land vs. Private Property: What's the Difference?" *Arizona Journal of Real Estate and Business* (2000), 1–3.

Cronon, William. "The Trouble with Wilderness: or, Getting Back to the Wrong Nature." *Uncommon Ground: Rethinking the Human Place in Nature*, ed. William Cronon, 69–90. New York: W. W. Norton and Co., 1995.

Davidson, Sara. *Loose Change: Three Women of the Sixties*. Berkeley: University of California Press, 1997.

Delgado, Richard, and Jean Stefancic, eds. *Critical White Studies: Looking behind the Mirror*. Philadelphia: Temple University Press, 1997.

Deloria, Philip J. *Playing Indian*. New Haven: Yale University Press, 1998.

Denker, Lisa, and Charlotte Lagarde, dirs. *Heart of the Sea*. Swell Cinema, 2002.

Diaz, Vicente M., and J. Khaulani Kauanui. "Native Pacific Cultural Studies on the Edge." *The Contemporary Pacific* 13.2 (2001), 315–42.

Dirlik, Arif. "The Global in the Local." *Global/Local: Cultural Production and the Transnational Imaginary*, ed. Rob Wilson and Wimal Dissanayake, 21–45. Durham: Duke University Press, 1996.

Douglas, Theo, and Elizabeth Glazner. "Gidget is 40! The Real Gidget." *Wahine* 5:2 (1997), 20–33.

Duane, Daniel. *Caught Inside: A Surfer's Year on the California Coast*. San Francisco: North Point Press, 1996.

Dubowski, Cathy East. *Luna Bay #7: Board Games*. New York: Scholastic, 2003.

Duclos, Jeff. "In Trim: Women of Malibu." *Longboard Magazine*, May–June 1999, 50–58.

Echols, Alice. *Daring to Be Bad: Radical Feminism in America, 1967–1975*. Minnesota: University of Minnesota Press, 1989.

———. *Scars of Sweet Paradise: The Life and Times of Janis Joplin*. New York: Henry Holt, 1999.

———. *Shaky Ground: The Sixties and Its Aftershocks*. New York: Columbia University Press, 2002.

Edut, Ophira. *Body Outlaws: Young Women Write about Body Image and Identity*. Seattle: Seal Press, 2000.

Ehrenreich, Barbara. *The Hearts of Men: American Dreams and the Flight from Commitment*. New York: Anchor, 1983.

Ehrenreich, Barbara, and Arlie Russell Hochschild, eds. *Global Woman: Nannies, Maids, and Sex Workers in the New Economy*. New York: Henry Holt, 2004.

Evans, Sara. *Personal Politics: The Roots of Women's Liberation in the Civil Rights Movement and the New Left*. New York. Vintage, 1979.

Farber, David. *The Sixties: From Memory to History*. Chapel Hill: University of North Carolina Press, 1994.

Findlen, Barbara. *Listen Up: Voices of the Next Feminist Generation*. Seattle: Seal Press, 1995.

Finnegan, William. "Playing Doc's Games-I." *New Yorker*, 24 August 1992, 34.

———. "Playing Doc's Games-II." *New Yorker*, 31 August 1992, 39.

Finney, Ben, and James D. Houston. *Surfing: A History of the Ancient Hawaiian Sport*. San Francisco: Pomegranate Artbooks, 1996.

Fletcher, Dibi. "The Pipeline Posse: She's Surfing's Boswell, a Woman Who Can Tell You Everything You Ever Wanted to Know about the Sport, Its Heroes, and Its Villains." Interview. October 2004.

Ford, Nick, and David Brown. *Surfing and Social Theory: Experience, Embodiment, and Narrative of the Dream Glide*. New York: Routledge, 2005.

Fraiman, Susan. *Unbecoming Women and the Model of Development*. New York: Columbia University Press, 1993.

Freeman, Carla. "Is Local:Global as Feminine:Masculine? Rethinking the Gender of Globalization." *Signs* 26.4 (2001), 1007–37.

Gabbard, Andrea. *Girl in the Curl: A Century of Women in Surfing*. Seattle: Seal Press, 2000.

Garrison, Edne Kaeh. "U.S. Feminism—Grrrl Style!: Youth Subcultures and the Technologics of the Third Wave." *Feminist Studies* 26.1 (2000), 141–71.

George, Rosemary Marangoly. "But That Was in Another Country: Girlhood and the Contemporary 'Coming to America' Narrative." *The Girl: Constructions of the Girl in Contemporary Fiction by Women*, ed. Ruth O. Saxton, 135–52. New York: St. Martin's Press, 1998.

———. *The Politics of Home: Postcolonial Relocations and Twentieth-Century Fiction*. Berkeley: University of California Press, 1999.

George, Sam. "Five Hundred Years of Women's Surfing." *Surfer Magazine*, July 1999, 112–23.

Giddens, Anthony. *Runaway World: How Globalization Is Reshaping Our Lives*. New York: Routledge, 1999.

Glazner, Elizabeth. "Lisa Andersen: Recollections of a World Champion." *Wahine* 1.1 (1999), 6–9.

Golson, Barry. *Gringos in Paradise: An American Couple Builds Their Retirement Dream House in a Seaside Village in Mexico*. New York: Scribner's, 2006.

———. "La Vida Cheapo." *AARP: The Magazine*, March–April 2004.

Gordon, Avery F. *Keeping Good Time: Reflections on Knowledge, Power, and People*. Boulder, Colo.: Paradigm Publishers, 2004.

Gore, Ariel. *The Hip Mama Survival Guide: Advice from the Trenches on Pregnancy, Childbirth, Cool Names, Clueless Doctors, Potty Training, and Toddler Avengers*. New York: Hyperion, 1998.

Gottesman, Jane. *Game Face: What Does a Female Athlete Look Like?* New York: Random House, 2003.

Gottlieb, Joanne, and Gayle Wald. "Smells Like Teen Spirit: Riot Grrrls, Revolution, and Women in Independent Rock." *Microphone Fiends: Youth Music and Youth Culture*, ed. Andrew Ross and Tricia Rose, 250–74. New York: Routledge, 1994.

Guidikova, Irena, and Lasse Siurala. "Introduction: A Weird, Wired, Winsome Generation: Across Contemporary Discourses on Subculture and Citizenship." *Transitions of Youth Citizenship in Europe: Culture, Subculture, and Identity*, ed. Andy Furlong and Irena Guidikova, 5–40. Strasbourg: Council of Europe, 2001.

Guzman, Isabel Molina, and Angharad N. Valdivia. "Brain, Brow, and Booty: Latina Iconicity in U.S. Popular Culture." *Communication Review* 7, no. 2 (2004), 205–21.

Hamilton, Bethany. *Soul Surfer: A True Story of Faith, Family, and Fighting to Get Back on the Board*. New York: Pocket Books, 2004.

Handley, William R., and Nathaniel Lewis. *True West: Authenticity and the American West*. Lincoln: University of Nebraska Press, 2004.

Harris, Anita, ed. *All about the Girl: Culture, Power, and Identity*. London: Routledge, 2004.

———. *Future Girl: Young Women in the Twenty-First Century*. London: Routledge, 2004.

———, ed. *Next Wave Cultures: Feminism, Subcultures, Activism*. New York: Routledge, 2007.

Hartmann, Susan M. *From Margin to Mainstream: American Women and Politics since 1960*. Philadelphia: Temple University Press, 1989.

Harvey, David. *A Brief History of Neoliberalism*. New York: Oxford University Press, 2005.

———. *Spaces of Hope*. Berkeley: University of California Press, 2000.

Hau'ofa, Epeli. "Our Sea of Islands." *A New Oceania: Rediscovering Our Sea of Islands*, ed. Epeli Hau'ofa, Eric Waddell, and Vijay Naidu, 2–16. Suva: School of Social and Economic Development, University of the South Pacific, Beake House, 1993.

Henderson, Margaret. "The Big Business of Surfing's Oceanic Feeling: Thirty Years of *Tracks Magazine*." *Growing Up Postmodern: Neoliberalism and the War on the Young*, ed. Ronald Strickland, 141–68. Lanham, Md.: Rowman and Littlefield, 2002.

———. "A Shifting Line-Up: Men, Women, and *Tracks Surfing Magazine*." *Journal of Media and Cultural Studies* 15.3 (2001), 319–32.

Hereniko, Vilsoni, and Rob Wilson, eds. *Inside Out: Literature, Cultural Politics, and Identity in the New Pacific*. Lanham, Md.: Rowman and Littlefield, 1999.

Herman, Matt. "Literature, Growth, and Criticism in the New West." *Western American Literature* 38:2 (2003), 49–76.

Hernández, Daisy, and Bushra Rehman. *Colonize This!: Young Women of Color on Today's Feminism*. Seattle: Seal Press, 2002.

Heywood, Leslie. *Pretty Good for a Girl: An Athlete's Story*. Minneapolis: University of Minnesota Press, 1999.

Heywood, Leslie, and Jennifer Drake, eds. *Third Wave Agenda: Being Feminist, Doing Feminism*. Minneapolis: University of Minnesota Press, 1997.

Heywood, Leslie, and Shari L. Dworkin. *Built to Win: The Female Athlete as Cultural Icon*. Minneapolis: University of Minnesota Press, 2003.

Hill, Trevor, dir. *The Women of Paradise: A Surf Documentary*. Fish Bowl Media Arts Production, 2005.

Holt, John Dominis. *On Being Hawaiian*. Honolulu: Topgallant Publishing, 1974.

Hull, Gloria T., Patricia Bell-Scott, and Barbara Smith, eds. *All the Women Are White, All the Blacks Are Men, But Some of Us Are Brave: Black Women's Studies*. New York: The Feminist Press at CUNY, 1982.

Irwin, John. "Surfing: The Natural History of an Urban Scene." *Urban Life and Culture* 2 (1973), 133–46.

James, C. L. R. *Beyond a Boundary*. Durham: Duke University Press, 1993.

Jameson, Fredric. *Postmodernism, or, The Cultural Logic of Late Capitalism*. Durham: Duke University Press, 1991.

Jameson, Fredric, and Masao Miyoshi. *The Cultures of Globalization*. Durham: Duke University Press, 1998.

Jiwani, Yasmin, Candis Steenbergen, and Claudia Mitchell, eds. *Girlhood: Redefining the Limits*. Montreal: Black Rose Books, 2006.

Jones, Nikki. *Between Good and Ghetto: African American Girls and Inner City Violence*. New Brunswick, N.J.: Rutgers University Press, 2009.

Juno, Andrea. "Interview with Kathleen Hanna." *Angry Women in Rock*, 219–45. New York: Juno Press, 1996.

Kampion, Drew. *Stoked: A History of Surf Culture*. Santa Monica, Calif.: General Publishing Group, 1997.

Kaplan, Caren. *Questions of Travel: Postmodern Discourses of Displacement*. Durham: Duke University Press, 2000.

Kauanui, J. Kehaulani. "Hawai'i in *and* out of America." *Mississippi Review* 32.4 (fall 2004), 145–50.

Kearney, Mary Celeste. "Girlfriends and Girl Power: Female Adolescence in Contemporary U.S. Cinema." *Sugar, Spice, and Everything Nice: Cinemas of Girlhood*, ed. Frances Gateward and Murray Pomerance, 125–40. Detroit: Wayne State University Press, 2002.

Kelly, Anna Keala. "A Kingdom Inside: The Future of Hawaiian Political Identity." *Futures* 35 (2003), 999–1009.

Kempton, Jim. "Margo Oberg: A Profile." *Surfer*, July 1981, 36–44.

Kindlon, Dan. *Alpha Girls: Understanding the New American Girl and How She Is Changing the World*. Emmaus, Penn.: Rodale, 2006.

Klein, Naomi. "Blanking the Beach: 'The Second Tsunami.'" *The Shock Doctrine: The Rise of Disaster Capitalism*. New York: Alfred Knopf, 2007.

Kohner, Frederick. *The Affairs of Gidget*. New York: Bantam, 1963.

———. *Cher Papa*. New York: Bantam, 1960.

———. *Gidget Goes Hawaiian*. New York: Bantam, 1961.

———. *Gidget Goes New York*. New York: Dell, 1968.

———. *Gidget Goes Parisienne*. New York: Dell, 1966.

———. *Gidget Goes to Rome*. New York: Bantam, 1963.

———. *Gidget in Love*. New York: Dell, 1965.

———. *Gidget: The Little Girl with Big Ideas*. 1957. New York: Berkley Books, 2001.

Kollin, Susan, ed. *Postwestern Cultures: Literature, Theory, Space*. Lincoln: University of Nebraska Press, 2007.

Kolodny, Annette. *The Land before Her: Fantasy and Experience of the American Frontiers, 1630–1860*. Chapel Hill: University of North Carolina Press, 1984.

Kripal, Jeffrey J. *Esalen: America and the Religion of No Religion*. Chicago: University of Chicago Press, 2007.

Kurungubaa: A Journal of Literature, History and Ideas from the Sea. Ed. Alex Leonard Stuart Nettle and Clifton Evers. Sydney, Australia.

La Chapelle, Peter. "'That Mean Ol' Boogie': Country Music, Migrations, and the Construction of Whiteness in Southern California, 1936–1969." PhD diss., University of Southern California, 2003.

La Feber, Walter. *Michael Jordan and the New Global Capitalism*. New York: W. W. Norton, 2002.

Lagarde, Charlotte, dir. *Swell*. Swell Cinema, 1996.

———, dir. *Zeuf*. Swell Cinema, 1994.

Lantz, Francess. *Luna Bay #1: Pier Pressure*. New York: Scholastic, 2003.

———. *Luna Bay #2: Wave Good-Bye*. New York: Scholastic, 2003.

———. *Luna Bay #3: Weather or Not*. New York: Scholastic, 2003.

———. *Luna Bay #4: Oh, Buoy!* New York: Scholastic, 2003.

———. *Luna Bay #5: Hawaii Five-Go!* New York: Scholastic, 2003.

———. *Luna Bay #6: Heart Breakers*. New York: Scholastic, 2003.

Leblanc, Lauraine. *Pretty in Punk: Girls' Gender Resistance in a Boys' Subculture.* New Brunswick, N.J.: Rutgers University Press, 1999.

LeMenager, Stephanie. *Manifest and Other Destinies: Territorial Fictions of the Nineteenth-Century United States.* Lincoln: University of Nebraska Press, 2004.

Lewis, Jordana. "New Wave of Surf Girls." *Newsweek*, 19 July 2004.

Lipsitz, George. *American Studies in a Moment of Danger.* Minneapolis: University of Minnesota Press, 2001.

———. *The Possessive Investment in Whiteness: How White People Profit from Identity Politics.* Philadelphia: Temple University Press, 2006.

Lipton, Lawrence. *The Holy Barbarians.* New York: Messner, 1959.

Lundburg, Sally, and Elizabeth Pepin, dirs. *One Winter Story.* DVD. Frank Films, 2006.

Lynch, Gary, and Malcolm Gault-Williams. *Tom Blake: The Uncommon Journey of a Pioneer Waterman.* Ed. William K. Hoopes. Corona del Mar, Calif.: Croul Family Foundation, 2000.

MacFarlane, Scott. *The Hippie Narrative: A Literary Perspective on the Counterculture.* Jefferson, N.C.: McFarland, 2007.

MacGillivray, Greg, and Jim Freeman, dirs. *Five Summer Stories.* DVD. MacGillivray Freeman Films, 1972.

Mafisa Media (in collaboration with the World Conservation Union), producers. *The Healing Power of Nature: Perfect?* South Africa, ABC3, September 25, 2005.

Maira, Sunaina, and Elisabeth Soep, eds. *Youthscapes: The Popular, the National, the Global.* Philadelphia: University of Pennsylvania Press, 2005.

Marcus, Ben. "Lisa Andersen: Still Looking for a Home." *Surfer*, February 1996.

Marsh, Ann. "Surfer Girls." *Forbes*, 9 July 1999, 1–4.

Marshall, P. David. "The Surf, Cultural Production, and the Value of Cultural Studies: How the Web Leads to a Tidal Shift in Orientation." Paper presented at the Cultural Studies Association of Australia Conference, Brisbane, 4 December 2000.

Marshall, Wende Elizabeth. "Remembering Hawaiian, Transforming Shame." *Anthropology and Humanism* 31.2 (2008), 185–200.

Martin, Joni. "The Woman Who Rides Mountains." *Wahine*, 5.3 (1999), 37–40.

Mascheroni, Giovanna. "Global Nomads' Network and Mobile Sociality: Exploring New Media Uses on the Move." *Information, Communications, and Society* 10.4 (2007), 527–46.

May, Kirse Granat. *Golden State, Golden Youth: The California Image in Popular Culture, 1955–1966.* Chapel Hill: University of North Carolina Press, 2002.

Mayer, Margit, and Roland Roth. "New Social Movements and the Transformation to Post-Fordist Society." *Cultural Politics and Social Movements*, ed. Marcy Darnovsky, Barbara Epstein, and Richard Flacks, 299–319. Philadelphia: Temple University Press, 1995.

McBride, David. "Death City Radicals: The Counterculture in Los Angeles." *The New Left Revisited*, ed. John McMillian and Paul Buhle. Philadelphia: Temple University Press, 2003.

McParland, Stephen. *Cowabunga! Gidget Goes Encyclopedic.* North Strathfield, Australia: CMusic Books, 2001.

McRobbie, Angela. *The Aftermath of Feminism: Gender, Culture, and Social Change.* London: Sage Publications, 2009.

———. "Four Technologies of Young Womanhood." Paper presented at the Zentrum für Interdisziplinäre Frauen und Geschlechterforschung, Berlin, 31 October 2006.

———. "Postmarxism and Cultural Studies: A Postscript." *Cultural Studies*, ed. Lawrence Grossberg, Cary Nelson, and Paula Treichler, 719–30. New York: Routledge, 1992.

———. *Postmodernism and Popular Culture.* New York: Routledge, 1994.

Meadows, Susannah. "The Rise of the Gamma Girl." *Newsweek*, 3 June 2002, 44–51.

Michaels, Lisa. *Split: A Countercultural Childhood.* New York: Mariner Books, 1999.

Mignolo, Walter. *Local Histories/Global Designs: Coloniality, Subaltern Knowledges, and Border Thinking.* Princeton: Princeton University Press, 2000.

Miranda, Marie Keta. *Homegirls in the Public Sphere.* Austin: University of Texas Press, 2003.

Moretti, Franco. *The Way of the World: The Bildungsroman in European Culture.* London: Verso, 2000.

Moser, Patrick, ed. *Pacific Passages: An Anthology of Surf Writings.* Honolulu: University of Hawai'i Press, 2008.

Murray, Yxta Maya. *Locas: A Novel.* New York: Grove, 1998.

Nam, Vickie, ed. *YELL-Oh Girls!: Emerging Voices Explore Culture, Identity, and Growing Up Asian American.* New York: Harper, 2001.

Nash, Ilana. *American Sweethearts: Teenage Girls in Twentieth-Century Popular Culture.* Bloomington: Indiana University Press, 2006.

National Coalition for Women and Girls in Education. *Title IX at 30: Report Card on Gender Equity.* Washington, D.C.: American Association of University Women, 2002.

Nicholson, Joy. *The Tribes of Palos Verdes.* New York: St. Martin's Press, 1997.

Noll, Greg, and Andrea Gabbard. *Da Bull: Life over the Edge.* Berkeley, Calif.: North Atlantic Books, 1989.

Norwood, Vera, and Janice Monk. *The Desert Is No Lady: Southwestern Landscapes in Women's Writing and Art.* New Haven: Yale University Press, 1987.

Oberg, Margo. "Strategy for Females." *Competitive Surfing: A Dedicated Approach*, ed. Brian J. Lowdon and Margaret Lowdon, 83–94. Torquay, Victoria, Australia: Movement Publications, 1985.

Okamura, Jonathan. "Aloha Kanaka Me Ke Aloha 'Aina: Local Culture and Society in Hawaii." *Amerasia* 7.2 (1980), 119–37.

Okihiro, Gary Y. *Island World: A History of Hawai'i and the United States.* Berkeley: University of California Press, 2008.

Ong, Aihwa. *Neoliberalism as Exception: Mutation in Citizenship and Sovereignty.* Durham: Duke University Press, 2006.

Orlean, Susan. "Maui Surfer Girls." *Women Outside*, fall 1998.

Osborne, Mary, and Kia Afcari. *Sister Surfer: A Woman's Guide to Surfing with Bliss and Courage*. Connecticut: The Lyons Press, 2005.

Pearson, Kent. *Surfing Subcultures of Australia and New Zealand*. St. Lucia, Queensland: Queensland University Press, 1979.

Pennybacker, Mindy. "Surfin' Surfari." *The Nation*, 7 September 1998, 38–41.

Peralta, Stacy, dir. *Dogtown and Z-Boys*. Sony Pictures Classics, 2001.

Pipher, Mary. *Reviving Ophelia: Saving the Selves of Adolescent Girls*. New York: Ballantine Books, 1995.

Podmore, Julie. "(Re)Reading the 'Loft Living' *Habitus* in Montréal's Inner City." *International Journal of Urban and Regional Research* 22.2 (1998), 283–302.

Preston-Whyte, Robert. "Constructions of Surfing Space at Durban, South Africa." *Tourism Geographies* 4.3 (2002), 307–28.

Radner, Hilary, and Moya Luckett, eds. *Swinging Single: Representing Sexuality in the 1960s*. Minneapolis: University of Minnesota Press, 1999.

Reed, Jennifer. "Roseanne. A 'Killer Bitch' for Gen X." *Third Wave Agenda: Being Feminist, Doing Feminism*, ed. Leslie Heywood and Jennifer Drake, 122–33. Minneapolis: University of Minnesota Press, 1997.

Reiss, Fred. *Gidget Must Die: A Killer Surf Novel*. Santa Cruz: Fred Reiss Comedy Productions, 1995.

Rohrer, Judy. "'Got Race?': The Production of Haole and the Distortion of Indigeneity in the Rice Decision." *Contemporary Pacific* 18.1 (2006), 1–31.

Sai, David Keanu. "American Occupation of the Hawaiian State: A Century Unchecked." *Hawaiian Journal of Law and Politics* 1 (2004): 46–81.

Sassen, Saskia. *The Global City: New York, London, Tokyo*. Princeton: Princeton University Press, 2001.

Schilt, Kristen, and Elke Zobl. "Connecting the Dots: Riot Grrrls, Ladyfests, and the International Zine Network." *Next Wave Cultures: Feminism, Subcultures, Activism*, ed. Anita Harris, 171–92. New York: Routledge, 2007.

Schneir, Miriam. *Feminism in Our Time: The Essential Writings, World War II to the Present*. New York: Vintage, 1994.

Schwarzstein, Alisa. "Qualifying Times: The 1995 Women's Pro Surf Tour." *Wahine* 1:1 (1995), 5.

Shields, Rob. "Surfing: Global Space or Dwelling in the Waves?" *Tourism Mobilities: Places to Play, Places in Play*, ed. Mimi Sheller and John Urry, 44–51. London: Routledge, 2004.

Silva, Noenoe K. *Aloha Betrayed: Native Hawaiian Resistance to American Colonialism*. Durham: Duke University Press, 2004.

Smith, Lissa, ed. *Nike Is a Goddess: The History of Women in Sports*. New York: Atlantic Monthly Press, 1998.

Smith, Neil. "New York City, New Frontier: The Lower East Side as Wild, Wild West." *Variations on a Theme Park: The New American City and the End of Public Space*, ed. M. Sorkin, 61–93. New York: Hill and Wang, 1992.

————. "Of Yuppies and Housing: Gentrification, Social Restructuring, and the Urban Dream." *Environment and Planning D: Society and Space* 5.1 (1987), 151–72.

Soja, Edward W. *Postmodern Geographies: The Reassertion of Space in Critical Social Theory*. London: Verso, 1989.

————. *Thirdspace: Journeys to Los Angeles and Other Real-and-Imagined Places*. Oxford: Blackwell, 1996.

Spurrier, Jeff. "A Generation of Gidgets." *Atlantic Monthly*, April 2002, 109–11.

Starhawk [Miriam Simos]. *The Spiral Dance: A Rebirth of the Ancient Religion of the Great Goddess*. San Francisco: Harper, 1999.

Starr, Kevin. *Embattled Dreams: California in War and Peace, 1940–1950*. New York: Oxford University Press, 2002.

Stedman, Leanne. "From Gidget to Gonad Man: Surfers, Feminists, Postmodernisation." *Journal of Sociology* 33.1 (1997), 75–90.

Stell, Mariam K. *Pam Burridge*. Pymble, Australia: Angus and Robertson, 1992.

Stillman, Deanne. "Introduction." *Gidget*. New York: Berkley Books, 2001.

————. "The Real Gidget." *Surf Culture: The Art History of Surfing*. Laguna Beach, Calif.: Laguna Beach Art Muséum, 2002.

Stockwell, John, dir. *Blue Crush*. Universal Studios, 2002.

Tatum, Stephen. "Postfrontier Horizons." *Modern Fictions Studies* 50.2 (2004), 460–68.

————. "Spectrality and the Postregional Interface." *Postwestern Cultures: Literature, Theory, Space*, ed. Susan Kollin, 3–29. Lincoln: University of Nebraska Press, 2007.

————. "Topographies of Transition in Western American Writing." *Western American Literature*, 32:4 (1998): 310–53.

Thomas, Albie. *Surf Movies: The History of Surf Film in Australia*. Sydney: Shore Thing Publishing, 2000.

Tihanyi, Izzy, and Coco Tihanyi. *Surf Diva: A Girl's Guide to Getting Good Waves*. New York: Harcourt, 2005.

Touraine, Alain. *Can We Live Together? Equality and Difference*. Trans. David Macey. Cambridge: Polity Press, 2000.

Trask, Haunani-Kay. *From a Native Daughter: Colonialism and Sovereignty in Hawai'i*. Monroe, Maine: Common Courage Press, 1993.

Tsing, Anna Lowenhaupt. *Friction: An Ethnography of Global Connection*. Princeton: Princeton University Press, 2005.

United Nations. *Pathway to Gender Equality: CEDAW, Beijing, and the Millennium Development Goals (MDGs)*. New York: United Nations Development Fund for Women in cooperation with the Federal Ministry for Economic Cooperation and Development, Germany, 2005.

Walker, Rebecca. *To Be Real: Telling the Truth and Changing the Face of Feminism*. New York: Anchor, 1995.

Warshaw, Matt. *Encyclopedia of Surfing*. New York: Harcourt, 2003.

————. "Paperweight." *Surfer's Journal* 6.3 (1997), 1–10.

———. *Surf Movie Tonite!: Surf Movie Poster Art, 1957–2004*. San Francisco: Chronicle Books, 2005.

———. *Surfriders: In Search of the Perfect Wave*. New York: Collins Publishers, 1997.

Whitney, Allison. "Gidget Goes Hysterical." *Sugar, Spice, and Everything Nice: Cinemas of Girlhood*, ed. Frances Gateward and Murray Pomerance, 55–70. Detroit: Wayne State University Press, 2002.

Willard, Michael Nevin. "Duke Kahanamoku's Body: Biography of Hawai'i." *Sports Matters: Race, Recreation, and Culture*, ed. John Bloom and Willard, 13–38. New York: New York University Press, 2002.

Wilson, Rob, and Wimal Dissanayake, eds. *Global/Local: Cultural Production and the Transnational Imaginary*. Durham: Duke University Press, 1996.

Wiseman, Rosalind. *Queen Bees and Wannabes: Helping Your Daughter Survive Cliques, Gossip, Boyfriends, and Other Realities of Adolescence*. New York: Crown Publishers, 2002.

Young, Nat, and Craig McGregor. *The History of Surfing*. Palm Beach, Australia: Palm Beach Press, 1983.

Zappa, Moon Unit, and Chelsea Cain. *Wild Child: Childhoods in the Counterculture*. Seattle: Seal Press, 1999.

Zimmerman, Jean, and Gil Reavill. *Raising Our Athletic Daughters: How Sports Can Build Self-Esteem and Save Girls' Lives*. New York: Doubleday, 1998.

Zukin, Sharon. *Loft Living: Culture and Capital in Urban Change*. New Brunswick, N.J.: Rutgers University Press, 1989.

Index

Page numbers in italics refer to illustrations

Krista Comer is an associate professor in the Department of
English at Rice University. She is the author of *Landscapes of the
New West: Gender and Geography in Contemporary Women's
Writing* (1999).

Library of Congress Cataloging-in-Publication Data

Comer, Krista.
Surfer girls in the new world order / Krista Comer.
p. cm.
Includes bibliographical references and index.
ISBN 978-0-8223-4789-7 (cloth : alk. paper)
ISBN 978-0-8223-4805-4 (pbk. : alk. paper)
1. Women surfers—United States.
2. Women surfers—Mexico.
3. Surfing—Social aspects—United States.
4. Surfing—Social aspects—Mexico.
I. Title.
GV839.7.W65C664 2010
797.32082—dc22   2010009123